THE
SPORT
IS
STEROIDS

One Athlete's Quest to
Set World Records and Win

Jim Rutter

Cover design by germancreative
Cover image courtesy of

For Lydia and Christine and Tara
and Cheryl and Maude and Kate
and Jenny and Mattie
and Wes and CJ and Harrison
and every lifter that's competed clean
and won at the highest levels.

Table of Contents:

Introduction

During the summer of 2017, Pat and Taylor Mendes generously invited me into their Kensington home each Sunday. They had moved to Philadelphia that April. Pat took a local position with Vivint and Taylor began training at Philadelphia Barbell Club.

Like many weightlifters, I knew Pat's story from the outside looking in and remembered seeing his massive lifts on YouTube before hearing of his doping offences in 2012 and 2015. I considered myself a fan of his lifting. No one with an open eye to this sport imagines any senior World record holder setting their marks without performance-enhancing drugs.

While the coach in me condemned Pat's methods, the journalist in me wanted to hear Pat's story. And then publish the truth. To that end, I recorded over 30 hours of interviews, most with Pat and Taylor together, some separately. I also interviewed dozens of coaches, athletes and officials and read hundreds of articles and books about the history of doping in Olympic and professional sport.

The following pages offer Pat's story as a lens through which to view the use and abuse of drugs, not just in weightlifting, but in all sport. Pat was not alone in his quest; most organized teams, sports, federations and countries, and even anti-doping organizations all sought the same goal: to set world records and win. Throughout this book, I present my own thoughts within the context of Pat's narrative. Most of these reflections begin or end each chapter. These sections state my arguments about how doping has affected weightlifting as a sport and how sports-governing bodies have used weightlifting in particular to deal with the problem of drug use.

I regard Pat as a highly competent individual. It's about the best compliment I can give. No matter what activity Pat tries, he succeeds beyond expectation. Pat learned to snatch with an empty barbell and within 20 months hit a weight never achieved or equaled by an American. He never sold alarms door to door yet earned sales Rookie of the Year for an industry leader.

I possess tremendous respect for him as an individual and successful adult member of society.

That said, I understand if readers don't feel great sympathy for Pat or his ban from the sport to which he devoted much of his early life. However, I do believe the Court for Arbitration of Sport should void his positive test for HGH, and any positive HGH result that resulted from the same test they declared invalid for Andrus Veerpalu. As this book's research shows, Pat has real justification to sue WADA for faulty tests and to sue the IWF for banishing him from the sport. What that would mean for Pat's ability to return to the weightlifting in any capacity remains to be decided.

As for the title? I choose something intentionally hyperbolic and which overly condemns weightlifting. The title should proclaim "All Sport Is Steroids." Every athlete seeks an advantage. Pat's story shows that some athletes take that quest too far.

July 2020
Philadelphia, PA

"The primary reason for the apparent lack of success of the testing programs does not lie with the science involved. While there may well be some drugs or combinations of drugs and methods of which the anti-doping community is unaware, the science now available is both robust and reliable.

The real problems are the human and political factors.

There is no general appetite to undertake the effort and expense of a successful effort to deliver doping-free sport. This applies with varying degrees at the level of athletes, international sport organizations, national Olympic committees, national anti-doping organizations, and governments. It is reflected in low standards of compliance measurement, unwillingness to undertake critical analysis of the necessary requirements, unwillingness to follow-up on suspicions and information, unwillingness to share available information, and unwillingness to commit the necessary informed intelligence, effective actions, and other resources to the fight against doping in sport."

Dick Pound, founding President of the World Antidoping Agency (WADA)
"Lack of Effectiveness of Testing Programs"
WADA document, May 13, 2013

"The changes to the policy we're all really excited about. It's a great evolution of the program and we're actually hopeful other sports who are interested in protecting clean athletes more effectively and creating fairer systems, this will be the model for it and something we've been pushing both the World Anti-Doping Agency (WADA) and other programs for the past couple of years to try and do something along these lines."

USADA CEO **Travis Tygart**, announcing a new drug policy for The UFC that provides acceptable thresholds of multiple steroids and substances banned by the WADA code.
Interview with MMAFighting.com, November, 2019

Prologue:

Salt Lake City: May 2016

I made my last backstage appearance at USA Weightlifting's 2016 National Championships. My wife Taylor and I entered the warm-up area set up behind the three competition stages. The officials hadn't yet brought the athlete attempt cards to the Marshall's table, but they let us into the back, and we picked out a platform.

Some of the other athletes for the 63kg A session started to filter in—not any of the medal contenders—but Taylor liked to get a platform early. Nationals was Taylor's first big meet since taking bronze in the snatch at the 2015 University Championships. As I watched her foam rolling on the floor, I knew she was nervous, even if she wasn't showing it.

I felt some of the other coaches watching me, the ones that knew anyway. The sport of weightlifting had grown significantly since 2011, thanks mostly to Crossfit, and many new coaches knew only two weightlifters, if any: Dmitri Klokov and Jon North. That, and being noobs most likely coaching for the first time at a national meet, they were over-focused on their lifters, worried and worrying the shit out of their own athletes.

But I had newfound notoriety. That past fall, I flew to Houston for my hearing with the disciplinary board of the International Weightlifting Federation (IWF), regarding my alleged positive test at the 2015 Pan American Games. The hearing had not gone well.

Some of the old guard coaches stared openly. Rumors spread fast in this sport and people love to gossip. I should've worn a baseball cap, and definitely not an Average Broz t-shirt.

My suspension from the IWF amounted to a death sentence. I could start weightlifting again at age 33, eight long years from 2016, and almost more time than I had spent in this sport. After their decision, I thought, I'm done, it doesn't even matter to me. A few years later, I wound up going head to head with Ilya Ilyin at a local seminar and beat him because I could still snatch 183kg, eight fucking kilos more than Wes Kitts 175kg American record at the time, and less than my first attempt at several international meets. I can only guess what I could hit at 33.

I draped a sweatshirt across Taylor's back as she sat in a chair. The rest of her competitors had filtered in. About 20 feet away, the technical controller yelled out names of the athletes in the session, calling them to lineup for introductions. I flashed a smile as Taylor headed to the platform and then laid out weights so we could load her bar quickly during warm-up attempts.

After the introductions, Taylor started moving. First with the bar, then muscle snatches at 35 and 40kg. She looked fast and snappy. Her eyes and face bloomed with confidence. I grabbed a pair of yellow plates to put 45kg on her bar. And then someone tapped my shoulder.

It was Phil Andrews, CEO of USA Weightlifting. "Pat, you can't be back here," he told me forcefully.

"What are you talking about?" I replied, moving my body in between him and Taylor's line of sight. Inside I felt my stomach drop. This is going to fucking suck.

"You're sanctioned. You can't be in the back. You have to leave." His words shot out machine-gun fire.

"Pat, what's going on?" Taylor's voice, now worried.

"Let's go Pat." Phil insisted.

"I have to leave," I mumbled.

Taylor's face crumpled into angry tears. "I'll get someone," I called back as Phil escorted me from the warm-up room. But she was already on it. Taylor might get upset, but never rattled enough to delay action. I looked back as I passed through the doorways and she was typing furiously on her phone to find a coach to count the rest of her attempts.

A few hours later, in the privacy of our hotel room, Taylor broke down, screaming at me. Billy Bybee, who owned Crossfit Las Vegas, had run down to help count her attempts. Despite me getting kicked out, she smoked all three snatches, taking Bronze with an 86kg lift that beat Cecily Basques' same attempt (Taylor weighed less). Her clean and jerks fizzled out; she only hit her opener at 99kg, and finished 8th in the total, nowhere near the performance we expected.

Could she have done better with me in the back? Maybe. I wanted to help Taylor. To give her the kind of support I never got navigating this sport. To let her understand the bullshit politics that baffled me, and provide her with better coaching than I received, so that she could avoid the pitfalls of a novice coach offering guidance while taking advantage of internet fame.

And now I couldn't help her at all.

I believe in taking responsibility for what I've done and will never shy away from it. By the time you finish this book, you'll hear all the drugs I took and the dosages I used. These pages detail my training and all the scandals in my competition history. For years, I struggled in vain to outwit a testing system that required institutional support to defeat. I planned to take on the athletes in the state-sponsored doping nations, win world championships and set world records, and I did whatever it took to achieve those goals.

So pay attention: I plan to drop names and call people out for their shit. But there's one thing I want you to know right from the start:

In seven years of weightlifting I accomplished more than 99% of all lifters that ever touch a barbell. Two World Championships. Two Pan Am Games. Representing two different nations. I'm still the only American male to snatch 200kg and all you motherfuckers know I snatched more than that.

But because of how I achieved my goals, I can't even help my wife when she needs me. And that's my biggest regret in this sport. Not getting popped twice. Not the bomb outs at big meets. That because of a pair of bullshit tests, I can't take care of my own when it matters.

Eventually, what I tried to achieve would cost me everything.

One:
The Decision

"Ok, then. I'm going to take steroids."

I made that decision less than two months into this sport.

I didn't dwell on it or need to sleep on that choice. I had one conversation about how weightlifters in other nations used drugs and said right then and there: I'm in.

In other countries, those with state-organized doping systems, this doesn't happen. The decision I mean. No one decides yes or no, compliance or refusal. You want to be in the program, you do what your coaches and doctors tell you. Buying in means travel, fame, some money. You refuse and you go back to your shitty village, small college, or family business. With limited prospects.

The East Germans built the model for this system during the heyday of the drug-fueled Olympic era that lasted from the invention of Dianabol in 1951 to the widespread use and abuse of Turinabol and Stanozolol in the 1970s and 1980s. From 1968 until 1988, East Germany alone won over 400 medals in the summer Olympics despite a relatively weak economic system and a population of only 17 million (plus another 110 Winter Olympic medals during the same period).

In his book *Faust's Gold*, Steven Ungerleider[1] detailed an East German system that identified talent, segregated those kids into separate schools, and then as early as 13, began daily doses of steroids, mostly Oral Turinabol. We know all this information because the East Germans kept meticulous records, notating doping schedules, dosages, and results seen in performance. Most of the drug abuse concerned swimming, track and field, and weightlifting, which along with cycling, still contribute the most doping cases that persist today.

Students that asked questions were told the tablets or shots contained vitamins or "supporting substances" that helped recovery. When kids first arrived at these schools, the administrators sent letters to the parents, letting them know not to worry about their children taking pills each day, because the medications contained extra vitamins. The explanation: the schools couldn't afford enough fruit to provide developing athletes with the nutrition their growing bodies needed, so they had to give them pills instead. If a child complained or refused, they received disciplinary measures ranging from extra laps to push-ups, and in extreme cases, were sent home. If an athlete caused enough of a problem, the Stasi (the East German secret police), created a file on them and their family.

The same tactics, the same systematic organization of doping persists well after the cold war, both here and abroad. Kazakhstan shot to the tops of the international ranks after developing a weightlifting program in the early 2000s that led to multiple gold medals at the 2008 and 2012 Olympics. In 2016, the World Anti-Doping Agency (WADA) used new methods to indicate the presence of anabolic drugs and their metabolites in the urine "B" samples from lifters in that country (and 17 other nations). Four of Kazakhstan's gold medalists lost their medals: Zulfiya Chinshanlo, Maiya Maneza and Svetlana Podobedova, along with Ilya Ilyin, the latter widely considered the greatest weightlifter of all time.

In the United States, the pro-cycling team U.S. Postal/Discovery used Stasi-like tactics to enforce a code of silence and ruin the future cycling careers of anyone that threatened to talk or disclose what USADA (the US Anti-Doping Agency) called "the most sophisticated, professionalized and successful doping system" the sport has ever seen. US Postal cyclist Christian Vande Velde testified to USADA that Lance Armstrong pressured him to stick to a program of doping designed by team doctor Michele Ferrari, that included regular use of EPO and testosterone. When Vande Velde left and joined Liberty Seguros, he found they administered an organized doping program as well. That team referred to their doping as "recovery injections" and you either took them or you didn't ride.

WADA caught US weightlifter Norik Vardanian in those 2012 re-tests as well. Like his legendary weightlifting father Yurik, Norik started lifting at a young age. He grew up partly in America, with his father as his coach, but decided to compete at the 2012 Olympics for his dad's native country of Armenia. In one training video posted on YouTube, Norik snatched 180kg and clean and jerked 220kg, wearing a t-shirt overtop his unstrapped singlet. The current American records in the 94kg class at the time stood at 166 and 208; Norik opened heavier than these numbers at the 2012 Olympics and later set the snatch record for the United States at 172kg when he began competing for this country again.

Anyone in these countries, including Vardanian's Armenia, took drugs because they were given drugs. In a podcast with "The Two Doctors" in September of 2017,[2] Norik recalled that the doctors and teammates there referred to the steroids as "supplements," and no one "asked" him to take them. Doctors and trainers set the timetable, and dosages. Coaches, lab technicians and scientists helped to cover up tracks by tapering the athletes off of drugs by calculating half-lives and making sure certain "masking agents" helped hide any lingering indicators of performance enhancing drugs.

But no state-sponsored program asked me to use performance enhancing drugs. I started taking steroids because I won a high school power clean meet.

Las Vegas: 2005-2007

Every year, more than 30 high schools in Vegas competed against one another in a pair of meets that tested the bench press and the power clean. The competition took place in April or May and divided athletes into year in school (freshman, sophomore, junior, senior) and a rough assortment of weight classes.

The summer before my freshman year, my family moved from a small town in Massachusetts to Las Vegas. My stepdad Ken took me to the high school to check out the football schedule. I played football for years in Massachusetts, mostly as a fullback. But when I moved to Vegas, I encountered a whole new level of athleticism. Because of the warmer weather, kids could play, practice, and compete year-round. Despite my speed and quickness, the coaches at Del Sol, my new high school, moved me to offensive guard.

Our township had just built the Del Sol high school. Like much of the country in 2005, Vegas rode the high of the housing boom, with new developments springing up everywhere. Del Sol took advantage of a massive influx of residents, and featured brand new equipment, including a weight room filled with platforms and bumper plates.

Being dumb high school kids, we only used them for bench press, power cleans and back squats. And some deadlifts. But mostly bench press and power clean.

At Del Sol, the physical education department coordinated with the sports programs. In Massachusetts, the bullshit PE classes made us run or play dodgeball, even during weeks where we had games. In Vegas, one of my PE teachers asked if I played football. When I replied yes, he asked "Ok, instead of going to gym class every day, do you just want to lift weights?"

My eyes lit up and I think I said something ridiculous like "that would be the greatest thing ever." And that's how I started serious weight training. Which in Massachusetts had not gone well at all.

In eighth grade in Massachusetts, I was a horrible kid who suffered a lot of disciplinary problems. One of my friends went to a different middle school that fielded a standout football team.

Because the state offered school choice, I transferred there. Entry to the high school football program consisted of a combine that tested athletes in the 40-yard dash, jumps, cone drills and bench press. I remember kids banging out 275lbs for 2reps after smoking 225lbs for 12. My weak ass struggled to get 115lbs. When they tested my squat, everyone laughed because I could only do 115lbs, the lowest weight for an eighth grader.

The problem? I couldn't stand the pain of the bar on my neck, a far cry from ten years later when I blew up on Instagram with my squat 600lbs-a-day challenge. Ever since that eighth-grade embarrassment, I obsessed over squatting and getting my legs strong. The apartment complex where we lived didn't have any barbells, but the gym there included a leg press. which like a madman, I used every day that summer.

After we moved to Vegas, I hit the weight room with the freshman team. The first time I squatted in front of everyone I lifted 315, which at 14 years old, blew everyone's mind. I know Travis Cooper tells a story about maxing out for the first time at that age and doing 405lbs, but he had a coach that taught him how to squat. I went from a kid that couldn't even rest the bar on my back without pain to doing leg presses all summer in my apartment's gym, and then as a freshman out lifting some of the juniors and seniors in the high school.

The football and baseball teams had us perform power cleans, which I struggled to learn. But by the end of my freshman year, I power cleaned and benched 225lbs, squatted 405lbs, and realized I could be really fucking strong. Only two kids out lifted me: a pair of freshmen from Samoa that squatted 455lbs and benched 275lbs. But they were massive, unlike me, who went from a skinny 150lb guard to just over 200lbs body weight by the end of my freshman year. Now I only wanted to get bigger and stronger. Mostly bigger.

During ninth grade, I started on the freshman squad. But I really stayed with football to keep lifting weights. During the winter, I trained with the baseball team, but gave up baseball after one season. I remember talking to my stepdad Ken that summer and reflecting on playing a different sport each season. Even as a 14-year-old, I searched for a purpose, something I could excel at. I told him "you know what my problem is Ken? I'm good at baseball, I'm good at football, but I'm not great at either." And right then I decided to specialize, focusing on football as a way to keep lifting, and lifting weights to become great at football.

My sophomore year I started varsity and lifted year-round. I also competed in the power clean meet for the first time. Over 30 high schools in Vegas, and that May I took second overall in my weight class, competing in the 220lb category and power cleaning 290lbs. By the end of the school year I raised that number to 310, which matched my best bench press, and capped it off with a 550lb squat (in fairness, I only squatted to parallel).

During eleventh grade, I took supplements for the first time. I need to specify what I mean here. Jared Fleming's father Dave tells this great story about how he coached Jared at the 2011 Junior World Weightlifting Championships in Malaysia. After Jared snatched 158kg, a new American Junior record in the 94kg class, one of the Chinese coaches asked him "what supplements does your son take." Dave, understanding he meant "steroids" replied, "nothing."

When I say "supplements" I don't mean steroids either. I mean legal and quasi-legal products like NO Xplode, creatine, and pro-hormones. I began using the latter during the summer between tenth and eleventh grade.

I took NO Xplode for the first time my sophomore year, which I obtained from Mike, my "supplement guy" who owned Optiva Nutrition, a store near my high school. Mike sold me products, and I then sold them to everyone else in my high school, often carrying in five or six of the red bottles to school on any given week. My nickname was "Pat, the NO Xplode guy."

Some of the teachers knew about supplements—which meant they had a lot of wrong ideas—and called out the kids who took creatine and NO Xplode as cheaters. But fuck them. The first time I used NO Xplode, I was hooked. Winter of sophomore year, I trained with a one of the best juniors, who could lift more than me. In our coach's program, everything tailored off your one-rep max in the squat, power clean and bench, so he could do the 280lb progressions and I had to do the 250lb workout. But that morning, before weightlifting class, I took NO Xplode for the first time and I said to him "Hey, I'm going to do your workout." And I got it done faster. Moreover, I liked that NO Xplode made me feel jacked and unstoppable. So I sold it to my friends and teammates to pay for my own supply.

Mike sold me pro-hormones during the summer between my sophomore and junior year. Today everyone knows them from Mark McGuire and Barry Bonds. The second Bush administration ultimately banned them in the US, although plenty of distributors found ways to keep selling them. Despite the baseball controversy and the DEA regulations, no one definitively called them steroids, nor did anyone draw a hard-moral line around whether or not they constituted cheating.

But they sure made you strong. Initially, I took two products called H-Drol (Halodrol) and S-Drol (Superdrol). Each morning, I trained at school. In the evenings, I lifted with my little brother at a regular gym because he was too young for the school's weight room. I bench pressed every day that summer, packing on serious upper body mass. And every single day I felt stronger.

When football started I hadn't grown an inch from my 5'9" height, but now weighed 225lbs. We practiced from 7am to 12 every day, then a second session in the afternoon. After that, I ate and then worked out in my garage, where I kept a bench press and metal plates. Even during pre-season, I bench pressed and power cleaned, lowering the weights to the floor after every clean. That summer alone, my bench shot up from 310 to 405lbs.

It baffled me how much my bench press numbers plummeted when I stopped taking pro-hormones and stopped training during football season. We capped off a great fall with a strong win-loss record, and I earned all-conference and all-division honors my junior year. But my bench dropped to 345lbs. In my head, I thought, I'm going back on pro-hormones, because why should I waste my time training without them when I can just take them.

I always had this mentality. The only reason I played football is because I knew that I couldn't afford to go to college unless I earned a full ride, which was probably the only way I was gonna go to school at all. I saw these supplements as a way to get bigger and stronger than everyone else and have a way better shot of getting to the next level. And I knew that other kids in my school took them too, because for a lot of them, I was their "supplement guy."

The power clean meet my junior year changed everything.

That previous Spring, Billy Winn destroyed the old Vegas power clean record of 315lbs by lifting 330lbs. You might know Winn's name because he plays defensive line for the Denver Broncos. Back when I lifted against him, he competed for a rival high school and ranked among the top football recruits in the country. As a senior, he stood 6'6 and weighed 265lbs with sportswriters calling him the greatest prospect to ever come out of Vegas high school football.

And I wanted to take him down. We already fielded a kid in the 220 and 242lb weight category, and although I only weighed 237lbs, I volunteered to lift in the superheavy class against this mountain of a high schooler who already locked up a D-1 ride.

Over 3,000 screaming football players and their families packed the indoor arena at Las Vegas High for that power clean meet. I didn't lift in front of that many people again, nor that exciting of an audience until the 2011 Pan Am Games. Luckily for me, Winn didn't know who I was, and opened his power clean at a pretty comfortable 290lbs. Competition rules gave each of us three lifts, and a fourth attempt if we broke the state record.

Until that meet, I had only power cleaned 320lbs. But my coach told me to open at 330lbs, to fucking beat this guy, and I listened (notice that I already follow coach's orders). I crushed 330lbs, then went 340lb to tie his second attempt (and win on bodyweight). Then I smoked 345lbs to match him again, even though he benefitted from a controversial call. Since he attended Las Vegas High, who held the meet, they ruled in his favor after he racked 345lb just above parallel, and then spun a full 360-degrees trying to stand it up as it threatened to slip off his shoulders. Someone touched one of the plates during the lift, but they still gave it to him.

When I took 345lbs, no referee needed to give me the lift. I set up, drove hard and pulled. In the blink of an eye that bar shot to my shoulders. The entire crowd erupted, screaming and yelling, it was the fastest power clean I've ever done, I got it on my chest in an instant, it flew from my hips to my shoulders with no controversy. That day, I felt strong enough to clean over 400.

The next year, I returned as defending champion. And met John Broz for the first time.

My senior year of high school passed quickly. I started at guard for the third season in a row. After my junior year, the coaches and my teammates looked to me to step up, to lead the team on the field, the locker room and the weight room, and to bring everything I had on Friday night.

That year I made all-state at guard, and all-conference at defensive end. Despite that success, and my coaches pressuring college recruiters on my behalf, I only received one D-I NIAA scholarship, from Midland Lutheran in Nebraska. Because of NCAA rules, they offered me a partial ride, then an academic scholarship on top of it. The tuition still amounted to 37k a year, which my family couldn't afford. I don't blame any schools for overlooking me; given my 5'9" height and 272lbs bodyweight, I didn't fit the mold of a D-1 lineman, or defensive end.

In hindsight, I might have amounted to something more than a good high school football player if I stayed at fullback. We tried to impress recruiters at the combines, where I ran a 4.75 40-yard dash. I could move and cut and hit and set cone times faster than all of the bigger guards.

And I easily out lifted all of them. At one combine, I benched 455lbs, and smoked 225lbs for 37 reps. I squatted 600lbs, and could have lifted more, but during my junior year, I basically squatted 100lbs more than the next best guy at my school, so the coaches told me not to push the squat, because I didn't' need to be any stronger in that lift. I could squat 585lbs any time I wanted, all the way down, ass to grass.

At this point, I still hadn't executed a full clean, and power cleaned with a fist-grip (no hook) while wearing Nike high-tops.

Frustrated, I began skipping school and went to the gym all day to prepare for one last triumph at the power clean meet. Las Vegas high scheduled the competition for May, and in addition to attending intramural football practices to keep a bit of conditioning, I lifted weights every day for about 2 hours a day. At our school we followed an upper-lower split. On the core lifts of power clean, bench and squat, I did the 6, 6, 4, 4, 2, 2 program that consisted of 6 at 70%, 4 at 80%, 2 at 90%. I did these progressions for years. Boring, routine, regular. The perfect preparation for the Bulgarian method that dominated my training for a decade. Later, I understood just how perfectly Broz' method and this program aligned, both very powerful and very destructive.

I also didn't know that Broz saw me lift the year before. He had never recruited anyone from the power clean meets. That year though, he came looking.
Let me say a few early words about John Broz. He's just under 6'3 and weighs 260lbs. But he doesn't just walk into a room. He imposes himself on it. When he stands, no matter anyone else's height or size, he towers over people, dominating them in a way.

Once, after I had trained with Broz for years, this guy from California showed up. He talked a big game about wanting to train as a weightlifter, go full-Bulgarian, bought his own Eleiko bar, said he would devote his whole life to training. But he lifted like a pussy, and clarked the bar constantly on snatch attempts. One day we found out that he planned to open his own gym and was using Broz for months so that he could learn to teach weightlifting and say he trained there.

When Broz learned his secret, he backed the guy into a corner and in an even, low tone told him "Look. You are gonna snatch 135kg today and if you don't, you're out of the gym. And then you're going to pay me $250 for every week you've been here and I'm keeping your Eleiko bar." You could hear a pin drop in a room where nobody noticed 200kg cleans falling. We all thought Broz would bloody the guy's nose at any minute, when in reality, he never even raised his voice. But terrified, this dude paid in cash, fled back to California, and Broz kept his barbell.

So when I met Broz, it wasn't the traditional "hey, how you doing, I'm John, I own this gym." He shoulder bumped me and said, "think you'll clean 400lbs this year?" It wasn't a question so much as a challenge, and I said something stupid like "yeah, maybe when I'm the world's strongest man." I had no idea that teenagers younger and much lighter than me could regularly clean and sometimes snatch that weight. At that point, I didn't even know what a snatch was.

The competition passed in a blur. I won, easily setting the state power clean record again. Afterwards, Broz stopped by and talked with me, my friend Taylor Smith, and Rob Addell, who played football for a local school and who I trained with at a globo gym. Taylor and Broz exchanged phone numbers and Broz invited all of us to this gym-like area he set-up at his granite business. Broz told us he could get us stronger for football and improve our technique as well.

On June 13, 2008, the three of us dropped in at Broz' granite business. Broz showed us some Iron Mind videos of people lifting, and I saw a snatch for the first time. Until then, I never knew weightlifting was a sport, let alone an Olympic one.

But I bought in quickly. With no football scholarships and no real prospects, I decided to start weightlifting. Every day, like I had been, now just more focused, and with different lifts.

Broz immediately started me on two-a-day workouts and by August, I trained twice a day every day. In the morning, I worked up to a 250kg back squat for one single. I racked up hundreds of mornings where I squatted 250kg or more that first year. If John stayed in his office that day and could watch me, I performed some light lifts. Otherwise, I tried to improve my mobility. Years of bench pressing left me with rigid shoulders, tight traps and lats. It took months before I could rack a bar on my shoulders in the clean, front squat or jerk without pain. Literally. That 365lb power clean? I caught it with open hands about four inches above my chest. And held it there as a stadium full of people screamed at me.

With the exception of the squats, I learned the lifts with an empty bar or PVC pipe. Most days, Broz showed me videos, of Bulgarian world champions or of Hossein Reza Zadeh clean and jerking over 550lbs. Clip after clip of these massive lifts that I couldn't imagine doing. Every night I went home and watched more videos on YouTube. My friends smoked weed each night, and I used to join them. But one comment from Broz about pot being bad for lifting, and I stopped instantly. When John said get a pair of weightlifting shoes, I ordered them that night.

Broz impressed me tremendously as a person. He owned his own business, he succeeded in multiple fields and then as an entrepreneur. He lifted a fuck ton, had married a smoking hot former model and he fueled this desire in me that had always wanted to break records.

When I was a kid, I owned a framed, signed photo of Emmitt Smith, who held all the NFL rushing records. And I wanted to do that. To set records. Once I started breaking high school records as a freshman, I worked to beat the sophomore records, then the school records. I obsessed over these objective numbers. Weightlifting suited that mindset perfectly.

Rob and Taylor quickly dropped out of training, but I pushed through double sessions. Once I understood basic technique, in the afternoons John and I both worked to maxes in the snatch and clean and jerk. Six days a week, plus squatting, true Bulgarian method.

Broz first talked to me about my prospects in weightlifting when I back squatted 195kg for a fast triple. He had this theory that whatever you could back squat for a triple in under 5.0 seconds, you could clean and jerk. Once a week we worked on those fast triples; his best was 190kg. Broz was very emphatic about speed squats, and when I hit five kilos over his best, he told me I had potential.

I talked to John about pro-hormones in August, two months into training with him as my coach. That summer, a friend of mine from high school started bodybuilding and began taking steroids. He kept trying to sell me the same drugs, mostly to fund his own usage, and I responded with "dude, I'm not taking steroids, that's fucking crazy." But he argued back that I had already trained on pro-hormones, which amounted to the same thing. "Bullshit," I told him, "you can buy pro-hormones in a store; steroids you go to jail just for owning them."

So I asked Broz about it. I want to be very clear, that I initiated the conversation, asking him what he thought about pro-hormones and steroids.

Broz has this talk he gives to any new lifter he works with, about goals and records, and what to shoot for. Say you walk into his gym and you're Angela Parra and you can snatch 85kg as a 58kg female lifter. He will tell you that doesn't mean anything because even though the national record is 90kg (at the time), the world record stands at 116kg. And when you begin weightlifting, your goal can't be to just qualify for National Championships or win that meet or set American records. Your goal is the world records; otherwise, whatever else you do in the sport doesn't mean shit.

During that conversation, Broz let me know in no uncertain terms that every person I saw in those Iron Mind videos, whether Russian, or Bulgarian or Chinese or Greek, they all used steroids. Every world record was set by a drug user.

The guy winning the gold medal? On steroids. The women too. That's the sport.

"The sport is steroids."

If you want to compete with them, if you want to break someone's records, you have to do what they did. You must take steroids. He laid it out very black and white; he was never going to lie to me and say "if you just work real darn hard, you can do it without drugs" Broz isn't like that.

Years later, talking about that conversation with my wife Taylor, we discussed whether he should have engaged in that conversation with an impressionable 17-year old kid. She argued that she would have appreciated his honesty. That when she got to the world level, she would have wanted to know well ahead of time the truth, so that she didn't sit there and wonder "why do I suck so bad" and question her work ethic or training. After all, the world record in the 48kg category is a 98kg snatch, a full 15kg heavier than the US national record. Morghan King, the American who snatched 83kg, can barely compete on the same stage, in the same A-session. In Taylor's mind, she wouldn't want to compare herself to someone who's playing a game in a way that she's not playing it.

My feelings are mixed. I don't resent what Broz told me that day. If I have a son, I won't' tell Pat Jr, at age eight that you need drugs to do this sport. But I will tell him when he's old enough.

While Broz didn't sugarcoat the sport, he also didn't say "You have to take this and this." The conversation asked: "If you want to compete at the highest level, if you want to break world records. Then yes, you will need to take steroids."

And I just said "OK"

In my mind, that is. That conversation didn't end with me asking Broz where to buy drugs. It didn't end with "How can I get away with this?" I heard what he said, and I internalized it as a clear decision: "I'm going to take steroids. I don't know when, I don't know how. But I'm going to figure out how to get this done."

At this point, I'm 18 and John is a 40-year old man that I've only known for two very intense months But I'm ready to fire on all cylinders. I've set my sights on world records. In my head, that now means I'm ready to start taking steroids. The decision has been made.

If you want to know how I arrived at that choice so easily, you only need to know how I grew up and how I planned to get out of there.

Two:
Origins

You want to know my history and what drove me? When I was 17, a guy passed away in our living room. My junkie mother stood there and gaped, pill-crazed out of her mind as I performed CPR on him. I heard his ribs crack under the force of my fists. For over five minutes, I pushed into his chest until the ambulance showed up. The EMT's had to pull me off the guy, and I collapsed in disbelief and exhaustion as he died on the floor in front of me.

That episode sums up my childhood. And it's just one incident. A lot of other athletes in weightlifting grew up in shitty backgrounds. When asked what led him to weightlifting, Chinese World Champion Lu Xiaojun claimed in an interview that he saw a promotional reel about the sport as a child. The video showed the weightlifting athletes eating beef. He never ate beef regularly, so he went into weightlifting to get some.

Other weightlifters grew up with money. Brazil's Fernando Reis? Wealthy. Dmitri Klokov? His family is loaded.

In a question and answer at the 2016 USA National Championships, four-time Olympic medalist Pyrros Dimas told a story about being pulled out of an orchard where he was stealing fruit. The guy turned out to be a weightlifting coach and took him to training to "keep him out of trouble."

The background drives the athlete. I was no different.

During the height of the Cold War[3] between the USA and the Soviet Union, physician Robert Goldman formulated a survey question: Would you take an undetectable performance enhancing drug if it guaranteed Olympic gold but would kill you within five years? He asked elite American athletes that question, and with surprising regularity for a social science questionnaire, the average "yes" answer hovered at over 50% for more than 15 straight years.

Goldman's dilemma, as it were, might be unnecessary, at least in terms of the well-documented consequences of performance enhancing drugs. Athletes that use PED's experience a host of detrimental side effects. In follow ups with the female athletes from the East German system, the author of *Faust's Gold* reported effects ranging from menstrual pain and ovarian cysts to infertility; many former East German athletes gave birth to children with clubbed feet and early-onset heart disease.

And still, athletes from East Germany won 176 medals in the 1976 Olympics, while their genetic brethren from West Germany scored a paltry 39. In a decades-later follow-up that detailed the health consequences, some of the athletes' Ungerleider interviewed took the attitude of "Who cares? We won, didn't we?"

In men, anabolic steroids can cause acne, hair loss, gynecomastia (male breast development) and mood swings, especially when coming off drugs. Those are the minor effects. Major complications include liver disease, Peliosis hepatis (formation of blood-filled cysts in the liver), high blood pressure, kidney failure and heart disease. All of those can kill you. And yet…

If you asked me Goldman's dilemma now, the answer is obvious and clear. I'm 30, I own a beautiful home in Texas and have a bright future as one of my industry's top national salesperson.

But at 17 when I made the decision to use? Back then I shared one thing in common with Dimas: sports became that thing in my life that gave me direction and showed me success. At the time, it was the only path leading to *any* possible future.

Massachusetts and Las Vegas: 1996-2007

My wife Taylor is probably the first person I could talk to about my rotten upbringing. Before I met her, if someone asked me about my childhood, I replied "it was pretty good." But after many late-night talks with her, I started realizing that most kids don't go through shit that I did. Most kids had a parent that could guide them. And few, after hearing my story, would look back and think *"yeah, my childhood was pretty normal."*

My mom worked endlessly. She was the breadwinner, and a good one, earning six figures as a nurse, mostly at hospitals. From the age of six, my memories consist of seeing her leave for work each morning wearing scrubs, putting on make-up at the breakfast table, drinking her coffee, basically passing by us kids in life as she went off to work. Between her commute and the long shifts, she returned home 12 to 14 hours later and went to bed.

She worked in nursing homes and hospitals, and eventually became director of nursing for a senior center. That job provided stability when I was a kid, and income wise, it was way above most parents in our neighborhood. Until I turned six, I primarily remember one home, in Marlborough, Massachusetts. Wherever we lived, we always stayed in the biggest house on the block. This one featured skylights over enormous rooms, way more space than we needed, and I remember liking it right up until we moved. We must have lived in half a dozen homes before I turned 13 and we moved seven times between my freshman and senior year of high school.

Why did we move so much? Besides being a little stir crazy, my mom indulged in terrible spending habits. She never saved money, always overleveraged herself and never paid down her debt. She lived paycheck to paycheck, and to keep up with bills and constant purchases, my mom always held more than one job—sometimes in violation of nursing regulations, and always without the hospitals knowing. And she worked way too many hours. No matter where we lived, my parents never owned because neither of them had the credit for a mortgage.

We moved from Marlborough to Northborough, and when I turned seven, we stayed at a house in Hubbardston. I remember this house as the last time my dad lived with us. He was Brazilian by birth, which gave me dual citizenship in that country—a huge benefit after my first doping sanction. Dad worked weird, odd jobs; at one point he delivered newspapers, and sold phone cards to mini marts. I often accompanied him on his newspaper route.

When certain birthdays or anniversaries arrive, and I get angry about the past, my wife reminds me that my dad was the only person I ever felt love from as a child. He displayed affection in a family where I never really saw my mom for more than five minutes at a time, and more than anything as a kid, I wanted his love and approval.

While dad frittered about with his side-gigs, my older brother and sister looked out for me. They were both stepsiblings, each from a different dad, with my younger brother and I descended from the same father. My one brother was five years older than me, and my sister seven years older. They had to fend for themselves but helped with my homework and studying. I think they played a big role in my aptitude for learning; I would do math with them as a kid, and they'd teach me to read, how to learn quick, and studied right along with me.

Like a Montessori school in an insane asylum.

My parent's marriage unraveled after we moved to Hubbardston. I was seven when the police arrested my dad on the front lawn of our house. He drove drunk with us in the car, and we peered through the front window as they put him in cuffs. Between his drinking and my mom's over-working, over-spending and eventual bipolar diagnosis, our house didn't provide a safe environment for anyone.

When I talk to my dad now, and when I briefly stayed with him while training for the Brazilian National Team, he told me her spending habits led to the divorce. Her need to overwork to cover debts prevented him from pursuing a career or earning anything resembling an adult living. Back then, we just thought mom worked, and dad did odd jobs to stay at home with us. Maybe that's the only thing I had in common with other kids: that my parents kept secrets to maintain that thin veneer of normalcy over the tempest beneath the surface.

Once dad moved out, I transformed from conscientious good student into a thug. Teachers couldn't get the last word; the bus driver threw me off for fighting. I raged for attention, disrupted class, put gum in someone's hair. Once, I tied a kid to his bus seat and he missed his stop and cried for an hour.

I was that child that wanted to make sure people knew who I was. I threw rocks at passerby, beat up neighborhood kids, spray-painted and vandalized, and had the cops called to our house on more than one occasion. Because of my outbursts, I stopped playing sports for over a year.

That break cost me. As a teen, I buried all my problems in sport, centering my focus on whatever game I played each season. I did that since age six, when my dad introduced me to soccer. Being Brazilian, it mattered to him that I play the game. But when my parents divorced, I took a year off, mostly because my mom worked too much and couldn't take me to practice.

My dad moved to Worcester, into this shitty 450 square-foot apartment with little room for us kids. My three siblings and I stayed in Hubbardston, along with my mom and my great grandmother (who I also watched die in our house). Initially, I saw my dad every weekend. Then every other weekend. Then once a month turned into every two months, then three times a year, until over time, we looked forward to seeing him at Christmas. To his credit, he never missed a child support payment.

Soon enough, my mom met this guy Ken, who worked at her hospital. Ken had a nursing degree and demonstrated a ridiculously accurate memory for trivia. We watched Jeopardy at night and Ken rattled off the answers before Alex Trebek finished reading the questions. But he never managed to pass his nursing boards, which perfectly suited the way my mom needed a man in her life.

Mom and Ken married within a year of dating. Ken was lazy and later revealed some nasty habits of his own. But he introduced me to baseball, where I displayed a natural athleticism. About a half hour before my first practice, Ken told me about the tryouts. "I don't have a glove" I mumbled. Ken pulled one from the trunk and we threw a baseball around for 30 minutes.

Massachusetts organized baseball like the only sport worth playing. Kids as young as eight competed for spots on teams organized around talent and ability, and tryouts reflected that hyper-competitive culture. They divided little league into the majors and the minors; at the first practice, I was one of only two third graders selected for the "major" team.

Ken reintroduced me to sports. He stabilized our home life and was the difference maker for a long time. Even though I didn't settle down in school, sports at least wore me out. I started American football at age nine, played basketball each winter, and baseball during the spring. One season I competed for three different baseball teams, leaving home at 7AM and not returning until after 9PM. Sports provided an outlet for my anger, an object for my intense focus, and a way to bury emotion. I continued this three-sport schedule for years, until we had to move because my older brother burned some poor dude's face off.

I wish I could make this stuff up.

My older brother was the black sheep of the family, a super nice guy always falling under the influence of the wrong people. He started smoking at 18 and had to repeat his senior year because he missed graduation by one credit. The next fall, he re-enrolled in high school, but one day he stole my grandmother's Ativan and took a handful. That morning, mom and Ken forced him to go to school and he passed out in the hallway. The school suspended him for 10 days after which he said, "fuck it" and dropped out entirely. My mom's nursing home hired him. As a "smoking supervisor."

Again, not kidding. His job entailed lighting cigarettes for the residents, which paid $13 an hour (in 2005). My wife and I still can't believe that was a real position. Unfortunately for one unlucky patient, his granddaughter came to visit, and she lit his cigarette for him, not realizing the tubes running into his nose circulated oxygen.

The guy's face caught fire, causing severe burns and disfigurements. His family filed a lawsuit against the hospital, against my mom and against my brother. Mom lost her nursing license in the state of Massachusetts, and that's how we ended up in Vegas.

At least that's the reason she gave us. Mom picked Vegas as a destination because her voided nursing license didn't count against her employment in Nevada. She also picked Vegas because three years earlier, she and Ken bought a timeshare on an impulse purchase, and the next summer, the entire family traveled there for a two-week vacation.

That vacation lasted four days. When mom met Ken, he was a recovering alcoholic, long-time sober, but with an itch to scratch. Mom gave Ken the food expense and spending money for the entire two weeks. Ken blew it all in one night at the casino. We didn't know where he went, couldn't reach him for a day. His losses left us stranded in Vegas with no money, trapped in a timeshare, and no funds to change our flights.

Vegas real estate still sold cheap then and mom and Ken headed out there to potentially buy a trailer. That week, I get a call—I'm a teenager, mind you—and my mom asks, "Hey Pat, what do you think about moving to Nevada." And I replied "Well, if it's Vegas, let's do it."

Once we settled in, Ken took me to the high school to sign up for football. That summer, I worked out every day in our apartment complex gym, mostly leg presses and benching. I took my little brother along. It helped me bond with him; he was chubby then and idolized me. To this day, he's still the only member of my family that has ever seen me lift.

In Vegas, I excelled at football, and gave up other sports. Mom maintained her old habits of overworking and began self-medicating. She would quit or get fired from one job and quickly get another. Pilfering pills became second nature. Ken turned a blind eye, staying home and cleaning and baking long after we needed him to care for us, just so he could avoid getting a job.

In school, I earned high marks, even without trying. I've always possessed an excellent memory, and my single-mindedness let me study one thing for a long time, until I felt like I mastered it. Our high school named me student of the semester, and the teacher that recommended me wrote this article saying I would go places and become this modern Renaissance Man, because I could rack up 20 tackles in a single game and do calculus.

Vegas' transient culture didn't encourage high expectations…

I didn't always do my own schoolwork. A cute girl that liked me wrote a few of my book reports and one of the football players worked as a student aid for a teacher and changed her record books to ensure that the entire team got A's. School guards caught my best friend Jason and I leaving the grounds for lunch; they punished him with "school beautification." Because I started varsity, my "punishment" was to head to football practice.

Mostly, I kept up my grades for eligibility, and my mom and Ken didn't give a shit about anything else. My friends and I partied and smoked weed on the weekends. I could crawl into bed after drinking myself to oblivion. As long as I earned A's or B's, no one cared.

Despite this success, I almost didn't graduate. The summer between my junior and senior year, my mom and Ken fought constantly over his lack of income. Ken convinced my mom that his brother would give him a job in Texas, and he could work, and she could stop putting in 70-hour weeks to pay bills.

Of course, there was no job. But I had to decide between finishing my senior year in Vegas or move to Texas. My friend Jason solved the problem: I could stay at the house he shared with his brother and his mother, Virginia.

Virginia became a real mom to me. She held me accountable, forced me to take the SAT's and apply to colleges. Jason and I both thought about enrolling in San Diego State, which his brother attended, and where I could play football as a walk-on.

Living with Virginia helped me realize I could have a future. My wife Taylor couldn't understand why I thought I had a pretty decent childhood, but I owe that sentiment to Virginia. All the shit that's happened to me: the divorce, the drunken dad and pill-popping mom, everything that everyone else might see as a negative, I've always put a positive spin on. If I didn't live with Virginia the first time, I would have quit studying after football season; I wouldn't have applied to any colleges at all, or even thought about going in that direction.

When my mom and Ken moved back in February after their jobs fell through in Texas, I made a huge mistake and moved back in with them. I only needed one class to graduate, so even though I enrolled in AP Calculus, I dropped it. In the morning, I drove to school and stared at the building, unable to force myself to go inside. Instead, I headed to Lifetime fitness, and lifted weights to prepare for the power clean meet.

My senior year, my mom transitioned into home health nursing, a mandatory career change because hospitals kept firing her.

Medicine would go missing and she was the prime suspect. Instead of fighting the charges, she switched jobs, then fell into home health nursing because it eliminated any boss or investigator looking over her shoulder. Now she could take an insane amount of drugs—mostly opiates—and still work.

She ended up caring for Mark Eddleston. He was a millionaire who traded stocks and bonds over the Internet from his trailer. And he was absolutely the most disgusting person I've ever encountered. At 5'2", he weighed 365lbs.

He hired me to take care of his wounds. Not bedsores. Open, festering wounds on his legs.

Despite being loaded—I saw his bank statements—he acted cheap. Mark initially hired my mom to provide him care, but something happened with his insurance; the coverage expired, and he didn't want to pay the $90/hour my mom charged, so he paid me $45 per visit instead.

My mom never took us to the doctors when we were kids. She always performed any medical care we needed, and if we required drugs or antibiotics, she stole them from the hospital. I learned from her how to clean and dress cuts, and how to administer CPR. Mark suffered from these massive, open sores on his legs—the result of edema—and he had congestive heart failure from obesity and water retention. He knew he was going to die.

While my mom lived in Texas, I took care of him, driving to his trailer multiple times each week to dress and clean his injuries. For two or three hours of work, I earned $135, great money for a kid staying in his friend's basement.

When mom moved back, Mark asked if he could move in with us, because he didn't want to die alone. She took him in—in part because he promised to leave her all his money—and also because he paid us $1000/month in rent. He stayed in his own room in our new house, and boom, now Ken has a job because Mark paid him for home health care. For three months, Ken fed him and wiped his ass and cleaned his sores. Despite Ken's care, the longer Mark stayed in our home, the more disgusting he became; between his bedsores and his general smell and not being able to bathe, he just reeked of this constant foul odor.

One night we heard Mark pacing. He couldn't sleep. Mark told us he had a premonition that if he went to bed he wouldn't wake up and he didn't want to fall asleep and die. Mark slipped and fell in his room. Ken and I raced over to help him. During the stress of trying to stand and the anxiety of fearing death, he suffered a massive heart attack. Ken and I tried to lift him into bed and Mark started convulsing. He shit himself, his heart exploded, and he slipped out of our grasp onto the floor.

Ken called 911, and I started CPR. But Mark was gone. An ambulance came and took the body. The police arrived, but we gave them a great cover: my mom's a nurse, he's her patient.

That's how a guy died in my house senior year. Pretty normal, right?

While he stayed with us, Mark drove around on this $5,000 electric wheelchair, and after his death I had some fun with it. I rode it to the grocery store, and people asked if I needed help getting things off the shelf. Picture this 270lb kid that can back squat 600lbs driving a dead man's wheelchair around the local Acme.

I can joke about it now, but his death changed the course of my entire life. For the next two weeks, I fell asleep to the echo of Mark's ribs cracking under my fists. I shot up in bed, woken from dreams about botched CPR, staring into Mark's eyes, watching the life disappear from them. His death occurred right when I tried to figure out what to do with my life. One of those nights I decided that hey, I'm not attending school anymore.

At age 17, Goldman's dilemma stared me in the face with obvious consequences: Live how you want or die with regrets.

Mark's death taught me that I'm only alive for so long and could die at any time. I had two choices: live a shitty life along the path others set out for me or find one thing that I really want to do and pursue it with a singular passion. Ever since this guy died with me literally breaking his ribs trying to save him, I have never looked back on my decision. I have always done whatever I wanted, to the nth degree, and with a point on it.

So when I decided to do steroids, I went all in No matter the consequences.

Three:
Learning to Lift

July 2017: Nat Arem—the owner of Hookgrip—sat down in a Massachusetts diner to interview Ilya Ilyin, Kazakhstan's two-time Olympic and four-time World Champion.[4] Nat asked Ilya to give a timeline of the weight he lifted in the snatch and clean and jerk.

A Vegas bookie could place odds on the time Ilya began using performance enhancing drugs. And make no mistake. Two re-tests in 2016 indicated that Ilya took steroids for years.[5]

Ilya first picked up a barbell at six and started serious training at age eight—not uncommon for a future international caliber weightlifter. At 11, he weighed 44kg and in competition snatched 42kg and clean and jerked 60kg. By age 13, he progressed into the 69kg weight class and hit a 105kg snatch and a 142kg C&J. These results earned him the title "Master of Sport," a level in the former-Soviet ranking system that indicated a lifter's technical mastery and progress relative to benchmark totals.[6] Armenian legend Yurik Vardanian accomplished this feat by the same age; I've heard that Russian World record holder Tatiana Kashirina matched that timeline as well.

At 14, Ilya won the 2003 Asian Youth Championships by snatching 117kg and clean and jerking 165.5kg to set a new Asian Youth record in the 14-15-year-old, 69kg bodyweight category. (Note that this is a 152lb, 14-year-old boy pulling 370lbs from the floor to his shoulders and then locking it out over his head.) By the next year's Asian Youth Championships, Ilya bulked up to

85kg, and took gold by pairing a 142kg snatch to a 187kg clean and jerk.

The next year (2004) he smashed the Junior World records in the 85kg category by snatching 170kg and clean and jerking a SENIOR world record of 216kg at that year's World Weightlifting Championships. He won this meet at 17, destroying men 10 or more years his senior. His Junior World record total of 386kg still stands, 16 years later.

Bookies could set decent odds on 2004 as the year Ilya began taking steroids. He was 15-16 at the time. Again, there is no doubt that Ilya at one point ingested performance enhancing drugs. The International Olympic Committee stripped him of both his 2008 and 2012 Olympic gold medals in 2016 after re-tests of his urine samples from those Games indicated the presence of long-term metabolites of the steroid hormones Oral Turinabol and Stanozolol,[7] the latter notorious as the substance that disqualified Canadian sprinter Ben Johnson from his Gold-medal, world-record performance at the 1988 Seoul Olympics.

Several other Kazakh lifters tested positive during the re-examination of the Olympic samples, including Mariya Grabovetskaya, Maya Maneza. Svetlana Podobedova, Irina Nekrassova, Vladimir Sedov and world-record holder Zulfiya Chinshanlo.[8]

While multiple Kazakh lifters testing positive doesn't *necessarily* confirm the presence of a state-sanctioned program, a smart gambler wouldn't stack the odds against it. And yes, 14 or 15 seems young to begin administering steroid hormones and other performance-enhancing drugs to international caliber youth athletes.[9] But Kazakhstan could find good company; young teens from Thailand, India and Egypt have all tested positive recently, and Ilya wouldn't rank as the youngest.

At the 2011 Youth Weightlifting World Championships, seven teenagers from Thailand tested positive, including future 2016 Olympic Gold Medalist Sukanya Srisurat (then 16). During the

2017 African Youth and Junior Championships, seven Egyptian weightlifters tested positive for banned substances, including two 14-year-old girls and three teenage boys. I should note that at the supposedly "clean" 2017 Weightlifting World Championships, Thailand bested all countries for most medals won (Srisurat took silver). Second place Iran took 14 total medals; they've clearly advanced from 2006, when nine of 11 athletes at their national training facility tested positive for steroids after doping agents showed up unannounced.[10] And Egypt scored six medals total, including a gold and bronze place podium finish.

Toward the end of the Hookgrip interview, the waitress dropped off the check, telling them to "enjoy the rest of their night," oblivious to the camera and microphone, and without any knowledge that she waited on one of the greatest strength athletes in history that night (no doubt she would have recognized Tom Brady or Kobe Bryant).

I don't mention Ilya's positive drug tests to bash him. In my opinion, he is the true GOAT, the best lifter ever, period. I competed against him in the 105kg A-session at the 2014 World Championships, and even now I consider him a colleague.

I bring up Ilya's dramatic increases because I know what it's like to undergo those same rapid progressions. What he achieved in his mid to late teens, I experienced in about 20 months' time (from age 18 to 20). But while Ilya benefited from a country that poured millions of dollars into its national federation's structured, systemic approach, I had to figure out doping all on my own. And I erred often, and costly in the process.

Las Vegas: Summer and Fall 2008

I didn't jump right into steroids, like some couch potato who thinks a pill will magically transform him into a *Men's Health* cover model. I needed to learn how to lift. In hindsight, I realize how stupid that sounds; few athletes start learning weightlifting with a 600lb back squat and a 365lb power clean. I could have muscle snatched 100kg my first day if Broz didn't insist on me learning the lifts correctly.

By August of 2008, I stopped taking the pro-hormones, but ramped up the volume of training considerably. About six weeks into training, Broz started me on two-a-days, with morning and afternoon sessions. We kept the intensity light at first; he took the attitude of "hey, just get into the gym more than once a day, to warmup, and work on your mobility."

And I had a lot of mobility work to do. During the entire summer, I arrived at Broz' gym in the morning early. Every day, Broz worked me up to a 250kg (550lb) back squat. I didn't hit that number on Day One. Broz puts a lot of emphasis on being a good squatter and by his standards, I sucked at squatting. High school football programs don't always emphasize full depth or speed, and Broz demanded both.

Initially, my squat went down as I worked on range of motion and mechanics. During my first squat session with Broz in July, I did 220kg (484lbs), but not to full depth. By August I had squatted 240kg for a triple, then 255kg, then 260kg for a few singles during different workouts. Broz didn't typically go in for volume in the squats except as back off sets; the goal was to get to the heaviest weight in as few sets as possible, hit a single there, and then do drop sets or move on. If a rep looked slow, that was it, you were done for the day.

Slow in the squats means something specific for Broz. After a few months of daily squatting, John pulled out a stopwatch. "We're going to do triples, as fast as you can. If you can finish the entire set in under 5.2 seconds, we'll try a heavier weight." When I did 195kg (430lbs) for a triple in under that 5.2s time cap, Broz got excited.

In all his years of training, Broz had never done more than 190kg that fast. Two months of just squatting and now he's telling me I had potential. (Years later, Nat Arem would show the Kazakhstan head coach a video of me squatting 250kg for a triple in less than

5 seconds. The Kazakh coach said it was the most impressive strength feat he had ever seen.) After the 195kg triple, Broz blurted out "that's unbelievable." He wanted to put more weight on and continue testing my ability to produce force rapidly.

We talked for hours that day about my future. I remember two things distinctly and thought about them for years. Broz said, "some people are born to lift weights, some aren't," and "some people want to lift weights, but they can't." To my 18-year-old mind, those words signified a challenge, a promise and a moral imperative. I began to envision a destiny. And I had to fulfill it.

While I learned how to squat fast singles each morning, I barely used any weight in the snatch or C&J. In many interviews, Broz discussed how he trains a new lifter. He gives them a PVC pipe or has them work with an empty bar for a month. His goal is to instill a mental engram, a pattern of movement over 1,000s of empty bar reps. Lifters that undergo this process will develop a feel for a good bar path and proper mechanics, uninhibited by their strength.

I also think that method weeds out people who might waste Broz' time. It definitely built upon the discipline that football and daily weight training already gave me. That summer after my senior year, all my friends partied, prepared for college and hooked up. Me? I lifted in a sweaty gym for six hours a day, concentrating on learning a complex movement with an empty barbell for rep after rep after rep. Hundreds and thousands of reps that first six months.

Through July and August, we gradually added weight. By the end of August, I squatted every day, twice a day. I worked to a fast single each morning then performed full lifts and more squats in the afternoon. If Broz couldn't watch, I didn't go heavy, just accumulated reps.

By October 2008, four months after learning what a snatch was, I smoked 137kg, and cleaned 182kg. That's when Broz scheduled my first competition.

And then the meltdown happened.

We planned for a local meet on Halloween, with me, Broz, my football buddy Taylor Smith and one other lifter. I use the term "other lifter" generously, because it was this guy Tyler, who basically just hung around the gym. Broz knew him for years; Tyler was a 30-year old barback, who left the Marines, lived in a shitty studio apartment and trained sporadically at Broz'. We considered him a true ABGOG (Average Broz' Gym Original Gangster)—what we eventually called the nucleus of people that formed today's well-known brand at Average Broz' Gym.

A few weeks before the competition, Broz tore a rotator cuff muscle. When I met John, he still considered himself an athlete. Getting myself, and my football buddies Taylor Smith and Robb Addell to lift at his gym gave him training partners first and athletes to coach second. (In fairness, plenty of well-respected coaches have formed clubs with the same approach.)

Broz lifted with us whenever it fit his schedule. One day he challenged me to see who could hit a heavier clean. I weighed about 120kg, Broz about 110kg, so we judged weight over bodyweight. He smoked 150kg, I took 160kg. He cleaned 155, I went to 170. Then I pushed up to 182 and Broz ripped 160 from the floor and misracked it, his lats flaring out like a turtle's shell as he struggled to stand up. A loud "pop!" rung from a snap in his upper back. Broz yelled and dropped the bar. His shoulder tore and the swelling prevented him from lifting his arm over his head the rest of the day. But we planned to compete on Halloween, and he pushed through and trained what he could.

The competition was held in Utah, a few hours' drive. Broz rented a minivan and told us to meet at the gym Halloween morning. Fifteen minutes go by, then a half hour, and me, Taylor and Tyler just stood on the pavement outside Broz' granite business waiting for him. An hour later Broz finally showed. He looked like he got hit by a bus.

Any other time, Broz strode into a room like a wall of granite, imperious like an emperor and standoffish like a statue. But that day I saw his shoulders slumped, and he could barely eke out a whimper when he spoke.

That morning, his then-wife surprised him in his driveway with divorce papers. I didn't even know they separated, aside from occasional comments about "problems" and what a bitch she was. Whenever she stopped by the gym, we all gaped, responding in cracked, squeaky voices to her cordial questions. Picture hulking teenagers humbled by a hot girl, like straight out of a teenage rom-com.

To us, she was just Broz' super-hot wife. A former model, now a service-industry girl in Vegas that pulled in serious bank. Broz met and married her when they lived in Minnesota, and she moved to Vegas with him. They spent almost a decade together. Later I heard that Broz hired a private investigator, dug up some real dirt. Another man had been involved and that morning she just wanted out. To my knowledge, Broz never saw her again.

Broz insisted we do the meet. So here we are, two teenagers (and this weirdo Tyler) super amped to compete and now sitting silently in the back of a minivan like punished children while "dad" drove us to Utah. Felt just like my childhood.

We arrived at the venue, a high school gymnasium in Utah. Rusty water fountains, bathrooms with the stall walls cut in half, and the warm-up area…basically 8x4 plywood sheets screwed together for the day. Random and mismatched plates littered the floor, like the meet directors asked every local lifter to bring their shitty bars and ratchet weights. People who just joined USA Weightlifting cannot fathom the difference in local competitions from just 10 years ago.

This meet took place before Crossfit, and three years into YouTube. Instagram didn't exist, and kids just started adding profiles to this relatively new site called Facebook. No one watched weightlifting, less people promoted it, so I just accepted it as the reality of a local comp. Shit, I just learned how to snatch with an empty barbell four months earlier. We weighed in, grabbed a platform and warmed up.

Broz explained how a weightlifting competition functioned. All lifters received three attempts in the snatch, and three in the clean and jerk. The highest total in each weight class won that category. If a lifter succeeded on an attempt, they could go up, by as little as 1kg. A lifter that missed a weight with attempts remaining could repeat or add weight to the bar. A one-, or two-minute clock governed the amount of time between each attempt, dependent on if any other competitors asked for the same weight.

Although I had lifted 137kg and 182kg in training, I opened conservatively and snatched 125kg and C&J'ed 160kg. Not bad for a rookie. Broz destroyed my total, despite his torn rotator cuff. I don't know if anger or despair put the numbers on the bar for him that day, but looking back on a decade of competition, I know one thing held true: no matter what other shit goes down in life, the barbell, it centers you. You grab it with both hands, and the knurling shakes your hand right back. The iron reminds you of who you are, where you've been and what you know you can do. Its touch obliterates all other considerations, and the setup locks you in to a mindset of ferocity and determination. Broz screamed with fury on every lift, smoking a 135kg snatch and matching me in the C&J at 160kg.

That day left me hungry. In 2008, those numbers qualified me for Junior Nationals and Senior National Championships in the 105kg+ weight class. I got my first taste of a pursuit that dominated the next decade of my life. And I loved it. Weightlifting gives you the chance to express your strength—using a number that ranks and levels all men and women. And this sport asks you to do it with two movements that require supreme athleticism and technical perfection.

We drove home in a much different mood. Broz still took the wheel, but now the four of us laughed, spoke excitedly about the lifts we made—and missed—and Broz told us war stories of past competitions and living with and learning from Antonio Krastev when they roomed and trained together in Minnesota. Like I said, there was no YouTube, but we all knew Krastev and his lifts (thanks to some Iron Mind VHS tapes that Broz ran on repeat at the gym). At that point, no one had snatched more than the Bulgarian superheavyweight's lift at 216kg.

I wanted that distinction for myself. One local meet in, and I was pursuing records, first national marks then international ones. High school had ended. There would be no more football seasons, no more power clean competitions. It was time to chase after the one thing in life that offered me a chance at greatness.

The four of us returned to Vegas late that night. The next morning I called one of my old friends from high school to ask him what drugs I should take.

Four:
Learning to Dope

In 1974, East Germany's Central Committee approved State Plan 14.25,[11] which instituted a systematic approach to doping for the entire nation. This plan used the country's network of sports-schools to mandate the administration of steroids to nearly 10,000 athletes preparing for national and international competition (some as young as 11).

East German physicians and researchers in applied biochemistry, sports science. medicine and endocrinology thoroughly studied the use of steroids and performance enhancing drugs. Titles of dissertations indicated their exhaustive approach; one PhD was entitled "For the Effective Use of Anabolic Steroids to improve Athletic performance in the athletic jumping events." Harmut Riedel authored that study. He later became head doctor of the East German Athletics Federation [12]

State Plan 14.25 relied heavily on one drug in particular: Oral Turinabol, a potent anabolic steroid hormone derived from testosterone and widely used by bodybuilders and athletes to this day. East German company Jenapharm developed it as a pharmaceutical drug in the 1960's. Turinabol increases lean muscle tissue without estrogenic side effects such as water retention, bloating or gynecomastia. (Until very recently, it rivaled stanozolol/Winstrol as the drug of choice for sprinters, weightlifters and cyclists.)

The East German's use of Oral Turinabol enabled that nation's incredible success. At the 1976 Montreal Olympics, East Germany took home 90 total medals, including 40 golds, a vastly disproportionate total to its small population. (By contrast, the USA won 34 golds and the Soviet Union tallied 49 golds.) Montreal was also the first Olympics to institute systematic doping testing, and Turinabol's short detection time added another benefit.

Werner Reiterer's book *Positive*[13] alleges that after the fall of the Iron Curtain and the dissolution of the Soviet Republic, many of these steroid researchers fled to the Middle East and Southeast Asia. No surprise which nations began to dominate the Olympics a decade later.

We know which countries began using these substances along this timeline because their athletes began testing positive for Oral Turinabol (among other PEDs) in international competition shortly after. In weightlifting, the success of nations like Russia and Bulgaria bled into satellite states in the near East: Azerbaijan, Albania, Armenia, Turkey and Iran; across to China, Thailand, and now North Korea and India.

East Germany first succeeded by leveraging the will and fierce nationalism of a centrally organized political system through a network of sports schools for teens and children. Doctors in both the military and academia conducted research into the performance enhancing effects of drugs on athletes in specific sports. This research informed further experimentation with each new crop of students, tracking dosages, optimizing training schedules and enabling athletes to peak for specific competition along the quadrennial plan of the Olympics. A tiny nation won hundreds of Olympic, World and European medals by marshalling its intellectual power and political will to achieve a single goal: drug-enhanced victory.

How did I do it? Like any teenager, I trusted two sources: my friends and the Internet. Looking back, I don't know why I thought I could game the system so easily.

Las Vegas: November 2008

I also have no idea why Broz stuck around, to be honest. The coach-athlete relationship we developed didn't function like high school football or baseball. Maybe the individual sport element set different boundaries, but over the next two years, we became friends in a way that I never developed with any past coaches or mentors.

Broz underwent rotator cuff surgery in November. He was still depressed from his divorce. I spent a lot of time that month driving him to physical therapy appointments, changing bandages, cooking and sharing meals with him. Meanwhile, I'm an 18-year-old kid and he's over 40.

I continued training twice a day and on December 14, I started my first cycle of steroids. The weekend before, Broz and I travelled to Phoenix to watch the American Open, one of two senior-level (age 18-34) national events that USA Weightlifting continues to host. Although I qualified, I didn't compete. Broz just wanted me to see a national level competition.

It's where I saw Caleb Ward lift for the first time. In 2008, everyone in USAW viewed Caleb as this star-child, future of the sport. He held the Junior American record in the snatch at 165kg and I think to this day is still the youngest American to have C&J'ed 182kg (400lbs) in competition.[14] Watching Caleb lift, I thought two things: I can beat this kid, and I want the *Junior World record* of 206kg in the snatch, not just some national mark 40kg less.

So I called a former football teammate who had gotten into bodybuilding. This guy was a true freak; 6'5", 320 pounds with a 7-foot wingspan and a 5.2 40m time. More than a dozen D-1 schools recruited him to no avail. He hated school, lost eligibility his senior year because of grades, then switched over to bodybuilding. And through bodybuilding, steroids.

My first cycle, he put me on 375mg Sustanon a week, a 50mg tab of Dianabol daily and 100mg of Equipoise weekly. Sustanon contains a blend of four different testosterone esters, a combination designed to keep testosterone levels high for a long period and produce various short and longer-term muscle and strength gains. Veterinarians prescribe Equipoise for animals, and breeders and horse owners have employed it to enhance the performance of their racehorses. In hindsight, I committed a mistake by taking a long-detectable drug like Equipoise; but my bodybuilder friend used it and I followed the same protocol.

Whatever. By the end of December I snatched 150kg. Ten kilos on my snatch in a few weeks sounds like a "magic pill" effect. But I benefited the most from just a lack of skill; six months into snatching and I still operated on the steep part of the learning curve. Most people also won't understand what an insanely low dose of steroids I took. Bodybuilders take anywhere from 3-5 grams (3,000-5,000mg) of testosterone a week on some cycles. When superheavyweight weightlifter Gerd Bonk competed for East Germany, he took 11,550mg of oral Turinabol *and* testosterone over a 12-month period from 1978-1979.[15] My amount seemed paltry in comparison.

Christmas came and went, and my mom and Ken caused no shortage of problems. I kept training, kept pushing for heavier numbers, kept taking the drugs. By February of 2009, I broke the American Junior record in the snatch by smoking 166kg one afternoon. Caleb Ward held that record officially at 165kg and Broz planned for me to compete at the 2009 Arnold Championships, where they didn't mandate drug testing.

The Arnold hosts competitions in dozen of sports and has featured a weightlifting championship since 2003. The weekend centers around the Arnold Classic bodybuilding show, and today includes a professional strongman championship (one of the premiere events in that sport). Over the course of the weekend, more than 20,000 athletes compete and over 90,000 fans descend on Columbus, OH to gaze and gawk at the muscled gods and goddess that stride the halls of the Columbus Convention Center.

In 2009, weightlifting at the Arnold offered one of the few American meets where lifters could earn cash prizes at all levels: Youth, Junior, Senior and Masters (35+). Broz and I flew out there with the goal of winning that junior prize money and beating Caleb Ward head to head. Even though my front rack still sucked due to my shitty mobility, I had already C&J'ed 200kg in training and knew that I could best Ward in the snatch.

Juniors competed on Sunday, the last day of the competition. The Arnold Classic Bodybuilding event took place the night before, and the next day, the venue at the Columbus Convention Center flowed with rivers of people. Hundreds packed the spectating area for weightlifting. After all the lifters in our session finished their three snatches, only Caleb and I remained.

Caleb opened at 147kg, which he saved after leaving it a little out front. His coach, Glenn Pendlay pushed him up to 152kg, and Broz moved my opener ahead of it to 153kg. We thought about opening as high as 160kg just to humiliate him but wanted to post one safe lift to secure a total and a chance at the cash.

Ward pulled 152kg off the ground but left it forward again. This time it cost him. The bar crashed to the floor for a no-lift. Since we already changed to 153kg, Ward got a two-minute clock, and Pendlay burned the clock for a minute to give Caleb some rest, then bumped him to 153kg. I sat near Ward in the pre-staging area and watched as Broz, stone-faced, unfolded his arms and went over to the marshal's table to change my opener to 155kg, which forced Caleb to take his last attempt before my opener. Broz leaned toward me and whispered "fuck that guy" as Caleb walked past us toward the platform. The mind games in this sport are vicious.

The crowd cheered when Ward saved a shaky snatch at 153kg. I stunned them into silence when I smoked 155kg on my opening attempt (you can see the battle on YouTube). Of course they were surprised. Coaches and weightlifters regarded Pendlay as one of the best in the business and his athletes won dozens of national championships and earned spots on multiple international teams.

No one even knew me. The Arnold was my second competition, but on my first attempt I led the Junior National Record holder by two kilos.

Broz chipped away at my two-minute clock with small increases on each of my weight changes. With about 50s left, I strode out to take 160kg for my second attempt. It went down just as easy as the first attempt. Now the crowd showed its enthusiasm, its hushed oohs and ah's turning to full cheers and chants. We entered 166kg for my third attempt, an unofficial Junior American record (official record attempts require drug-testing). I drove hard with my feet and moved fast under the bar. But I underpulled and the lift fell to the floor in front of me.

No matter, we led by 7kg going into the clean and jerks, a sizable margin even though Ward could destroy some big lifts. He opened with an easy attempt at 180kg and Broz bumped me to 185kg for my first, which I made just as soundly. Each of us had locked in a total and now the game was on. Clean and jerks function like the second half in football; a whole new ballgame that really decides the outcome of the competition.

Ward weighed less than me at the time and listed 192 as his second attempt. Under the rules in 2009, the lighter athlete won if both lifters totaled the same amount. He and Pendlay banked on that outcome. Caleb looked rocky on his second jerk, dropping his head a little in the lockout, but his elbows held solid and he brought his feet together slowly and surely for a good lift, moving into first place in the total (with a tie at 345kg).

I heard someone scream "wow" as I manhandled my second clean at 195kg and then stumbled my way through a successful jerk that probably should've gotten at least one red light. My lead surged to 10kg, 355kg to his 345kg. To his credit, Ward gave the clean at 200kg a valiant effort, driving onto his toes and diving under the bar in an attempt to win gold in the C&J. But not that day. The weight tumbled through his arms and it was over. I tried 205kg on my third attempt, pulling it to my hip before dropping it, having wrapped up the win on my second lift.

A close battle in weightlifting gets decided by 1-3kg. Many meets at the time ended in ties, with the lighter athlete purposefully matching his opponent to win on a lower bodyweight.[16] Getting beat by 10kg? That's like a 30-point blowout in football. It's an embarrassment. Like the other guy just let you hang in the snatch knowing all along that he would bust your cap in the C&J's.

I knew Ward felt that embarrassment. A few days after the Arnold, I received a message on Myspace (2009, remember?). Whoever was dating Caleb's sister messaged me to say "thanks." Apparently, Caleb lived with his sister and her boyfriend at the time and the two of them didn't get along. The boyfriend told me that Caleb moped around for a week, lying in bed crying and acting miserable. And he told me "thanks for bursting his bubble of ego."

Looking back, I feel bad about it now because Caleb never lifted the same after that year's Arnold, and who knows how bad he took the loss. I would have eventually outlifted him, even without steroids. While I enjoyed my victory—and the $800 payout for Best Junior Lifter—I took little delight in reading that Myspace message.

With that win under my belt, Broz planned my next competition for the 2009 National Championships in Chicago. Which meant I had to clean out for the first time.

I didn't know anything about tapering off steroids and neither did my bodybuilder friend. His sport didn't test at all. And I couldn't ask Broz about it. Some days I could barely find him.

By mid-2009, the recession devastated Las Vegas and the surrounding "sand states." Broz owned a granite business, which had laid off everyone and did little business. He lived off his savings, and still dealt with the divorce. A year earlier, we ate dinners out most weekends. But now, the rare night we headed to a TGI Fridays, the place echoed with our lone conversation. No one in Vegas had money to spend on anything but surviving.

During the day, I ground away at two-a-day training sessions. In four months, my back squat shot up from 265kg to 310kg. That May I snatched 170kg for the first time, a 20kg increase over my numbers in December. The C&J plateaued. I hit some monster PR's in the deadlift and bench and a few other strength lifts, but my horrible front rack impaired me from attempting heavier cleans. Every time I racked the bar it crashed, and I winced in pain before dumping it.

National Championships rolled around quick, and Broz and I flew out last minute to Chicago for the competition. Even as his business tanked, Broz paid for my flight, hotel and meet registration. My anxiety spiked upward, and my training began to derail. Broz and I never saw eye to eye on having a true plan going into a meet. Sure, he paid for everything, but I wanted to have the tickets booked and a hotel reserved at least a month ahead of time to avoid worry (my OCD is a real thing). Broz wouldn't tie up these details until a week out (at best) which irritated the shit out of me and threw off my training.

After lifting six hours a day, I spent my nights digging around the Internet. I posted on forums to ask for advice, and crunched numbers on spreadsheets to calculate half-lives and detection times based off information from popular websites. Very little information I read on the Internet validated my experience coming off drugs. Four to six months detection window for Equipoise? Yeah, try six to eight months. And way longer for those long esters of testosterone. I didn't discover testosterone suspension—a true game-changer—until 2014, too late to help me the first time I cleaned out.

We arrived in Chicago and stayed at the venue hotel. Time peeled by like paint drying; Broz insisted I relax in the room ("conserve energy" as he put it), and absolutely forbid me from watching any of the competition (as that added emotional stress). I never experienced any of this before, and Broz didn't give me advanced warning. My anxiety gnawed like a toothache.

Sunday, June 7, I competed in my first nationals. I weighed in, my warmups moved crisp, but I felt nervous on the platform. My pull lacked aggression, and I bombed out in the snatch for the first time in my career.

The legendary Shane Hamman retired in 2005 after winning nine straight national championships. By 2009, no one filled his shoes at superheavyweight. My first national meet and Broz opened me at 160kg in the snatch, the highest opener that session. I'm 19, going up against veteran lifters as old as 30 who missed 160kg on their second and third attempts, and Broz opened me there. A made attempt at 160kg would earn silver in the snatch and total. But I hadn't slept, couldn't think straight, and left the bar out front. No lift.

Second attempt: despite my protests, Broz bumped me up to 165kg. I sat there fuming as Jason Starks missed his second attempt at 160kg, Patrick Judge made his second at 160kg, Starks missed again and then Matt Rue botched his final attempt at 162kg. At least five minutes passed and now I'm furious *and* cold. I failed 165kg out front.

Judge decided on 165kg for his third attempt, robbing me of my two-minute clock. And still, Broz increased my attempt to 166kg! For what? To say that I "took a shot at" the Junior American record? None of that historical bullshit matters if you miss, and I went out there and just fucking missed it. No strategy, no total, no attempt at placement. Just three failed snatches to commemorate my first National Championships.

I clean and jerked 186kg then pushed 195kg forward twice, a number I handled decently three months earlier at the Arnold. All that work for one lift at 186kg, which finished fourth in the C&J after two other guys bombed out.

In retrospect, bombing out probably helped my career. While I tapered off Sustanon and Dianabol a bit earlier, I only stopped taking Equipoise six weeks out from Nationals and would have been 100% positive for that steroid.

If USADA had bothered to test me at Nationals, my story would end right here.

But they didn't, and I flew home with a plan to retire from competition for the longest stretch of drug use in my life.

Five:
The World's
Strongest Teenager

The documentary *Icarus* scandalized[17] the West with its account of systematic, state-led doping amongst Russian athletes, coaches and sports federations. Two years before Bryan Fogel premiered that film, the German news agency ARD released *The Doping Secret: How Russia Makes its Winners*, in which journalist Hajo Seppelt detailed the methods employed by RUSADA and the Russian Federal Police (FSB) at the 2014 Sochi Olympics.[18] Seppelt's expose provoked international outrage and spurred a WADA-led investigation that culminated in the McLaren Report, and the partial ban of Russian athletes from the 2016 Olympics.

Icarus gave an insider's account of a state-run doping program in Russia that helped that country dominate the 2014 Winter Olympics and raised consciousness of that nation's cheating (especially for American audiences).

But it began by showing how Grigory Rodchenkov, head of Russia's anti-doping laboratory (RUSADA), helped amateur cyclist Fogel to improve results through PED usage while also beating the tests.

Fogel doped in preparation for the Haute Route, a punishing seven-day amateur bike race in the Swiss Alps. Rodchenkov's protocols provided precise amounts of drugs to take, when to take them, and how to taper off the drugs in time for competitions. This sophisticated understanding relied on Rodchenkov's connections to financial and institutional support, including access to testing facilities, suppliers of (untainted) performance enhancing drugs, and protection from valid doping control authorities—or at least an informed awareness of when supposedly random tests would take place. It also required the *accurate* detection times for each PED, and for Russian athletes, funds to bribe officials to either not report or invalidate positive drug results.[19]

The first 30-minutes of the film depict Fogel achieving many of these goals in secret, without the support of a federation or a team. Fogel claimed he wanted to expose the ease at which athletes beat tests and prove that current methods of doping control failed in cycling. Mid-way through filming, Rodchenkov flees Russia, two of his colleagues die mysteriously, and Icarus transforms into an expose of how Russia cheated at the Sochi Olympics, among other high-level competitions.

That's where Fogel's film finished, for sure, leading to an Oscar for Best Documentary, a celebrated book for Rodchenkov (now hailed as a "hero") and testimony for his lawyers in front of Congress. But Fogel had no idea his film would travel down that rabbit hole. He instigated the project to see just how much benefit doping conferred. Amateur or whatever, everyone's curious what the drugs can do for them as an athlete. I put Fogel's ideas into practice years before he made his film, which I found much harder as an American unprotected by a sports federation willing to look the other way.

In April, I turned 19. Barely a year out of high school. I convinced myself that I could beat the system, ingest massive quantities of drugs, improve my lifts by 40kg or more and then return to the sport clean. To do that, I needed to go underground. In 18 months I would age out of Junior contention. I had already attempted the Junior National record. I knew I could set the Junior world record.

The Iron Mind videos of Bulgarians, Greeks, Turks, Russians, and Chinese showed that a stratosphere of difference separated the achievements of their weightlifters from the results achieved by the USA. Through Broz I learned that all the countries fielding great lifters supplied their athletes with performance enhancing drugs.

In 2009, American weightlifters couldn't even tread water at a world-level meet, both the men and the women. The athletes of every medal-winning nation eclipsed our totals by 15-percent or more. I thought: "I'm a smart kid, determined and resourceful. I can figure it out." I planned to return to competition only when I understood how to use PED's without detection.

At first, I lacked the details to accomplish that task, but I did get good at it. Over the next six years, both USADA and WADA tested me almost two dozen times. I only failed twice (and both of those were bullshit). The success of the doping nations proved that what happened in *Icarus* could be done. I just had to be smarter for longer.

Las Vegas: July to November 2009

I officially retired from USA Weightlifting a few days after nationals. The process was simple; I emailed USAW and said, "hey I don't want to be a member no more." Since I didn't total at my only National meet, didn't even come close to eligibility for a stipend or an international squad, and never even registered for the Out-of-Competition Testing Pool, it was that easy. If anyone at USAW noticed they probably shrugged and thought "great, sorry you didn't enjoy your three weightlifting meets."

After Nationals, I took a few weeks to stay clean and train light. In Broz' system, backing things down meant training three to four days a week, twice a day, with morning squats up to 220kg (instead of my usual 250kg), along with some light lifts to warm up. When I dove back into full training, the program intensified, and so did my drug regimen. I decided to ditch Dianabol. I never felt that it added to my training or recovery.

Trenbolone,[20] on the other hand…

Farmers worldwide inject Trenbolone (Tren) into beef cattle. Tren increases feed efficiency—meaning it takes less grain to produce a greater amount of future steak. Regulations specify a certain time before slaughter when farmers must stop administering Tren to their cattle so that it doesn't contaminate the meat sold at the butcher's shop. But that doesn't always happen.[21]

Tren improves nitrogen synthesis in muscle, adding lean mass without conversion of the hormone to estrogen (which happens with testosterone and leads to fat storage). It also activates the androgen receptors with up to five times the potency of testosterone. The androgen receptors in the myonuclei of muscle cells contribute to greater recruitment of muscle fibers.[22] Farmers may not care how much their cows can clean and jerk. But for strength athletes, tren is a game changer.

Starting in August 2009, my weekly regimen consisted of 300mg of Tren and 375mg of the testosterone blend Sustanon. Testosterone remained important for building muscle and enabling faster recovery. Weightlifters that train as hard as I did need to recover for the next day's punishing workout.

I occasionally injected Equipoise, which was stupid as tren gives basically the same effects with a shorter detection window. I also started taking 20mg of Oral Turinabol each day, which over time I upped to 40mg a day. Once I added oral steroids to the mix, my progress skyrocketed.

By September 2009, I snatched 175kg, C&J'ed 200kg again and my back squat shot up to 320kg. In October I back squatted 280kg for a set of six, snatched 185kg and C&J'ed 210kg. Broz told me to eat constantly, but only my body composition changed and the weight on the scale barely budged.

My legs exploded with muscle. I didn't take measurements, but not even sweatpants fit anymore. And since I stopped doing all the "bro-science" upper body and bench pressing, I now looked like a weightlifter, with a massive upper back towering over giant quads, glutes and hamstrings. Picture the hulk of a cathedral upended and stacked on the columns of a Roman aqueduct.[23]

In November, I snatched 185kg and clean and jerked 220kg for the first time. Every week in November I snatched 180kg. I was 19. Ward held the Junior snatch record at 165kg, and Shane Hamman's senior snatch record stood at 197.5kg.

From Monday to Friday, I trained twice a day, every day. Saturdays and Sundays I squatted. Weekday mornings I back squatted to a heavy single, then lifted light. Afternoons I snatched to max, or power snatched to a peak, then did cleans, power cleans or C&J's for a few heavy singles. Occasionally, I jerked from blocks. Afterwards, more back squats. Every day that month I snatched at least 150kg. Toward the end of November, I hit 300kg for a triple in the back squat. And they didn't move slowly. Broz wouldn't allow it.

Even though I snatched to max every afternoon, I rarely compiled a total (we did jerks separate from cleans often). But that November, I tested both snatch and C&J in the same session and hit a 400kg total. A year earlier, at the Halloween meet, I totaled 285kg...

I back squatted twelve times a week. We rarely front squatted. My knees couldn't handle it. If I worked more on front rack mobility, I think my clean and C&J would have improved as quick as my snatches. But any time I cleaned or front squatted, my knees screamed in pain. Racking a clean caused the most distress; the constant patellar and quadriceps tendinitis in both knees killed me. Any time I dipped in the jerk I thought "here's where my knee tears apart."

During the month of December, I added another 30kg to my back squat with a 350kg lift! In one year, I progressed from 265kg to 350kg. Eight-five fucking kilos when I already squatted over 600lbs. That same month I snatched 190kg for the first time. Now only 7.5kg separated me from Shane Hamman's Senior National record.

Whenever Broz supervised my training sessions, he analyzed the bar speed to determine if I should add weight on a snatch or clean and jerk. Most of the time, he used his naked eye to determine the bar speed. Today, coaches on Instagram use wires, electrodes on the end of the bar synched to computers or apps like Coaches Eye to track velocity. Hint: you want to develop a good eye as a coach? Rely on the two in your skull and watch a lot of lifts.

Broz never periodized my programming[24] with respect to modulations in volume or intensity or on a timeline relative to an upcoming competition. But there were general rules: you're going to snatch to max almost every day. Then push to heavy clean and jerks, cleans, power cleans or jerks. Then you squat again, also heavy. The more Broz watched me lift, the more progress I made. I can't value enough the quality of feedback he gave me during this training period, especially how he coached the mental game. Session after session, Broz reiterated and reinforced the goal and desire to lift heavy weights, to push *always* toward world record attempts, to close the gap on the world record. The only number that mattered.

When Broz's granite business kept him from coaching, I found the discipline to do the work. I relied on that single-mindedness that drove me to do leg presses and bench press every day for an entire summer. Some days I heard Broz' voice in my head, or let my intuition guide me. Other days I did as I pleased, snatching and squatting heavy, putting the C&J's on the back burner. Once, long after I snatched 200kg, I put together a casual 400kg total with a 200kg snatch…and a 200kg clean and jerk. Cue the lols and raised eyebrows.

One Saturday morning, I totaled while drunk, hitting 160kg and 190kg because I walked in still hammered from the night before. I drank too often to excess that fall, getting blackout drunk on more than a few weekends. Then one crazy night almost put an end to everything.

A few of my high school friends stayed in Vegas after graduation to attend UNLV and we hung out during their fall and winter semesters ("winter" in Vegas being a relative term). One of the Hispanic fraternities threw an off-campus house party. Me and four friends drove there in a pick-up truck, not looking to cause trouble, just wanting to hang out.

I remember walking in and noticing this imposing, gigantic bald guy holding court in the center of the room. "Damn, that's one big dude" I said to my friends. We grabbed some beers and talked to people we knew. A few drinks later and I hit on one of the girls partying there.

Next thing I know, I'm feeling eyes on me, and got a weird vibe from the room. I decided "hey, it's time to go." As I headed toward the door, the big ass bald guy followed me. Turned out that I talked to the wrong girl and he and his friend planned to jump me. "I need the keys to your truck" I told my friend, "this guy's following me, something's wrong and I gotta leave. Like now." I already fought someone a few weeks earlier and had no taste for it that night.

My buddy handed me the keys and I walked outside. Thirty people tailed me. Not all guys, some girls, basically this huge crowd that sensed a fight and wanted to see it go down. I reached the truck and stood on the passenger side, fumbling with the keys when the giant confronted me with his boy in tow. They both stood over six feet, weighed at least 300lbs and the bald guy said "Yo man, you talked to my homeboy's girl. That's fucked up, and we gonna fight."

I responded to him with "c'mon dude, I don't wanna fight you." Literally pleading with him to the point of tears because I really did not want to fight anyone. Almost ten of them had surrounded me now, with the truck to my back. And he wouldn't let it go.

A switch flipped. I swung in and blacked out completely. My friends told me the story after we left the hospital: I flew into a rage and fucked this guy up so bad that he didn't get any action on me or anyone else. The other big guy lunged at me after I dropped his friend and I threw him across the pavement. At this point, I was snatching 180kg every day, so I'm tossing these 300lb dudes around like rag dolls. A few smaller guys jumped on me and with one hand I threw them off one by one. Eventually, I worked my way around to the driver's side of the truck. I was covered with blood and howling with rage and I screamed "there's not a motherfucker here that can knock me out!"

Just then some dude flew through the crowd and superman punched me in the side of the head. I dropped down hard. More guys rushed me, and now one of my friends—who trained for the Olympics in boxing—started laying people out. Finally, some guy who lived in the house burst through the front door with a shotgun and fired it in the air.

The crowd momentarily dispersed and we piled into the truck. As we drove out of there, the mob regrouped and tore into my buddy's pickup. They kicked in his doors, the sidings, knocked the mirrors off. The cops eventually showed; they checked on me and sent me to the hospital. In the emergency room, blood poured out of my head, I trembled with rage, and my blood pressure spiked to 230 over 160. A doctor said my head should have exploded. I suffered a slight concussion but everything else appeared fine.

I saw Broz the next day and told him what happened. He didn't hide being pissed, but his advice stayed with me. "You can't mess with certain people" he told me. "Some of them have nothing to lose."

After that I stopped partying. In three months, I turned 20, my last year as a Junior. I buried myself in training. Broz increased the squatting intensity, so now I hit over 250kg for singles in the back squat every morning for three months in a row. Almost immediately I snatched 180kg again, and then smoked it regularly.

My PR's burned through the pages of my training log. Each day that month I snatched 180kg and C&J'ed 210kg. In March, I added Anadrol to my drug regimen. Anadrol is the nuclear bomb of steroids, and I immediately saw its effects. Plus, the detection time is short, so I felt uninhibited taking it.

Finally, I PR'ed my snatch at 191kg. Now 6.5kg off Hamman's senior record. During one week in March I snatched 180kg every single afternoon. Then I cleaned 230kg for the first time. That clean almost ripped me to shreds. On the first attempt, it crashed hard and I cranked my knee standing it up.

I cleaned 220kg on the rep before, then pushed right to 230kg. In the clean, I often hesitated, because I still dealt with some painful shoulder immobility. After pulling cleans off the floor, I regularly clarked the bar (pulled it to the hip and let it fall). At the time, Val Balison trained with us. He competed for Team USA in the 1980s and founded the high school power clean meet in 2004. Val bragged about the garbage lifts he hit 20 years ago (150kg and 190kg as a 90kg lifter).

Every time I clarked a clean, Val taunted me, and I couldn't stand that motherfucker, so I took 230kg again just to prove that hater wrong. And smoked it.

Some guys like Val knew how to push my buttons. And I pushed back. I always brought up my age, especially to old heads like Val. One of those days, while trash talking him, I let him know specifically that I planned to snatch 200kg before my 20th birthday.

April approached quickly. I turned 20 on the 22nd. A buddy of mine gave me some Adderall around this time; man did that give me an edge. The first week of April, I snatched 190kg twice—two singles on different training days. That Friday I PR'ed again, smoking 192.5kg. The next week I snatched 190kg every single day.

That weekend I crushed some of my biggest squats to date. On Saturday I back squatted 340kg (748lbs). Sunday, I did 220kg for two sets of five—a light day for once. Anyone who doesn't undergo this type of training can't imagine what it's like to train ten times during the week and then only squat on the weekend. Your body reacts like it went on vacation.

When I showed up that Monday, April 19, my body felt fresh. I was hungry. And I snatched 200kg for the first time. No American had ever achieved that feat before, not in training or competition. I wish I could say that camera bulbs flashed or ticker tape fell from the ceiling. Broz filmed it with his phone. Another lifter named Tim Sprague trained that day. He saw it. We all high fived and I don't think I've seen a smile replace Broz' scowl for a longer period.

In our tiny, two-platform gym in Vegas, this massive lift happened. It was mine. I owned it, and of every American weightlifter who ever put his hands on a bar, I'm the only one that's ever known the feeling of snatching 200kg. And I had to hold onto it and keep pushing for more.

Because while I made all these monster lifts, I was broke and my life was falling apart.

Six:
The Price of
Internet Fame

Over the course of eight years training and competing, I earned negative dollars as a weightlifter. I lifted for two nations, in two World Championships and two Pan American Games, but my net receipts bled red. Scars on my arms prove it.

Broz and I paid my entry fees for national competitions, most of my flights, the majority of my meals, transportation to the gym, membership in the federation and any shoes and gear I needed. During much of my lifting career, my internet fame skyrocketed. But I netted zero revenue from YouTube and lived on negative income from 2008-2012 and little more from 2013-2015. The only "big money" I reaped came when Broz said he would pay me $10,000 the day I snatched 195kg. I think he still owes me some of it.

Serious countries fund their weightlifting programs. They pay coaches, build training halls, organize teams, select and develop athletes within the middle and high schools. Kazakhstan fields multiple teams with independent training sites (for instance, Team Astana, for whom Ilya competed). Brazil also operates a club system, each with its own training halls and living quarters—one each in Rio de Janeiro and Sao Paolo.

Both Russia and China operate thousands of sports schools where athlete-students (that's the correct order) split time between athletics and academics. Cuba operates a smaller network of these schools that select outstanding athletes from across the island for enrollment and specialization in sport. In the mornings, they attend classes, then practice full-time

Russia organizes training camps. Colombia manages three training sites and splits the lifters among them (I've been told it's so the entire team doesn't all get kidnapped and held for ransom at once). They pay stipends, cover rent, feed them, buy them cars, offer them pensions for when they retire. Some nations give lifetime stipends for World and Olympic champions

Kazakhstan funnels funds from its oil and natural gas industry into a massive, state-organized weightlifting system. According to Ivan Rojas' book *Kazakhstan Weightlifting System for Elite Athletes*, before 2008, the Kazakh federation's membership included only 600 athletes. But in the 2008 Olympics, they won four medals. At London's 2012 Olympics, Kazakh weightlifters stormed the podium with four Gold medalists.

According to Rojas, any athlete can train for free at a weightlifting facility, which includes coaching. As athletes demonstrate ability, they are selected for clubs, which train separately (and get prioritized training hours). Elite youth athletes (17yo and under) receive stipends of $350/month to train; Elite junior athletes (under 20yo) earn $2,000 a month, with World Champions netting $20,000 in monthly stipend. Olympic Gold medalists take home a direct payment of $500,000 plus a car and apartment.

USA Weightlifting only began paying stipends in 1997, to a small group of weightlifters. The most they ever paid me was around $600/month. In 2013, the year I started competing for Brazil, USAW's total direct support to athletes amounted to less than $30,000/year.[25]

The adage, "you can't get full-time results from part-time athletes" implies a corollary for the governing body of any sports federation: you only get world-class achievements from athletes enabled to train full-time.[26] In many countries, doping plays a major role, but so does covering rent and groceries.

While Ilya benefited from a country that poured millions of dollars into its national federation's structured, systemic program, my approach took a more haphazard path.

Las Vegas: Winter 2009-2010

Like I mentioned, Broz recruited me at a high school power clean competition. The whole thing started by accident, with him saying "hey, I can teach you technique, I got this little gym," which really wasn't a gym but an office space in the back corner of his granite business. For the first few years, I trained with zero other people except Broz and some former lifters from the 1980s like Val Balison (born 1955) and Gary Savage (born 1960). Imagine lifting world class weights next to a pair of geezers struggling to clean 120kg.

Broz didn't even own real platforms. Not kidding. I learned to lift on carpeting surrounded by office mats. You know, the clear, bubbly surfaced mats that desk chairs roll over to avoid scuffing tile floor? Yeah. I snatched over 140kg pushing off carpet swatches and dropping the weights onto them. Even Broz preferred lifting at the Gold's Gym on Flamingo Ave.

To Broz' credit, he collected a ton of nice equipment over the years. He owned several Eleiko bars and an assortment of Eleiko, Uesaka and vintage York bumpers, plus a few other brands no longer in production. Shortly after I committed to two-a-days, he picked up some platforms as well. The National Strength and Conditioning Association (NSCA) hosted a conference in Vegas that August and put demo platforms in their booth. It cost them more money than expected to ship them back, so Broz arranged for us to take them…as a donation. He basically told them "I got some kids lifting out here now and we could really use some platforms." Broz usually gets what he wants.

At first, my friend Taylor Smith trained too, and we did our first meet together. But his interest waned quickly, and for the bulk of

2008-2010, I lifted mostly alone. Basically taking international-caliber lifts on donated platforms, with no training partners and a part-time coach. In the back corner of a granite showroom. Sometimes I still don't know what drove my training every day. Pure desire to achieve greatness at first, and most days, the benefit of habit. Young lifters should never discount the advantage of routine. Everything else in your life can suck and still, you get out of bed, you eat, you train.

Then you do it all again.

That's exactly how Broz said to simplify my life: "don't get a job, don't have a girlfriend, just rest, eat, and train and you will achieve great results." I heard that advice as a command and followed it. While I partied with friends on weekends and hooked up with my share of girls, my wife Taylor is my first girlfriend (and I met her in 2013). When Broz learned that some of my friends smoked pot, he told me it impeded recovery and I never smoked again.

I didn't hold a job either. Don't really know when I could, training an hour or so in the morning, eating beforehand, mobility afterward, driving home to nap and eat, then training three to four hours in the afternoon only to repeat the same process Monday through Friday. My mom let me live with her, still paid for my food, and she and Ken eventually supported my goals—once I started hitting bigger numbers and talk of the 2012 Olympics kicked in. I think they ultimately wanted me to go to college, but at the same time, they both took the attitude that I would succeed in whatever I did. As crazy and dysfunctional as they acted otherwise, they always believed in me and never held me back. Which was probably a good and bad thing.

Initially though, my mom took a cynical attitude toward how much time I spent with Broz. She can be very sadistic; she honestly thought John was fondling me for money. She saw John as a predator because in her mind, she couldn't fathom why I spent all this time with a 40-year-old man when I'm 18. She asked why he let me lift in his gym, why he invited me to his house, why we hung out like best friends? In some ways I saw her point. My wife still teases me about my relationship with Broz, how it was just me and this older man spending most of the day together.

But I can assure you, everyone kept their pants on.

For his part, Broz went out of his way to stop by and meet my parents, telling them they had a really special kid, and that I trained with greater effort and focus than any lifter he ever worked with, teenager or adult. Every once in a while, my mom gave me gas money; she still worked a crazy amount of hours and I occasionally caught her in a generous mood.

But most of the time, I paid for gas by donating plasma. I figured out a perfect system for exactly how much gas I needed each week and then calculated how many times I needed to sell plasma. In 2008 and 2009 I lived a mile from the gym. When Taylor Smith trained with us, I picked him up—he lived a mile in the opposite direction—so I mapped out how far I drove each day and how far I could drive in between plasma donations. Usually five miles of driving each day in a shitty 2001 Jeep with a busted driver's seat.

Once I started picking up Billy Bybee and Ian Droze (they began training in 2011), it doubled the mileage and almost bankrupted me. I couldn't give enough plasma to cover it. Sometimes at night, lying in bed with my wife Taylor, she'd trace her finger over the scars on my arms, which run along my elbow like ridges on a map. And I'll hear her sigh.

But what else could I have done?

I also needed to pay for steroids. Gregg Valentino—who inflated his arms with synthol[27] when steroids didn't grow them enough— once said that anyone taking steroids is also selling steroids. Back in high school I sold supplements[28] and continued afterward, using my network of high school football friends and making appearances at the National Power Clean meet. My buddy Mike sold me stacks of pro-hormones, which I peddled for higher prices at the high school. Those sales covered the real drugs I used.

Living at home helped with food bills. But that eventually came to an end towards December 2009. During the recession, our family moved around constantly. My mom still worked 12-hour days, five to six days a week, holding one job and moonlighting at another. Most of the houses we rented cost about $2000 a month, but nothing lasted. Even though my mom earned over 10K a month, her wild spending kept us on the move, always one step ahead of debt collectors.

On weekends, my friends and I drank all night and I often rolled in around dawn. My mom worked swing shifts at a hospital, and she arrived home one morning and immediately downed a bunch of pills. When I came home, she passed out, fell down the stairs and fucked up her shoulder. Complete dislocation, multiple torn rotator cuff muscles. It still doesn't function 100%.

I remember feeling disgusted, watching her lie there. I didn't even call an ambulance, just went to my room and slept. Her drug use spiked upward, and our relationship deteriorated with equal magnitude. I didn't even care that she was alive. The hospital she worked for began proceedings to suspend her license.

Then the economy tanked and the bank initiated foreclosure proceedings on our house. We needed to move again. My mom decided to buy a trailer on the outskirts of Vegas. We traded a huge house one mile from the gym to a shitty trailer almost 40 minutes away. I remember lying in my bed, unable to sleep and pacing, writing down things I planned to say to each of my family members when I finished with them forever. I couldn't stand living there, but I couldn't just up and leave either.

Mostly because my little brother still lived with us. In a few months he entered his senior year of high school and I thought "just suffer out this year until you can both get out." The gas bill for my car more than tripled, I didn't have any money and I wasn't going to quit, wasn't going to get a job. I upped the frequency of plasma donations. I lost sleep. Given all the steroids I took, I'm surprised I didn't experience more rage. Somewhere online I read that Tren caused insomnia. But I just welled up with so much hate for my family that it kept me up at night.

I stuck it out through the fall and then my best friend Jason came home for Christmas break. We hung out every day, partied on weekends. My senior year I stayed at his house and his mom kept a room ready for me. One night, I remember telling him "I just don't want to go home." And that's how I moved in with him and Virginia for the second time.

It doesn't surprise me that I put 30kg on my back squat that December. My stress levels plummeted once I no longer lived with a junkie and her fucked up husband. I stammered my way through the initial conversation with Virginia, because I really suck at asking people for things. That sounds weird now, given my success in sales, but if I can offer someone a straight exchange, then no problem. But to basically say "Hey, can I live at your house rent free?" and "can you pay my food and everything just so I can lift weights all day and not work?"

Virginia acquiesced without a thought. She knew from Jason that I trained for the Olympics, and that aligned with her idealistic views of helping young people. Her youngest son Evan still lived there; a year later, he graduated and attended Brown, where he competed in the decathlon and fulfilled his own Olympic dream in 2018.[29]

Every aspect of my life improved. I lived close to the gym, with a stable—if adopted—family, and hung out with my best friend each night. I shifted my mom's drug addiction to the back burner. My brother still lived there, and I checked in on him frequently, but only when I knew Ken and my mom weren't home.

Then I became famous on the Internet.

The New Year rolled around, and Broz uploaded videos of my lifts to YouTube. Since 2007, Broz put a few of his and other ABG athlete's clips online, but the uploads gained a lot more traction when he posted my strength feats. One video of me back squatting

300kg for a set of six got some attention. Then Broz posted me front squatting 250kg for a set of four. Comments poured in and the view count spiked into five, then six figures.

At the time, only Broz and Cal Strength promoted the sport online. That era's Cal Strength lifters included Donny Shankle and Jon North, a very promising Spencer Moorman, Kevin Cornell and a few others. Pendlay coached them in San Ramon, and they pioneered the use of the livestream on YouTube. Glenn asked viewers to donate in real time, with money going to whoever hit the biggest total or snatch or C&J that day. Some videos spanned three hours, and the view count blew me away. A real hunger for weightlifting content grew in America.

While Cal Strength capitalized on their viewers to raise money, Broz took a different approach. We didn't run an E-commerce store or secure a YouTube partnership. Today, people earn money hand over fist on YouTube; but Broz posted to inspire American weightlifters. He wanted to say, "Americans can hit big numbers, and lift just as well as Russia, China and Iran."

At night I scrolled through the comments and felt excited from the attention. I was just some kid in Vegas, not doing anything with my life, and athletes from all over the country shared and re-posted and commented on my videos. Some wrote about how I inspired their own athletic pursuits. View counts regularly topped six figures and comments numbered in the 100s, peanuts now for a professional YouTuber. But in YouTube's infancy it seemed huge. I pushed Broz to publish more videos, just to see the commentary, which became a little addicting.
Otherwise, what did I have?

The videos didn't bring in any money until Broz uploaded the "World's Strongest Teenager." That clip compiled my biggest lifts to date: a 250kg back squat triple done in under five seconds, a 320kg (706lb!) back squat set of five executed raw with no belt, knee wraps or spotters, a 230kg (507lb) bench press—again done raw. The capstone showed a 195kg snatch, a 230kg clean and the monster 200kg snatch still unequalled by any American. I achieved all these feats before my 20th birthday.

Broz posted that video and the very next day I received a call and a check from Charles Poliquin. Back then, Poliquin towered over the strength and conditioning world (which like everything else, was still developing in terms of branding, influence and the popularity contest that is social media). Poliquin trained athletes since the 1980s. His client list included NFL Pro Bowlers, NHL Stanley Cup winners, World Champions in multiple sports, world record holders, and medalists in 12 different Olympic disciplines. I don't care how many followers some gym bro or Insta-thot racks up. They'll never top Poliquin's level of actual success.

Poliquin worked with pro athletes and Olympic Champions and wanted to sponsor me! On the phone, he called me the future of American weightlifting. His sponsorship started with an investment of $2,500. In one phone call, I went from zero dollars to enough money to train for six months without donating plasma. Plus, he sent me an $800 gift card to Whole Foods every month! "I know you must be eating a ton, and I want to make sure its healthy food" he told me. It also meant I didn't have to sponge off Virginia as much.

Eventually, the sponsorship included Poliquin flying me to his New England facility to promote his work and for physical therapy. His therapists performed dry needling, acupuncture, massage and techniques to improve blood flow. From summer, 2008 until May 2010, I never had any work done on me. No chiropractor, no massages, nothing. I couldn't afford it.

The medical treatment came at the best time. After the 200kg snatch, and the high rep back squats, Broz dialed down my training. Little injuries flared up and magnified. My patellar tendinitis irritated me daily, my wrist stung when I turned over heavy snatches, and I felt a stabbing sensation in my shoulders. These nagging issues kept setting me back, bit by bit. People believe this myth, that steroids act like a magical recovery serum that lets you go heavy and hard 24-7 and nothing will hurt. But I suffered massive amounts of pain. Every day. Every training session. The only thing I took was ibuprofen.

I trained lighter through the summer and in August, Broz ramped up the intensity and volume again. Morning sessions I back squatted 300kg almost every day, followed by power snatch and power cleans. Most days I casually hit 140kg and 170kg. But one morning I powered 170kg in the snatch and crushed a 200kg power clean!

My squat volume increased on the weekends. During August I squatted 340kg at least five or six times. Broz still had me squatting 12 sessions a week, which sounds like high frequency for any movement. But to put it in perspective, the Bulgarians front squatted 15 sessions a week, with only Sunday off from training. Kazak lifters front squat up to 18 times per week. I think people hear about the frequency and think "only drugged lifters can do that," which to me sounds like an excuse. People can squat every day; I don't consider that unique at all. We can debate whether an athlete can sustain squatting multiple times per day forever, but Angelo Bianco trained the squat up to 22 sessions per week, and I **know** he didn't take any banned substances.

Saturday, September 4th, I back squatted 300kg for 21 total reps, split up into sets of two and three. Broz regularly picked a number on Saturdays, which indicated how many reps he wanted. I could divide it however I needed. It might take a few hours, but I got it done.

That next Thursday, I smoked 350kg (770lbs) for a fast single and attacked 363kg (800lbs) on the next set. But I dumped it behind. Friday, I trained snatch and C&J to max, and Saturday I strode into the gym with determination. We worked up as usual, 70kg, 120kg, 170kg, 220kg, 270kg, 300kg, then 330kg then 350kg again. All fast, solid quick reps. No belt, no knee wraps, no spotters.

On the next set I put 363kg on the bar for the second time and slam dunked it. Eight hundred pounds, raw, ass-to-grass weighing

130kg (286lbs). I don't need to mention how fast it look
can watch on YouTube.[30]

During the month of September, I snatched 190kg or more every afternoon. Monday to Friday, five times a week. I hit 200kg a few more times that month (lifetime, I've snatched that weight or more about 12 times). I was 20 years old, now chasing that 206kg junior world record snatch. In the mornings, Broz added full snatches, nothing heavy, but hitting 160kg or so each morning to work on my timing.

October rolled around. A hunger for bigger lifts consumed me. Monday, October 4th, I showed up, fresh from two days where I only squatted. I worked up to 200kg easy. Flat feet, bar behind my head, no wobble, no need to stand it forward, just straight up and straight down and a 200kg snatch like no one else in America has ever done before.[31]

Broz told me to jump to 207kg on the next rep. That was his mentality, always pushing for 5kg PR's or more, taking massive jumps, never these one-kilo baby steps. John got so hyped at these moments, he sometimes threw up from the excitement. (FYI: One kilo PR jumps are just fine.)

I put 207kg on the bar and the rest is history. Did I walk it a little forward? Yeah. Did I use straps? Sure. But I snatched greater than a world record, without a single miss in training that day. Broz filmed the lift on his iPhone. I think we high-fived; I can't really remember much about that day, no matter how much I re-watch the video on YouTube. But I can still sense that lift, me ripping the weight off the floor, the feel of my feet planting down on the platform, the forceful finality of locking my elbows out in the catch just before I stood it up. The moment I locked the bar out, I knew I had it, a fucking world record lift, something no American had done for over 50 years.

Now it was time to set some of these marks in competition. And for that I had to come off the drugs and clean out. Again.

Seven:
Pedigree,
Method and Myth

I just set an unofficial Junior World Record in training. Lifted every day, and twice on most days. Paid in blood to get to the gym. And less than two years in, I found myself wondering: was Broz fit to coach me?

It's doubtful that weightlifters in China, Russia or Kazakhstan ever asked the same question. Aleksey Ni rose to the position of Kazakhstan's weightlifting head coach in 1994.[32] After competing for 10 years and attaining the title Master of Sport, he retired and attended college, graduating in 1983 from the Kazakhstan State Institute of Physical Education. The next year, he began training youth and junior athletes at a local club in his hometown; three years later he coached for a club in Almaty, the nation's largest city. In 1990, the federation appointed him head Youth coach and then elected him top men's coach in 1994.

His career proceeded through a systematic process, where a federation, organized into competing clubs, recruited and selected not only their best athletes, but promoted their best minds and talents as coaches.

Ni never achieved greatness as a weightlifter. He entered the sport late after being expelled from his first love, soccer, when he was caught smoking a cigarette. Oftentimes, great athletes become great coaches when a retiring lifter fills a role in an existing system's hierarchy. Hossein Reza Zadeh's career followed this route when he stepped back from competing and assumed the head coaching position of the Iranian National team.

USA Weightlifting boasts more active members in its federation than any other country, even China. Athletes can join with a credit card and compete with a photo ID. Our federation actively encourages former and current participants from other sports (especially power-sports like gymnastics, track and field and football) to crossover to weightlifting well into their late teens and early 20s—a time by which other nations have already determined a weightlifter's prospects. Those that meet a certain total stipulated by USAW can compete in national level events. Lifting an even higher total provides eligibility for international teams. For example, Florida's Jason Bonnick qualified for and competed at his first world championships at 37, long after most internationally successful weightlifters have retired.

For coaches, USA Weightlifting keeps the barriers to entry just as low. Prospective coaches must invest in their own education; USAW offers two standardized certifications aptly called the Level One and Level Two. Anyone with $500 can sign up and USAW's education department designs the course material to ensure a high success rate on the exams.

In many ways, this setup reflects the decentralized nature of the free-market economy. The US doesn't shuffle promising kids into sports-schools like Russia, East Germany, Cuba, China, or South America.[33] Here, weightlifting relies on interest, seeing it on TV, or in the case of many prominent youth athletes—knowing a sibling or parent or friend that already competes. Even during the Olympics, Weightlifting receives scant television coverage.

Other countries organize the coaching of weightlifters from the top-down, with manuals periodizing training from the time a youth athlete first touches the bar until athletes pass through puberty, ascend the youth and junior ranks and achieve standards such as "Candidate for Master of Sport," "Master of Sport" and "International Master of Sport." These titles signify technical skill and a certain total in competition. Russia has produced and updated training manuals for weightlifting since they began studying the subject scientifically in the 1960s. Most of the Soviet states, including Cuba, adopted the Russian model. Lately, Kazakhstan developed its own systemized training plan—again, with the goal of organizing training by age, weight class and with the goal of qualifying athletes for international competition. It follows that these programs also weed out athletes that fail to obtain a certain level of progress.

In those countries' institutional structure, coaches often teach youth and junior athletes first. With success and recognition, they progress to senior lifters and then to members of international teams.[34] In the past, USAW employed an official head coach, but no longer.[35] Now, any coach, regardless of background in the sport or general education, can obtain a USA Weightlifting Level One Certification and immediately start coaching. Once they pass criminal background checks, and doping and SafeSport education, they can register a barbell club.

Then hang a shingle on the door:
Joe Weightlifting Coach, athletes welcome.

Las Vegas and Chicago: 2009-2010

In 2009, about a year after I started training, this dude from Ireland dropped into the gym to do a video interview.[36] He asked Broz, "how long you been weightlifting."

"Twenty-two years," John replied.

"And how long you been coaching," the interviewer followed.

"About a year."

About the same amount of time I had been weightlifting.

No systematic, institutionalized education or structure brought Broz into coaching. He just happened to work as a bouncer with one of the best lifters of all time.

For three years, Broz lived and trained with Antonio Krastev, one of the greatest snatchers in weightlifting history. Krastev snatched 216kg at the 1987 World Championships. No one touched that record for 30 years (when Iran's Behdad Salimi tied it at the 2016 Olympics).

Broz grew up in Cleveland and learned weightlifting from John Schubert, who coached Chuck Vinci, the last American male to win Olympic gold. Schubert taught Broz to lift but Broz didn't really take to the sport, or do any serious training until his late 20s, when he met Krastev.

Krastev medaled at five World Championships and won two in the 1980s, competing for Bulgaria at a time when that tiny nation produced the world's most dominant weightlifters. From Bulgaria, he travelled to Canada, then moved to Minnesota. When Broz met him, Krastev worked at a bar in the Mall of the Americas, checking ID's and bouncing.

I know, it sounds strange that a world record holder and two-time world champion wound up working an off-duty cop's job at a mall.[37] But a similar fate befell Krastev's teammate Aleksandar Varbanov. He won worlds three times, Europeans four times, took bronze at the 1988 Olympics and set 10 world records. Varbanov also emigrated to Canada, where a weightlifting fanatic—out shooting a round of golf—found Varbanov cutting the course's lawns.[38] The sport might pay now, but after the Cold War, the tide of history reduced many weightlifting icons to poverty.

Krastev coached weightlifters part-time at a local YMCA, and Broz moved to Minnesota to train with him. He and Broz hit it off, and the two became housemates. Broz told me he paid the rent and groceries in exchange for weightlifting coaching from the World Champion. Soon enough, Broz started working at the same bar, three nights a week to earn the bare minimum for expenses.

Over the next 24 months, Broz subjected himself to the Bulgarian method, as taught by one of its greatest pupils. During this time, Broz snatched 160kg in training as a light super, competed in national championships, and dated the woman that became his first wife. Broz and Krastev eventually fought, with cultural differences magnifying a small spat into a larger argument (Broz called him "weird" on many occasions). The two drifted apart.

Broz took what he learned from Krastev and applied it to me. With Krastev, Broz snatched, clean and jerked and squatted, and performed these three movements every day. Krastev held him to that single-minded approach for years, and Broz improved quickly.

But when Broz coached me with the same method, he made it seem like he implemented a pre-planned, fully articulated system of training. He encouraged others to believe that, first in the gym, then on YouTube videos, then in interviews.[39] The reality differs greatly.

My wife Taylor calls me "Broz's guinea pig," and reminds me that "Broz had no idea what he was doing and would never be the person to admit that." I think that Broz has since fine-tuned what he learned from Krastev (particularly regarding 2017 Pan Am medalist Angelo Bianco). But she was right; an exceptional athlete will make even a bad program appear better and enable a good program to achieve exceptional results. In interviews, Broz talks like my achievements confirmed some system already in place, but he's never replicated my success.

That success was me. My youth, my willingness to take drugs, my discipline and determination.

Every morning, I squatted to a heavy single, ranging from 250kg to 310kg. Each afternoon, snatch to max, then clean or clean and jerk to max. Eventually the morning sessions included heavy power snatches and power cleans, and then later, full snatches. Broz inducted me to this regimen as soon as I committed to lifting every day. This rushed introduction to the sport totally belies what he's said in interviews, about how an athlete needs to build work capacity over a significant period of time. But what Broz post-rationalized later, I didn't realize then, and trusted him. When the lifts looked fast, we added weight. When he watched me train, that is.

Otherwise, he didn't operate on a method. The Kazakh lifters go just as heavy just as often, but with structured daily workouts, defined loading and peaking phases modulated by volume and intensity, including tapers. But I only backed off when my injuries flared up; if I couldn't snatch or clean, I squatted more. If I couldn't squat because of my knee, Broz told me to do pulls.

If I missed a snatch or clean and jerk, I could attempt it again—up to six failed snatches and three or four dropped clean and jerks. Broz argued that each new weight on the bar resembled shaking someone's hand for the first time; you wouldn't know how it felt—or how to move the bar—until you actually grasped it. He told this story of the first time he snatched 150kg, how he missed it 52 times that day before he succeeded. Two hours of trying one weight on the bar until he locked it out overhead.

That never quit, never say die mentality is what Broz taught best. No sport demands more mental toughness than weightlifting. No activity punishes the body more. The competition lifts require years of practice toward mastery. Then add heavy squats, deadlifts, rows and presses to build the strength required to hit positions correctly and accelerate the bar at heavy weights.

Competitions give the athlete three attempts per lift. You fuck up three times and you're done. That stress alone compounds on lifters who spend hundreds of hours performing the same two movements for each attempt on the competition platform. Thousands and thousands of reps over months for six competition lifts. In a room, sometimes with no windows, often without other athletes; or on a team, always with the same small group of personalities all trying to fight and persist in the same stress-fueled manner.

Broz' mental approach applied most to pain and suffering. I heard the phrase "How you feel is a lie" only a few times before I didn't need to hear it anymore. Broz believed that something will always hurt, and that doesn't indicate injury or even that something happened or went wrong. Your body will lie to you. Pain will appear in one place one day and migrate somewhere else the next. Do you want to succeed? Don't listen to your body. Train through it. He insisted that athletes must train when things hurt. **And the lifter that can endure the most pain will be the most successful**. Even today, that last idea rings in my mind like a challenge, one that I still endorse and believe in.

For Broz, these ideas constituted the real work of a weightlifter. The bar feels heavy? No. It's heavy here (points finger to head). Something hurts? Ignore it and push through. You lack energy? Wait til you feel that way and still hit PR's. Then you'll know you're doing something right. And you'll achieve that fatigued state—which Broz called "the dark times"—only by training every day, twice per day if possible, 365 days out of the year. "There's no such thing as overtraining" I've heard Broz say. There's only under-recovery. Learn to fight.

So I listened. I learned. And I endured a hell of a lot of pain. In my head, I cultivated this myth, a narrative of what I was trying to do and my place in the universe. Think about it. My high school, Mike's supplement store, Virginia's house, and Broz' gym all lie within a one-mile radius. In a small town that happens all the time. But in the sprawl of Las Vegas, where people have to drive to their mailbox in some areas? If you stood on Virginia's front lawn, you could almost see all these important places from one vantage point. It felt like destiny.

And Broz, being taught first by Schubert, who coached the last American male to win gold at the Olympics, to then come under Krastev's tutelage? To coach me, after bumping into me at a high school power clean competition? A kid that possessed the determination and single-mindedness to leg press and bench every day for a summer? Broz later recruited other lifters from the power clean meets, but I was the first one. I thought, what are the odds?

I took a shower one day and started laughing. It just clicked. All these elements combined in my head into one big idea: that I was fated to be the greatest weightlifter of all time. I pictured myself lifting more than anyone ever. That was my goal. It would be my destiny.

That myth sustained me through a lot of early failures, and I relied on it whenever I questioned Broz, or his method, or his ability to coach me. And those doubts cropped up early: happening for the first time at the 2009 National Championships.

The Saturday night before I lifted at Nationals, I turned in around ten. I showered, got under the covers, read part of a book. Broz and I shared a room with two double beds. Eleven o'clock rolled by, Broz still hadn't returned to the room. I needed sleep and eventually found it.

Around 3:00 am, the door opened. Whispering turned into giggling, and I heard two voices, Broz' and a woman's. They closed the door and kept the light off. Streetlights shining through the blinds illuminated a mass of curly blonde hair falling over muscular shoulders. Pale white skin like a Viking. Sounds of kissing broke the stillness. I gripped the sheets in my fists, thinking "what the fuck?"

More whispering led to light moans, those obscured by the sounds of mattress springs creaking under the movement of two bodies. They're fucking in the bed right next to me. Broz and this girl who I later found out medaled at nationals that day and met up with him for drinks after. The noise went on for 20, 30 minutes. Then stopped, to be replaced by heavy breathing and more whispers. A few minutes passed and the door cracked open again. Through a half-closed eye I saw Broz sitting up in the bed, facing the door, his back to me.

Why didn't I flip out or say anything? Because Broz was my coach. He was the key to my myth, the gatekeeper to my future.

doubt the power an institutional structure exerts, especially over young boys, and especially over those devout, faithful, committed to a cause. Young men crave hierarchies as much as they rebel against them. The pecking order exerts one of the most powerful forces in human society. A real evolutionary force, which from a biological basis, builds forth into social structures. The most troubled youths can find their place in a rigid order; kids like me that cause trouble in class thrive on team sports, or later achieve positions in the military or corporate world.

It shouldn't surprise anyone with a basic grasp of evolutionary psychology why so many young men and women around the world unquestioningly let doctors and coaches feed them pills and inject them with syringes. What should really surprise is that any kids protest at all. Goldman's dilemma doesn't entice or decide, it exculpates later, long after the victories and the consequences and horrors that accompany them. Long before an athlete discovers himself, some adult with position and power presents him with opportunity, on a ladder leading up with fixed, measurable goals and rewards. Hungry athletes grab that first rung and climb.

Young people like me with no experience—and by definition, we have none—find an identity in sport and a place in the pecking order. We guard that identity fiercely, despite society's ethical objections, or possible punishments and stigmas. Ilya doesn't care that WADA labs popped him on retests. His country's doping program already enabled him to achieve unheard of feats: senior world champion at 17, world record holder in three different weight classes and two-time Olympic Champion. In that system, Ilya found his place in the world, his identity within a hierarchy, and he climbed the ladder until he was the Greatest Of All Time.

So while I wanted to scream and yell and curse out Broz for bringing some girl to our room the night before my first nationals, my position held me in check. In high school, my football coach could have told me to do burpees in full equipment until I threw up in my helmet. And I would have followed orders and obeyed. That's how hierarchies work. Not fear and reward, but position and privilege. Do what you're asked to earn your spot and you get to play the game.

To yell at Broz would have been unthinkable—to upset the natural order of things. I was 19. A kid. A grown man that held my future in his hands made choices that affected me. "Who am I to question him?" was never a thought. Because I was never going to question him. Period.

After the door closed and Broz went to sleep, I boiled inside. I bit into the pillow and balled my fists. The next morning, sleep deprived and still angry, I bombed out in the snatch.

Was Broz fit to coach me? I don't know. I soldiered on. Finding my place in the world as I went.

Eight:
A Cat and
Mouse Game, Part I

Countries, coaches and sports federations hold a vested interest in their athletes not testing positive for drug use. The state sponsored doping programs—though rife with highly publicized PED scandals—clearly succeed in evading the tests and testers year after year. Case in point: an anonymous survey[40] conducted at the 2011 World Championships for Track and Field revealed that over 30% of the competitors[41] used banned substances during the past 12 months. That number rose to 45% of respondents at the 2011 Pan Arab Games.[42]

During those 2011 Track and Field World Championships, doping officials tested *every single participant.* Yet less than one-half of one percent of them returned adverse analytical findings.[43] Thirty percent of the athletes surveyed at Worlds admitted using banned substances within 12 months of the event. But the testing of all athletes yielded less than 25 positive drug test results! Meaning: hundreds of the competitors got away with cheating at the 2011 Track and Field World Championships.[44]

Whether aided by state-sponsored doping programs, or acting on their own, the vast majority of athletes that use banned substances succeed in tapering off drugs and evading detection. These athletes then show up to competitions like World Championships and the Olympics in a drug-enhanced condition.

Cue the crickets.[45]

Researchers from Harvard Medical School and Germany's University of Tübingen conducted that study.[46] The scientists believed this survey showed doping remained widespread, and that despite the efforts of anti-doping organizations, few athletes got caught. Furthermore, these researchers believed the 30% figure underestimated the true nature of drug use in sport.

WADA initially refused to let the researchers publish their findings.[47]

In 2012, WADA administered over 267,000 drug tests worldwide.[48] This number does not include tests done by individual national doping agencies, such as USADA. Those 267,000 tests recorded only 3,200 adverse analytical findings that led to loss of competition results, medals or bans. That figure amounts to just over one percent of all athletes tested. The usual assumption holds that "most athletes train and compete clean." But the Harvard/Tübingen study suggests otherwise. More importantly, it indicated that most athletes that dope get away with it.

How do countries and athletes beat the testers? Historically, the state-sponsored programs tested their own athletes before *allowing* them to compete internationally.[49] According to Reiterer's *Positive*, at the 1976 Montreal Olympics, a boat bearing Russian flags moored in the city's harbor about a week before the games began. Soviet athletes landed in Montreal. and immediately headed to the docks. Not everyone who boarded the boat competed. Those in the know speculated that the ship contained a drug-testing laboratory. At the 2014 Sochi Winter Games, Russia one-upped these tactics, drilling a hole in the wall behind the drug-testing laboratory's refrigerator, then going in at night and swapping out clean samples of urine for the potentially doped ones.

East Germany passed State Plan 14.25 in part to keep random usage and the number of potential positives under control. The East German's operated on a strict schedule of doping, knowing how to bring the athletes off drugs so that positive results wouldn't embarrass the nation's sporting program. Xue Yinxian, a former doctor for the Chinese Olympic team, revealed in 2017 that China modeled its doping program on the East German success, and that over 10,000 athletes (as young as 11) were subjected to state-sponsored doping during the 1980s and 1990s. She added that China[50] tested its athletes before international competition, and these athletes only participated in an event if they passed China's own testing protocols.[51]

This type of pre-testing by national federations still occurs at the International level. The 2015 ARD Documentary *Doping—Top Secret: The Shadowy World of Athletics* exposed how it happens with Track and Field Athletes.[52] Filmmaker Hajo Seppelt presented evidence of Russian athletes, told of pre-competition testing. A still-positive athlete didn't travel to the meet.

Sometimes the athlete simply withdraws shortly before the start of a major competition (to avoid a potential sanction). The 105kg A session at the 2012 Olympics should have fielded the fiercest weightlifting session of the London Games. At the past year's World Championships in Paris, Russian lifters Dmitry Klokov and Khadzhimurat Akkayev fought lift for lift in an epic battle that Klokov lost by 2kg. The London Games should have pitted both against 2008 Olympic Champion and World Record Holder Andrei Aramnau (Belarus).

But a new rule[53] took effect for the London Olympics, that stipulated a lifetime ban for any athlete caught doping during the Olympic Festival (which is why Albania's Hysen Pulaku[54] can never compete in the Games). A few days before the start of the Olympics, Akkayev withdrew, citing a back injury; then Klokov bailed for "unspecified medical reasons." Aramnau also no showed. A test from earlier in 2012 returned a positive[55] finding for Akkayev, which is presumably why he didn't attend.

State-sponsored doping programs protect their best athletes, pre-testing them before the anti-doping agencies can catch them. If they've come off drugs in time, they compete. If not…well, just report some injury as cover and withdraw them from the event.[56]

That's what I did in 2010 on my return to competition. I bagged it, knowing I was still positive. Just like the state sponsored programs, I gamed the system to know if I came off drugs in time. Only I didn't have a federation or government backing me up. I had to be clever.

Las Vegas: 2010

I tapered off drugs even before I snatched 207kg on October 4. About a month earlier, I ditched all the injectables, including tren and all testosterone esters (I stopped taking Equipoise even earlier). I knew a guy in Vegas that stockpiled Testim—the testosterone cream—and I continued to use that daily, in addition to some of the orals.

Even as I cleaned out, I still crushed monster numbers in training, snatching 190kg nearly every day in September. I felt pumped and ready to compete at the 2010 American Open and obliterate the Junior National Records. That month I put together my best total to date, pairing a 205kg snatch with a 227kg C&J for a 432kg total.

I wasn't worried about the testosterone cream. At the time, testing for that hormone consisted of detecting a ratio of testosterone and epi-testosterone, a similar substance naturally produced by the body (usually in a 1 to 1 ratio with testosterone). Scientists have determined that in 90% of males, the ratio of test to epi-test does not naturally rise above 4 to 1; in the 99th percentile, it edges up closer to 6 to 1. WADA initially set the threshold at that latter number; anyone whose urine—analyzed by gas chromatography[57]—showed levels of testosterone to epitestosterone above 6:1 was considered to have administered artificial testosterone.

For instance, in 2006, cyclist Floyd Landis[58] showed a T/E ratio of 11 to 1; in 1996, American distance runner Mary Decker[59] displayed a level greater than 6 to 1 (which she blamed on birth control pills). As of this writing, WADA has brought the adverse level down to 4:1. If a sample's flirts with the 4:1 ratio, WADA uses a separate technique[60] to determine if the levels resulted from natural testosterone production or from pharmaceutical origins.

Here's a slight twist: many athletes of Asian descent show no variation in their T/E ratios when tested. According to Swedish doctor Jenny Jakobsson Schulze,[61] about two-thirds of Asian men possess a double gene deletion that causes them to not excrete *any* testosterone in their urine, **no matter how much testosterone they take exogenously or produce naturally**. Safe bet that national federations in some countries profile their athletes to detect this double gene deletion and then dope accordingly (about 10% of Caucasian-descended males[62] also have this gene deletion).[63]

I don't know if I possess that gene deletion or not, but I calculated that I wasn't using enough testosterone cream to surpass that magic 4:1 number.

Broz told me I needed to qualify for that year's American Open, and he picked the Nomad Open for its location and proximity to the end of the qualifying period. We arrived at the venue and I signed up with USAW that day, mostly to avoid giving them notice that I was competing (we knew the folks at USAW watched our videos on YouTube). The Nomad Open marked my fourth meet ever, after almost three years of training weightlifting.

Our plan: for me to lift just enough to qualify for the American Open. National meets in 2010 seldom fielded enough lifters for "B" sessions, especially in the superheavyweight category (some years, only five or six lifters competed). I opened at 170kg and smoked it. The small crowd didn't expect to see a monster lift that day and roared with enthusiasm. No one in the competition snatched anywhere near my opener, so Broz let the two-minute clock tick down a few seconds before bumping my second attempt to 173kg, then 175kg, and then stopped at 180kg. Even with my headphones on, I could hear the anticipation and excitement of the spectators.

On my second lift, I sat a little long in the setup. I had only snatched this weight without straps a few other times and wanted to sense how heavy it would feel in my hands. I rocked back in my heels then lifted my hips, gripped the bar and pulled hard. Luckily, the mistake didn't cost me the lift. The weight sailed up, almost too easily and I punched hard into the collars to lock it out overhead. Another successful lift down; one attempt to go.

Broz declared 182kg—400lbs!—just for the crowd to know we meant business, then increased my attempts to 185kg and finally 190kg. I had never snatched this weight without straps; shit, I almost never snatched without straps.[64]

I set up just as tight as 180kg, then ripped the bar off the floor, grabbing it so violently with my hands that the weight drug me forward. My legs drove the weight high enough, but I left the barbell just out front for a close miss. The crowd vented their disappointment, then cheered, knowing that only one other American—Shane Hamman—had even attempted this weight before. And they got to see it in person, at a local meet!

The crowd called and cheered for a massive clean and jerk to exceed the huge snatch attempts. But Broz and I took a different path. He decided that a 300kg total would suffice for me to qualify for the American Open, so I warmed up quickly with the empty bar in the back, then hit a single power clean and jerk at 70kg before declaring my first attempt at 120kg. I strutted onto the platform, power cleaned it easily, then drove it overhead for my only C&J of the day. We scratched my last two attempts and called it a day.

Maybe that pissed some people off, but whatever. By this point, we already attracted a good deal of hate online. Some YouTube comments turned negative. Broz generally responded to questions about training, but by mid-2010, posters began asking "when will Pat compete next" or worse, "how come he doesn't compete," insinuating that I'm a dirty lifter and Broz a dirty coach. Someone even pranked the gym, calling to ask if they could buy steroids before laughing and hanging up.

At home, Virginia pressured me to compete as well. From her point of view, I crushed all these big training lifts, but hadn't done a meet in over a year. Even though she let me live rent-free and supported my training, she asked questions, and I felt the need to pay back my debt. Plus, I really wanted to prove myself. It's not easy to train hard for over a year, hit massive numbers and never get anything out of it except likes and comments on YouTube. I knew I should compete and achieve my greater goals in the sport.

Two days after the competition, USADA knocked at Virginia's front door for the first time. Then two guys in lab coats barged into Broz' gym looking for me. At this time, Broz still ran his gym out of his granite business. He hadn't registered a club with USA Weightlifting and his company lay way off the beaten path as far as Vegas goes. No one knew the location, we never hung signs, listed in the phone book or ran a website. But someone called USAW, told them "hey, Pat's on drugs" told them *where we were*, and sicced USADA on me.

But when USADA arrived, I wasn't there. Any other Monday, I show up like clockwork for training, even two days after a competition. That morning, Virginia asked me to drop her at the airport. When I rolled in that afternoon, Broz looked like a ghost. We thought you needed to be on an international team or signed up for whereabouts for USADA to test you at their will. Before that weekend's competition, they couldn't test me no matter how many world records I shattered on YouTube.[65] I was a private citizen, lifting weights in a backroom of a granite business. Signing up for USAW put me back in their purview.

Now they lost the element of surprise. The lab guys didn't stick around. I wasn't in the registered testing pool so they couldn't demand me to be anywhere at any given time. They needed to catch me. Taking Virginia to the airport on that day, when USADA shows up randomly, played right into my myth. Now I believed even harder that it all had to happen.

I qualified for the American Open and planned to compete. But I needed a lab to drug test my urine before USADA forced me to give a sample. A quick search on the Internet led me to Redwood Toxicology Laboratory in Santa Rosa, California.[66] Even today, their website offers to test the full "WADA panel" of banned substances. They sent me double-sealed urine collection kits (the same used by USADA) with randomized numbers for anonymity; I could even tell them exactly which drugs to test for!

One catch: the company only provided services to accredited sports leagues or corporations. So I registered an amateur sports league and created a schedule of (non-existent) events requiring drug testing in the name of "clean sport." Now Redwood worked with me. Any time I wanted; I could submit my own urine as if it was a testable sample of one of the players in my phony sports league that we randomly selected for drug testing!

Redwood sent back the worst news: my urine tested positive for metabolites of trenbolone. If USADA tested me the Monday I took Virginia to the airport, it would have been game over. Those metabolites meant I couldn't compete at the 2010 American Open, the last meet of my career at which I could attempt Junior national records.

That news hit hard. I crumbled the letter from Redwood in my hands and cried. Cleaning out had wrecked me hormonally. All that hard work just to discover I didn't taper off drugs soon enough.

Ever since Broz posted the "World's Strongest Teenager" video, YouTube comments rolled in like a river of hype, hope and hate. I felt paralyzed, like I gotta break this record, I gotta do something. I was crazy tired of lifting all this weight in training, listening to people talk shit, and then not being able to capitalize on my efforts. My last meet as a junior and now I would miss it.

A slight pain nagged at my shoulder since August, and over the next few months, it crept into my elbow and wrist, radiating pain during heavy snatches. Someone Broz knew arranged for me to get an MRI and the imaging revealed a supraspinatus tear. Figures. I'm strong enough and technically proficient enough to snatch

190kg every day for a month with a torn rotator cuff but not smart enough to taper off tren in time.

The injury gave me an excuse. Something to tell Virginia, my friends and myself for why I couldn't compete at the American Open. And it gave me a motivation, to clean out for good. December 1, 2010, USADA dropped by Broz' gym again. I hid in a storage room, literally cowering behind a stack of granite tiles. Crouching on that cold floor, listening to a pair of voices demanding to know where I was, I made another decision: I had to find a way to do this sport without drugs. And for almost a year, I stuck to it.

NINE

LEGITIMACY:
THE ARNOLD & THE OTC

In the college football movie *The Program*, defensive end Steve Lattimer adds 35lbs of muscle "and an attitude to match" in one summer. The NCAA tests him rigorously, but he evades detection, in one case, substituting another athlete's urine for his own, much like Giants legend Lawrence Taylor did during the 1980s.[67] After Lattimer assaults a coed, the coach tells him to clean out, and that he (the coach) "is personally gonna watch him pee in that cup."

A few hours before his next drug test, one of Lattimer's friends administers "an oil change," inserting a catheter down his urethra to pump the doped urine out of his bladder before injecting clean urine back in. It sounds fictional, but in 2014, a group of football players at Pace University convinced nursing students to perform the same procedure on them.[68]

WADA's continually updated code bans many diuretics and masking agents that can flush out or hide the presence of PED's. That hasn't stopped athletes from engaging in some crazy schemes and antics to avoid drug detection. It's been rumored that one track superstar kept her bright fingernails long to surreptitiously pierce a pouch filled with clean urine that she hid inside her vagina before a race. For men, "The Whizzinator" was a rubber, customizable prosthetic penis sold with dried, drug-free urine. The wearer could re-hydrate the powder, pour it in the shaft, place it on his own unit and then relieve the contents before unwitting doping agents. Again, not Hollywood. A few high-profile athletes got caught with this device. Congress even held a hearing about it.[69]

One of the best ways to avoid detection is to never get tested at all. The IOC mandates out-of-competition testing (OOC) as part of Olympic qualification. National or sporting federations must show compliance and regularly test athletes in the lead up to each quadrennial's Games.

A 2019 documentary alleged that weightlifters don't consistently undergo that process. German broadcaster ARD aired Hajo Seppelt's *Lord of the Lifters*, which claimed that officials bribed drug testers in Moldova to accept an imposter's urine for an athlete's sample, that 2/3rds of Russian medalists at Worlds were not tested and that almost 50% of the total medalists from the 2008-2017 Worlds Championships and Olympics did not get tested after medaling. The ARD documentary also claimed that one four-time world champion was not tested at all while serving a suspension.[70]

It's not just weightlifting.[71] From February 2012 until that summer's Olympics, Jamaican Antidoping (JADCO) performed only one out of competition drug test on that nation's athletes.[72] Jamaican sprinters dominated those Games, winning 12 medals. In 2013, world record holder Asafa Powell and four other Jamaican sprinters tested positive for banned substances.[73] Whistleblowers in Russia described bribes and advance notice of OOC testing.[74] A doping officer claimed in 2018 that he tipped off three-time 1500m World Champion Asbel Kiprop about an OOC test, one of many incidents in that powerhouse running nation's problems with policing its drug use internally.[75]

Even at the 2016 Olympics, the IOC failed to execute almost 50% of their planned out-of-competition tests, because the testers *could not find the athletes* in the Olympic village![76]

But you have to compete to get caught. I learned that when I ditched the 2010 American Open.

I can all but guarantee USADA would have tested me at that event. They knocked on Virginia's door a few days after. My urine still showed tren metabolites, so I hid downstairs. I didn't know how to mask doping, and my youth and inexperience again hindered my success.

Las Vegas: December 2010

Not attempting the Junior records left me devastated going into the holidays. Virginia and her sons celebrated a traditional Christmas, far removed from the craziness of my childhood. I stopped by to see my mom and Ken on Christmas for the last time. My little brother found his own adoptive family, staying with friends until he finished high school.

Despite the normalcy at Virginia's house, my depression worsened. Internet forums and bodybuilder friends can only describe what happens when you clean out from steroids. The actual suffering transcends explanation. My testosterone levels plummeted. For over a year I substituted artificial hormones for my body's own production, which shut down in response. Smarter athletes avoid this problem with the help of doctors, and by taking drugs like Human Chorionic Gonadotropin and estrogen blockers that re-start normal testosterone production. Of course, WADA has also banned these drugs, so god forbid you get caught taking them.

Studies reveal that low testosterone in men causes a host of emotional problems, from bitterness and anger to depression. I had Redwood Labs check my levels: they asked if I mislabeled the gender on the sample.

Broz pushed me to prepare for next March's 2011 Arnold and the July 2011 National Championships. In January, I resumed training, seven days a week, two sessions a day Monday to Friday. This time without drugs. Friends still ask what motivated me, and honestly, I really liked weightlifting, and spending time in a gym. The routine often did the work that discipline couldn't. In the back of my mind, I figured something would happen, or I could learn how to dope strategically and attempt world records again.

Without testosterone, without access to methods that could re-engage my natural production, I trained as best I could and then moped around Virginia's basement. That was my life post-steroids. No PR's, few big lifts, lots of pain and lethargy.

But then an invite to the Arnold lit a fire under my ass and drove me to go heavy again. The 2011 Arnold featured a premiere session of six top USA male athletes pitted against the top men from the Oceania Weightlifting Federation. At the time,[77] organizer Mark Canella ran the Arnold as his discretion. He offered prize money for all age categories and invited international lifters Dmitri Klokov, Tatiana Kashirina and Lydia Valentin to compete alongside America's best. Each year the Arnold drew upwards of 90,000 spectators, giving the competition a prestige unmatched by even USA's National Championships.[78] Newer members of USAW are spoiled by how good American lifters have become. Back then, Canella flew in foreign champions to show us just how much weight a human could put over her head.

Canella hand-picked the athletes for what he titled the "Islands versus Mainland Challenge." Team USA included Olympians Chad Vaughn and Kendrick Ferris, national record holder Caleb Williams[79], Dutch Lowry, 2010 National Champion Phil Sabatini, and me! My YouTube "celebrity" finally paid off, granting me access to this event even though I had yet to post a total at a national meet. Oceania's roster listed athletes from the Pacific Islands, headlined by Nauru's superheavyweight Itte Detenamo, who competed at two Olympics and medaled at the 2006 Commonwealth Games.

Now I was fired up!

My squat still floundered; attempting max singles crippled my knees, and repetitive misses in the snatch wreaked havoc on my wrists, elbows and shoulders. Luckily, one of the guys at Broz' gym paid for Plasma Rich Platelet Therapy (PRP) on my shoulder, which alleviated the torn rotator cuff. I sent another sample to Redwood and boom! I was 100% clean and ready to go.

The minute I registered for the Arnold, I heard a knock on Virginia's door. I don't know how anyone had the stones to use a whizzinator. Once you make eye contact with USADA reps, you can't leave their sight. No way I could brew up some clean piss and put it in a prosthetic penis. Plus, under USADA rules, the dude stares right at your dick the entire time you're peeing. Some days it took forever for a trickle to come out, and I had to run water or imagine standing in a river. My wife Taylor has been drug tested nearly as often as me—guilt by association. whatever—and doping control agents won't even let females sit down on the toilet. They made her pee standing up as the woman squats down in front of her, staring at her vagina, no matter what time of the month or how unkempt it might look.

Saturday, March 5, 2011, we weighed in for the premier session at the Arnold. Before the weigh-ins, Team USA treated it like an exhibition match, offering cheery introductions and hearty handshakes. But once the ten-minute clock ticked down, we went to war.

Caleb Williams kicked off the snatches with an impressive 125kg lift (at 69kg, a few kilos shy of his own national record). Then Chad Vaughn smoked a 147kg snatch—then just 3kg under the National Record. Kendrick—who still competed at 85kg—flew under a 155kg snatch with a speed that outclassed everyone in the session.

In the clean and jerks, the Oceania lifters held a clear advantage. Some of their lighter athletes crushed massive attempts. Vaughn hit a solid second attempt at 183kg, and then attempted a national record of 191kg on his third. He racked the clean easily but couldn't stand it up for the jerk (why he never wore a belt baffles me to this day). Kendrick bombed in spectacular fashion, while attempting 197kg, 6kg under his own national record of 203kg.

Everyone on Team USA finished snatching when the loaders put 170kg on the bar for my opener. I smiled as Broz shook his head and increased the weight, forcing Detenamo to take 170kg for his *second* attempt. This guy outweighed me by at least 40kg, and after he made 170kg, I walked out for 175kg. The Arnold was my fifth meet ever and I opened heavier in the snatch than a two-time Olympian.

The bar felt light off the floor and I smoked my first lift for a 5kg advantage. Detenamo missed his third. On my second attempt, I threw 182kg behind then left 183kg out front. Going into the C&J's I maintained a 5kg lead (plus the bodyweight advantage).

Detenamo opened with 205kg, crushing his jerk like an unloaded barbell. Broz pushed me up to 207kg, which I manhandled; surprising the audience (and myself TBH) with a strong power jerk. That lift increased my lead to 7kg. Now the jockeying for placement began. Detenamo barely racked 215kg on his second lift but stood it up and jerked the bar like a broomstick. My next lift marked the first time that Broz' ego impeded a sound strategy in competition. Had I opened at 210kg, or matched Detenamo lift for lift, we could have pushed him into lower C&J attempts and kept a lead over him by bodyweight if nothing else.

But instead, Broz thought "beat him in the C&J too" and moved me to 217kg for my second lift. I crushed the clean but couldn't get my hands around the bar for the jerk. After driving it high, I struggled to push under it and lost it forward. Detenamo's coaches played it smart, letting his clock start on 217kg for his third attempt before moving to 220kg, which forced me to take 217kg again with less than a minute's rest.

Three months earlier, I would have stood that up on tired legs. But now, 217kg dragged me to the floor. I misracked it, giving Detenamo a 3kg margin of victory. I posted my first big total at 382kg and suffered my first loss as well.

My total would have won the past year's national championships, and I did it as a relative unknown, facing a two-time Olympian in a session with multiple Olympic competitors. Representatives from USA Weightlifting noticed and waited for me after drug testing.

"Pat, we'd like you to come out for a trial residency at the Olympic Training Center."

My jaw dropped. The federation created the OTC for weightlifting about a decade earlier, and only recruited the most promising lifters. An invitation conferred legitimacy and an affirmation of the athlete's potential.[80]

I accepted on the spot. They told me to enroll in RTP ("Registered Testing Pool") which required me to use the "Whereabouts" athlete tracking system. Every three months, I needed to give them a firm schedule of where they could find me 24-7.[81] If I traveled, I had to let them know. Ditto if someone died or I went to the hospital. If USADA showed and I wasn't there, they assessed me with a "finding failure" for evading the drug test. Three of those in an 18-month period and they could suspend me for two years.[82]

After three months in RTP I became eligible for international team selection.[83] I agreed to what RTP implied, because National Championships—the final qualification event for the Pan Am Games and 2011 Worlds—was three months away. I signed up for RTP the minute I returned to Vegas and Broz and I began planning for Nationals.

I scheduled my two-week tryout at the OTC a month later.

At the time, I still donated plasma for gas money. Even with my strong performance at the Arnold and the invite to the OTC, USAW didn't grant me a stipend. And unlike today, where athletes on the World Team earn a generous living allowance, USAW's stipend system paid little in 2011. At my peak, when I represented Team USA at Worlds, I received $600/month.

As much as I loved living with Virginia, I hated not paying rent. At the OTC, athletes lived in dormitories, with meals provided by a cafeteria. Several sports kept residencies there, including baseball, wrestling and USA Gymnastics. USAW picked up the tab for resident weightlifters.[84]

When I arrived, only a handful of athletes stayed there, including two of the top 63kg females: Carissa Gump and Natalie Burgener. They fought pitched battles at national meets, one snatching heavy, the other destroying big clean and jerks. Geralee Vega from Puerto Rico moved there and represented Team USA several times internationally before leaving the sport.[85] Jessica Gallagher (now Lucero) also worked out with the team, but not as a full resident.[86]

On the men's side, Donovan Ford lived there on a sizeable endowment from DeVry University. Colin Burns enjoyed a similar setup as Jessica Gallagher; at the time, his expenses weren't funded, but he resided locally and trained with us. He also didn't talk to me during my visit.[87] Jared Flemming dropped in at the same time, on a try out like me. Few athletes, not all of them the best in their respective weight classes; not necessarily the model for professional, team-based training at the level of Colombia, Poland or Kazakhstan.

Aside from the dorms and cafeterias, the OTC's real benefit was Zygmunt Smalcerz, the official Head Coach for USA Weightlifting.[88] While competing for Poland, he won Gold in the 1972 Munich Olympics (52kg category) and took Gold at the 1971 and 1975 World Championships. He withdrew from the 1976 Montreal Games due to injury and then embarked on a storied coaching career for Poland, where he produced world champions and Olympic medalists Szymon Kolecki, Marcin Dolega and Adrian Zielinski, among many others.[89]

Strangely enough, not every athlete there trusted Zygmunt. He replaced the popular Dragomir Cioroslan, an Olympic Bronze medalist from Romania. Zygmunt followed a volume heavy training plan adapted from what he used in Poland. His methods reportedly beat the shit out of the American athletes, but I loved it. And I loved working with him.

Zygmunt put me on a structured program from day one. The weightlifters woke early, ate breakfast, and then squatted. I managed to grind out a very painful 310kg one morning, to which Zygmunt muttered a barely approving "good." It was the heaviest weight I squatted all year. After one successful snatch session, where we worked up to doubles from the floor, he gave me a rare compliment, telling me that my snatches reminded him of three-time world champion Marcin Dolega.

Afternoon workouts included positional work in the snatch and clean. Almost three years into the sport and I had never lifted from the hang or from blocks. "Do four sets of four, 60 percent" he told me. After a long diet of heavy singles, I struggled to get my breath. We then switched to block work, doing doubles at 80 to 85 percent and fluctuating the intensity up and down on subsequent sets. He watched me critically, offered technical suggestions, and always encouraged my performance. In stark contrast to Broz, during the weeks I spent under Zygmunt, we didn't max out the snatch or clean and jerk a single time.

We still lifted heavy. When I arrived, I told Zygmunt and the other coaches that I was battling a nagging injury (I knew my YouTube reputation preceded me). Once, Zygmunt played a video of me snatching much heavier weights. Through a sly smile he asked, "where's this guy?" before quietly walking away. I blamed the injury and he didn't push me about it.

The general antipathy and unwillingness to trust Zygmunt's coaching confused me.[90] Some of the residents flat out refused to follow his programming; Bob Morris still held his appointment as USAW's official women's coach and a few of the athletes there worked primarily with him.

I loved Zygmunt. He said I possessed a fantastic base for training, and he liked that I followed his directions and didn't question things. I responded that I didn't understand why the athletes resisted his coaching. Zygmunt shrugged a similar disbelief. "I have suitcases full of medals," referencing the dozens of medals his athletes won at Europeans, Worlds, and the Olympic Games.

The Americans—perhaps rightly—didn't believe that his methods would work with non-doped athletes given that three of Zygmunt's prodigies (Kolecki, Dolega and Zielinski) all tested positive for steroids at one point.

During my stay, USAW hooked me up with a nutritionist, who ran a DEXA scan to measure bone density, bodyfat and other markers. He catalogued what I had been eating (which was terrible) and then prescribed a much better nutrition plan. It was easy to follow when I only had to eat, sleep and lift each day.

But not everything at the OTC facilitated the weightlifters' success. Sure, USAW covered dorms and meals, but they didn't foot any recovery methods and therapy. Want a massage? Pay for it out of pocket at prime rates. The baseball players and gymnasts could access new technologies like Normatec (their federations covered the cost), while we looked on dumbly and wondered how the compression felt. At very specific times, the lifters could sit in the ice baths and sauna, but we were clearly bottom of the barrel. With the number of times we trained per week, none of us could work to pay for treatment.

Otherwise, the OTC upgraded everything over my current life. If I moved there, I could live and train like a professional athlete. No more donating plasma. No more relying on Virginia or Poliquin for food. Not to take credit away from Broz, but the OTC gave me the opportunity to work with an international coach that produced medalists at multiple World Championships.

On my second day at the training center, USADA came looking for me, a little to the amusement of the athletes who watched them escort me the bathroom. All these tests turned into a blessing. After I cleaned out in November, I kept passing their drug tests and my clean record justified an invite to stay. A few days before my departure, some officials from USAW met with me for an exit interview.

I answered their questions casually and they offered me a full-time residency. "We want you to be the new face of USA

Weightlifting," they announced. My eyes widened then must have immediately contracted, because they added "We realize it's a huge change. Give it some thought, talk to your family about it."

Which meant talking to Broz about it.

The next day, I flew back to Vegas and drove to the gym for training. Broz was there; I could see him pacing up and down the back office when I drove in. The conversation quickly intensified. Even before I left, Broz told me repeatedly that he didn't want me to visit the OTC. I know he feared losing me as his athlete, that he feared losing this vicarious weightlifting dream of an Olympic Gold medal.

The moment we started talking, Broz sold me. His eyes watered and he said "I really don't want you to go. I know we can do this, I know we can get there." In hindsight, I see how delusional it sounds, and can't believe I fell for it. Broz lacked an international coaching background; he didn't earn a degree in chemistry or possess the finances to support me. Nothing substantiated his plans other than the fact that up to that point, I lifted a lot of weight. In secret.

Since the Arnold, a small team of lifters formed at ABG. Some of them, like Josh Gilbert and Jared Enderton, showed true promise. And my old football rival Rob Addell would put up monster numbers—at least on YouTube.[91] Tyler Thuente, Billy Bybee and Ian Droze all qualified for Nationals, and Broz laid out plans for a true team training environment supervised by him; a proper space, with a half dozen platforms and better equipment.

In my head, I knew it was the wrong move if I wanted to play it safe, have a journeyman's career in weightlifting. I understood the unspoken undercurrent of Broz' words. If I moved to the OTC, it meant never achieving international medals or records. I trained with the athletes that lived there; none of them came within 90% of their respective world records. From a national perspective, I produced solid numbers; the clean and jerk lagged a bit, but I needed to emphasize it more in training. But internationally? My best efforts would barely bump me into a B-session at World Championships.

Broz infected me early with this notion that only World Championships counted, and the only number that mattered was the world record. All those champions took drugs. All those world records required drugs to achieve. The alternative? Lift and train at the OTC and do well with Zygmunt as my coach but never medal at worlds and never hold a world record. No matter how hard I tried as a clean lifter in the United States.

So I relented to Broz' begging. I stayed in Vegas, slept on a borrowed bed, ate meals off another person's plate and continued to donate plasma for gas money. I could have escaped all of it. But I stayed and prepared for Nationals without any steroids to help me.

I chased the same big goals but with no understanding of how to achieve them.

Ten:
Winning 2011 Nationals and Lifting for Team USA

Name your favorite weightlifter. With few exceptions, odds are that he or she has tested positive for PED's. Lasha Talakhadze, Sohrab Moradi, Liao Hui, Toma Loredana, Ilya, Kim Un Ju, Marcin Dolega, Kim Un Guk, Boyanka Kostova, Aleksei Lovchev, Olga Zubova, Sukanya Srisurat, Nurcan Taylan, Nijat Rahimov. All World medalists, most world record holders, and all tested positive at one point in their respective weightlifting careers.

Critics will always single out weightlifting for its drug abuse. And the prevalence of doping cases might lead some to believe that the sport teems with unsavory characters. Especially internationally, where drug-free champions like Tara Nott, Christine Girard and Lydia Valentin are the true outliers.

In a few even rarer situations, some weightlifters win multiple World and Olympic medals, set one world record after the next, and never get popped. Sometimes, a superstar's entire national team tests positive but they're the lone exception.[92] Bribery and payoffs occur in lifting just as much as soccer and track and field.

Why do so many weightlifters get caught using performance enhancing drugs? Does the sport attract unethical competitors, or corrupt those who practice it?

Or does the better question ask why so many swimmers, cyclists, and track athletes test positive? Why did over 30-percent of the participants at the 2011 Track and Field World Championships admit using PED's in the 12 months before that event? Why do so many athletes in these sports ask for TUE's for asthma medication or blame positive stimulant results on cold medications taken in the middle of the summer? Why were marathoners Galen Rupp and Mo Farrah illegally given intravenous L-carnitine?[93]

It's because the iron does not lie. The stopwatch does not lie. The tape measure does not lie.

Every sport that measures results in kilograms, meters or seconds clearly indicates the superior athlete in competition. The metrics of weight lifted, times ran, swum or biked, height jumped, or distances thrown are objective measures. Measurable progress invites cheating just as much as influence of judges and referees invites bribery and fraud in other areas (figure skating, basketball, gymnastics, baseball). Where referees and judges can aid victory, you find coaches and athletes willing to pay or coerce.

No amount of corruption, bribery or diplomacy can sway the absolute judges of kilograms, meters and seconds. But performance enhancing drugs can affect those outcomes. And athletes use them to train harder, recover better, and enable those razor thin margins that determine a spot on the podium from those few hundredths of a seconds that finish fourth place.

It's human nature to push the boundaries and see what you can get away with. And yes, it's also human to fight against those impulses even when the disappointment becomes more feigned and the disillusionment more ignored with each idolized superstar that falls from grace.

Las Vegas: Summer 2011

My performance at the Arnold put Broz' gym on the map. Before that competition, mine—and Broz'—reputation rested on

YouTube videos. But I just hit a solid total, in a premiere session at the biggest sports festival in the country. Now people moved to train with me and Broz in Vegas.[94]

For the first time, I lifted alongside other young, hungry athletes. When Broz began coaching, he let anyone train with us, including masters athletes that he knew from Gold's Gym. Some days I ignored their lifting; other times I wanted to scream. Broz and I had to hype them up to take (and usually miss) 100kg C&J's. And I needed to turn my head away, cause their failures weighed me down like a stone when I tried to snatch nearly twice as much after their attempts.

Good training partners can set any room on fire with the energy that fuels monster lifts. If Rob Addell and Josh Gilbert trained with me during the 18 months that I doped, I have no doubt that I could've snatched 210-215kg with them pushing me. Especially on the days Addell cranked out rep after rep of 200kg cleans.[95]

Their presence after the Arnold was a godsend. Because I needed their motivation and support to plow through the hardest training period of my life.

There really is no end to the way in which training on drugs is better than training without drugs.

After knowing the alternative, training clean was the worst fucking thing in the world. I hated every second of it. Even today, I can't compare the sensations of doping and clean lifting. Sure, I suffered aches and pains when on steroids, but I recovered quickly from one workout to the next, and the much bigger numbers I hit always compensated for the discomfort.

Off drugs left me spinning my wheels the entire year.

Broz still asked me to train twelve sessions a week, but I couldn't handle the volume. He tempered some of the afternoon workouts with power snatches and power cleans, to keep the intensity lighter. But the average weight on the bar kept dropping. There was no plan to figure out how to adjust; Broz' attitude and method boiled down to "go train go train go train."

We spent most of 2011 trying to get my squat back up. Like a broken record, he repeated that I if I squatted heavier, then bigger lifts would follow. I didn't back squat more than 320kg the entire year, and I only hit that number once.

My hip bothered me, my shoulder flared up, and my weight topped 130kg—my heaviest yet—mostly from constant inflammation and water retention. I felt in horrible shape. Nonetheless, me, Broz and four other lifters trekked out to Council Bluffs, Iowa for National championships.

Our new team enjoyed immediate success. Ian Droze took third in the 69kg class behind Derrick Johnson and Caleb Ward. He snatched 116kg and C&J'ed 146kg. The next day, Billy Bybee finished fourth in the 77kg class with a 115kg snatch and 150kg clean and jerk (two missed lifts away from a medal). Jared Enderton lifted on an injured thumb, snatching 131kg and clean and jerking 166kg to take ninth in a stacked 94kg class. Tyler Thuente placed tenth in the supers.

On Sunday, I lifted in the final session of the competition. Spoiler alert: no one hung with me in either lift. Shane Maier and Cameron Swart took silver and bronze, respectively, but I attempted all of my snatches after they completed their own attempts. By this meet, my technique improved, and my mental game caught up as well.

When I wore straps every day, I just ripped the bar off the floor as hard as I could (imagine the strength required to snatch 207kg with that approach). Wearing straps never let me feel how light the bar actually is off the floor either. No athlete with a good squat and a strong back will ever put enough weight on the bar in the snatch for it to truly feel heavy. Never. I could deadlift 150kg more than I could attempt in the snatch, so 180kg should always feel light if I kept my back and lats tight.

With straps I could never achieve that sensation, but now without them, I finally learned to push with my feet. I didn't execute that way on my opener at 170kg, which explains why I missed it out front. But I smoked the second and third attempts (170kg and 177kg, respectively), giving me a 12kg lead.

Heavier jerks eluded me, mostly from constant pain in my knees and shoulders. I retained a sizeable lead after Maier, Swart and I opened (at 203kg, 205kg and 200kg, respectively). Maier tried to close the gap by taking 208kg on his next two attempts but missed both jerks. After Maier finished, Swart took a ridiculous 14kg jump to 219kg, setting me up for my second attempt. I cleaned 210kg easily but didn't lock out the jerk, then came back and crushed 212kg on my third attempt. Swart took two cracks at 219kg, but misracked both cleans.[95]

My teammates high fived me for winning my first national championship. Doping control corralled me after the medal ceremony, my sixth test in three months. The reputation at Broz' gym—completely undeserved at this point—preceded us to nationals. USADA representatives tested every single Broz athlete in the competition, including Tyler Thuente, who lifted in the B session and came nowhere close to medaling. In that regard, nationals was a huge success: we were all tested, everyone totaled, and no one got popped!

After the medal ceremony, officials from USAW approached me. Pending the outcome of my drug tests, they offered me spots on two International teams: the 2011 Pan Am Games squad going to Guadalajara, Mexico in October, and the World Championship Team set to compete in Paris that November. Broz patted me on the back as they discussed my prospects, and I felt stunned, and happy, the first signs of success I earned in three years of training.

In the back of my mind, I knew I wouldn't stand a competitive chance at Worlds that fall. None of the Americans would. All the top doping nations fielded full squads, and the usual suspects dominated: Armenia, Azerbaijan, Belarus, China, Kazakhstan, Russia, Turkey and Ukraine.

At the time, most of their athletes passed doping control by tapering off drugs in time, especially steroids like Oral Turinabol and Stanozolol. USADA tested me every few weeks, and on whereabouts, tracked where I lived, worked, trained and slept. They could find and test me at any time. I learned much later through personal conversations with foreign lifters—not to mention a German documentary—that athletes in other countries never faced such scrutiny.

How could I take drugs to keep up with them? Alleged BALCO mastermind Victor Conte once argued that "beating a doping test is like passing an IQ test." You're either smart enough to out-maneuver the system or you fall short. He advised—in a still available YouTube interview—that athletes in whereabouts could continue doping by manipulating the "failure to find" provision of the whereabouts testing.[97]

He calculated the likelihood of a USADA random test at 1 in 25 during any training period. In theory, athletes could dope on a pre-planned schedule. If USADA showed up during the doping period, the athlete would hide and accept a "failure to find." In 2011, an athlete could receive three of these in a 12-month period (since expanded to 18-months). On the third failure, athletes got a sanction (at the time, a two-year ban). An athlete manipulating the system in this way could dope for 12 weeks, banking on USADA not looking for them more than twice in that span.

In 2011, that strategy enabled someone to take testosterone suspension, growth hormone and orals like Turinabol, all of which possessed short detection times. The benefits of even a 12-week doping program on these drugs would improve results. If done long enough, I could—in theory—match the numbers hit by athletes in state-sanctioned doping programs. Or at least keep my numbers high enough to take a legit shot at medaling at World level meets. The better option, the one run by every sport not tested directly by USADA, involved the national federation alerting their athletes to the timing of a "random" out of competition drug test.[98]

But USADA targeted me with far greater frequency than twice in 12 weeks, leaving Conte's tactics off the table. Even clean, USADA handed me my first "failure to find" that summer. A few days after the team returned from Nationals, USADA knocked on my door to test me again. I thought, c'mon motherfuckers, you just tested me Sunday and it's not even Friday of the week after. But USADA suspected me of going right back on drugs as soon as I cleared testing at nationals. And they acted on an attitude of "make examples of these cheaters or harass them out of the sport." Let me reiterate that **at this point, I had never failed a drug test** and their scrutiny derived purely from speculation.

That day, I took a trip to LA and forgot to enter it in whereabouts. On the ride back, a USADA rep called my cell. He informed me that he was in Vegas, came to the gym, went to Virginia's house, and wanted to know where he could find me. "I'm driving and will be back around 3 or 4 o'clock," I told him, asking if he could wait. The rep replied that he needed to test members of a local soccer team, and he would swing back for me. Except that he didn't and a few weeks later USADA mailed me a "finding failure" letter. I appealed it, told my story, but the arbitration panel upheld the original decision.

Again, the circumstances validated the narrative I told myself whenever I doubted my ability to succeed in this sport. The day I received that finding failure, I visited Brazil's consulate in Los Angeles to pick up my Brazilian passport. Even as USA Weightlifting selected me to represent the country in two major International meets, I prepared my exit plan.

With their monthly testing, USADA taped a bullseye to my back. I could never beat a drug test with Conte's method; I could never compete seriously at Worlds against doping nations without using drugs myself.

My dad's nationality gave me dual citizenship in Brazil.

USADA's hounding gave me reasons to act on it.

Eleven:
The C Session
Stands for Crickets

An undetectable performance enhancer. That's the Holy Grail of drug cheats worldwide. On one of my visits to Charles Poliquin's facilities, he told me that scientists could create over 50,000 steroid molecules that drug tests couldn't detect.

For a brief period in the early 2000's, top athletes took The Clear,[99] a drug so potent it only required a few drops under the tongue. It passed every known test. Patrick Arnold[100]—whose passion to design drugs far transcended his college chemistry degree—first synthesized The Clear (Tetrahydrogestrinone, or THG) around 2001 at the request of Victor Conte. Conte wanted a new drug for his BALCO network of professional and top amateur athletes. These included Marion Jones, Barry Bonds, boxer Shane Mosley and NFL player Bill Romanowski.[101]

In the human body, THG binds to the androgen receptors in skeletal muscle, where it elicits both androgenic and anabolic effects. Scientists consider it 10 times more potent than trenbolone but with a bonus: it confers no estrogenic activity (such as bloating, fat gain, gynecomastia or roid rages).[102] For almost five years, athletes exploited The Clear with impunity. Marion Jones took home five medals at the 2000 Sydney Olympics. Barry Bonds won the National League MVP four years in a row (2001-2004). Shane Mosley held three world boxing titles from 2000-2003. Romanowski's team played in the 2003 Superbowl. No one detected the source of their success.

No one even knew it existed.

Human error—and in some cases, blind fortune—often leads to the gains made by the crusaders against the cheats. During the 1984 Olympics, Don Catlin—then head of the UCLA Olympic Analytical Lab—felt frustrated that his staff didn't possess a test for stanozolol, which he (rightly) believed many Olympians took to improve performance. He asked German chemist Manfred Donike for help.[103]

During the 1970s, Donike invented many of the tests and methods still employed to detect performance enhancing drugs in urine and blood. He told Catlin to swallow a stanozolol pill and then send him the next day's urine. Two years later, Donike had developed a detection method for stanozolol from Catlin's drug-tainted sample.

But with The Clear, the doping police simply lucked out. In 2003, Jamaican-sprinter turned track coach Trevor Graham anonymously sent USADA a syringe he "found" in a locker room trash can. Catlin's lab analyzed it and developed a detection method. History later revealed that Graham's athletes and their drugs of choice competed against athletes given The Clear at BALCO; Graham turned in that syringe to undermine his competition.[104] Graham, first hailed as a whistleblower, later faced felony charges[105] and received a lifetime coaching ban from USA Track and Field for his own doping involvement.[106]

Who knows how much drug-aided success Graham thwarted? Without Graham's involvement, athletes could still be winning gold medals, Superbowls and World Series by taking The Clear today. And even though the drug testers caught this designer drug, they only won one battle in a never-ending war.

Scientists continually invent whole new classes of molecules that act like steroids. In the 1990s, drug companies began to produce SARMS: Selective Androgen Receptor Modulators. These compounds mimic hormones like testosterone. But where testosterone operates globally in the body (affecting multiple systems and pathways), the "selective" in SARMS enables this class of drugs to target certain androgen receptors in specific tissues. Where testosterone builds muscle, improves bone density and enlarges the prostate, a SARM can combat osteoporosis without building muscle tissue (or without testosterone's negative effects on the prostate gland).

Human growth peptides are another novel class of molecules designed—and widely used by athletes—to mimic the effect of anabolic hormones, including Human Growth Hormone (HGH). Anti-doping agencies have developed tests to indicate their presence in urine and blood. But underground chemists like Patrick Arnold—whether working for-profit or for-state sponsored doping programs—develop the next class of drugs and the cat-and-mouse game continues.

Wait until geneticists start churning out CRISPR babies for sport.[107]

Las Vegas: Summer and Fall 2011

In April, Broz convinced me not to live at the Olympic Training Center. I gave up the chance to lift full-time without worrying about paying rent or groceries. Three months later, I won Nationals by a huge margin and USA Weightlifting selected me for its 2011 Pan Am Games and World Championships teams.

On the surface, things looked up for the first time since I tapered off steroids eight months earlier. With my enrollment in the Random Testing Pool (RTP), USADA could appear and test me any time, and they did. I had to train clean and stay clean. I didn't know of any other top athlete in *American* weightlifting that doped *and* consistently outwitted or passed their tests.[108]

When the team returned from Nationals, Broz told us that CrossFit Las Vegas agreed to provide 1,500 square feet of training space for our club. We built five platforms. Broz brought over his Eleiko equipment, CFLV purchased some new plates, and machines like a GHD. We moved from 600 square feet in the back of a granite showroom to a wide-open gym. The fresh environment immediately lifted everyone's mood. John put up Iron Mind photos, memorabilia from international meets and tons of weightlifting posters. It felt like a real training hall.

One of Broz' old training partners increased the excitement further. Gary Savage won nationals in 1986, and finished second in 1983, 1984 and 1987, hitting a 130kg snatch and 180kg C&J at 75kg bodyweight. After weightlifting, he embarked on a successful career as a business owner (he owned a stake in Chippendales, yeah, the male strippers), worked as a commodities trader, and ran an incredibly profitable subscription-only blog called Smart Money Tracker.

With just the click of a button, he sent an email blast to his subscribers and raised over $35,000, which he invested as a stipend system for the athletes at Broz' club. His generosity provided me a cash payout every month. For lifting! Shortly after, Broz sold his granite business; Savage called a huge spike in the silver market, and Broz tripled his money.

We were all winning.

John's personal life changed significantly that summer. Without really talking about it, he married again. No "hey, I'm dating someone" or "hey, I'm engaged" but more of a "she just came into the picture" and now occupied a major place in Broz' life.

Broz met Linoy through friends. She emigrated to America from Israel, and we heard rumors that he was paid to marry her, so she could become a citizen. In 2012, Broz turned 44, and Linoy was 23, *less than two years older than me* at the time. A few years later, Taylor talked to John about it; he said he wanted kids, felt lonely and filled with regret.

Me? I felt jealous. Linoy worked sales—in a job Broz set up—and she randomly dropped by the gym to occupy his time. "Show me how to do this" she whined, and Broz obliged her. She basically came to get Broz' attention, not to work out or train. By the end of the year, it didn't seem like he could do anything without her tagging along.[109]

But only some of that affected my story.

While Broz fucked around with his half-age bride, I returned to full-time training to prepare for the Pan Am Games and World Championships. A host of nagging injuries plagued me, from my shoulder to my knee to my wrist. Chronic inflammation tore up my joints, constant fatigue slowed down my lifts, and I couldn't recover from sessions that felt like a joke.

Charles Poliquin threw me a lifeline that August. He heard from Broz that I made two International teams and knew how I felt about not having access to the same type of care and treatment athletes received at the OTC.

Once a month, he flew me out to his facilities in Rhode Island. Paid for my plane ticket and had his specialists work on my health and recovery. Now I really felt like a professional athlete. I spent weekends in a posh hotel, and trained one-on-one with one of the best strength coaches that ever lived. Poliquin regularly charged $1,000 an hour for private consultations and he gave me his time as an investment. He published articles about me on his website, and connected me to Kim Goss, who edited *Bigger, Faster, Stronger* magazine. Goss wrote about my training and the Internet hype escalated all over again.

Poliquin showed me different recovery exercises, taught me to stretch and mobilize properly and ran a bunch of tests on me for supplement recommendations. The first time I visited his facilities I weighed 132kg with 32% body fat. But within six weeks, I dropped to 122kg and 22% body fat. His advice to stop eating gluten enabled faster recovery, and his supplement stacks helped even more with my health and body composition.

His supplements balanced out my hormones. Most of Poliquin's nutritional ideas addressed where the body held onto fat, as adipose storage indicated hormonal imbalances or deficiencies. He gave me one supplement stack to increase my testosterone (nothing illegal or banned), because my estrogen had shot up. His advice to cut gluten reduced my inflammation completely. My knees stopped hurting, I stopped retaining fluid, I moved better. Broz thought I looked too small and wanted me to keep eating but after eight months of suffering, I finally felt amazing.

The IWF calendar that year left only a two-week window between the Pan Am Games and the World Championships (they scheduled them similarly in 2019). But the honchos at USAW unwisely decided to send most of the same people to both events. On top of that, USAW mandated that the entire team attend a training camp in early October, about two weeks before the Pan Am Games. I had to train at their five-day camp, which culminated in a competition so they could see who was in shape for the Games.

I clean and jerked 215kg at their mock meet, hitting that number for only the second time in 2011. When off drugs, I could rarely hit maximal C&J's back to back. And in my head, it felt like I could only hit those peaks one or two times the entire year. That feeling wrecked my confidence in the clean, especially when I spent 2009-2010 going from PR to PR, week in and week out. Knowing I just used up one of my big C&J's threw me into an emotional tailspin.

After the camp, the team convened at the airport in Houston, and flew to Mexico as a group. The men's team included me, Chad Vaughn (77kg), Kendrick Farris (85kg), Jon North, Jared Fleming (94kg) and Donnie Shankle (105kg). On the women's side, Team USA fielded Kelly Rexroad-Williams (48kg), Hilary Katzenmeier (53kg), Danica Rue (69kg), Sarah Robles and Chioma Amaechi (both 75kg+).

Before the trip, USAW decked us out with a ton of swag: Oakley sunglasses and a backpack full of fresh gear from Nike, including new singlets. Police vehicles escorted our bus from the airport to the venue, where the Mexican federation built an entire village for the athletes. The resort included pools, restaurants, bars and cafeterias, and they handed us all condoms at check in. I got my own room, which was pimp and once again, I felt like I made it.

The Pan Am Games operates like a mini-Olympics, with countries from North, Central and South America competing in 36 sports. Over 5,000 athletes enter and live in the same compound. Most individual sports teams ate with their respective countries, and I met some cool people, including gymnast Shawn Johnson and Tommy Jones, a professional bowler I recognized.

Donnie Shankle and Jon North ventured out every night for a few drinks, and I could hear and see athletes from other sports and countries partying together. At the time, I was still brainwashed by Broz to do nothing but lift, eat and sleep and stayed in my room the entire week. Even after I trained, I didn't leave my room to lounge by the pools or hang out.

Weightlifting took place in an indoor arena, set up with stadium style seating and a raised platform. The entire team came together to watch any session with a USA athlete and people from all over Mexico filled the stands. Each time a big lift went down, 2,000 people stood up and cheered and hollered, waving flags and whistling. Jon North put his showmanship on full blast, working a crowd of thousands into chanting U-S-A, U-S-A! They loved him and he relished it.

On the men's side, Chad Vaughn, Kendrick and Donnie all took bronze in the total.[110] Jon North finished fourth; he was not yet the great snatcher he became a few years later. The then-dominant Cuban team cleaned up, and the Colombians presaged a weightlifting powerhouse in development. None of the women came close to medaling and Sarah and Chioma both bombed.

My session started well. I snatched 170 and 175kg and missed 178kg on my third attempt out front. Brazil's Fernando Reis beat me with his monster 185kg third lift, and I tied for second at 175kg (but was ahead on bodyweight) against Guatemala's Christian Lopez Bobadilla.

But I got crushed in the C&J, finishing eighth in a field of nine athletes with a miserable 205kg opening lift (missing jerks at 210 and 213kg). I don't want to speculate about what I could have hit if I kept that 215kg lift from a few weeks earlier in my back pocket. Reis obliterated everyone, opening at an international C&J personal best (211kg) and then clean and jerking 216kg and 225kg in a six-for-six performance.

Reis competed literally days after he finished serving a ban for a prohibited stimulant. In early 2011, Reis lived, trained and competed for Missouri's Lindenwood University. During the 2011 University National Championships, he tested positive for methylhexanamine, a popular and powerful amphetamine then found in products like Jack3d, Lipo 6, and Cellucor's C4 Extreme. Kids at my high school took it.

At University Nationals, Reis posted a 385kg total, snatching 175kg and clean and jerking 210kg. His previous best international competition total stood at 372kg (171kg snatch and 201kg C&J) from the June 2010 Junior Worlds in Bulgaria.

He received a six-month suspension that started April 24, 2011, then moved home to Brazil. Reis put on almost 10kg of bodyweight and added 15kg to each of his lifts in six months. His ban conveniently ended just in time for the Pan Am Games, where he destroyed the first and second place finishers by 17kg. How did he do make so much progress?

That total established Reis as a world-level competitor. I don't bring up his success to bash him or imply anything that's not self-evident. I trained and competed with him for Team Brazil in 2013 and 2014. He served his ban and worked hard, just as I worked hard during the 2009-2010 training period. That his results followed shortly after a suspension only further illustrates the complicated, shadowy nature of our sport's relationships to performance enhancers.[111]

I'll also never know how I would have performed if Broz attended the Pan Am Games. The silver market crashed, and Broz lost much of his investment. He sold his granite business, started coaching as a profession and earned income from a weightlifting-related website that sold lifting straps and t-shirts. When it came time to book tickets for Mexico, he said he couldn't afford it.

Two weeks later, he suddenly had money to travel to Worlds in Paris, even enough to bring his young wife along. I won't lie and say it didn't piss me off. He insisted that I stick around and train in Vegas, foregoing my opportunity at the OTC, and offered nothing but promises for my future. But when it came to the international meets, he turned into a different person.

In Mexico, half the team got sick with swine flu. It felt like someone poisoned me. Everything cramped up, I couldn't eat, no one functioned well. Plus, all of us had to return home and train for what—a few days—before jumping on another set of flights to Paris. It was an honor to represent Team USA at the Pan Am Games, but dumb of USAW to send such an overlap of lifters to both events. They should have picked two teams.

USAW sent a full team to Worlds, eight men and seven women.[112] On the men's side, we fielded Darren Barnes (56kg), Vaughn (77kg), Kendrick and Zach Krych (at 85kg), Fleming (94kg), Shankle (105kg) and me and Zach Schulender (at 105kg+). The women's team featured Katzenmeier (53kg), Amanda Sandoval and Rizelyx Rivera (at 58kg), Danica Rue (69kg), and Sarah and Chioma (75kg+).

The organizers held Worlds at Euro Disney, about 20 miles outside the city. It didn't even come close to the atmosphere in Mexico. Less athletes, only one event, but the best of the best from weightlifting powerhouses like Russia, Turkey, Azerbaijan, Ukraine, China and Bulgaria.

I got my own room and kept the same mindset as the Pan Am Games: eat, sleep, train. Didn't really hang out with Team USA either—half of whom didn't give a shit and spent the week partying. Most of the time, I followed the North Korean team around, even walked with them from the hotel to the training and competition venue. Security guards escorted them everywhere and I trained with them and sat in the cafeteria when they ate.

Team USA offered no organization. No regularly scheduled training, and no support staff to keep us accountable. If anyone showed up when another USA athlete competed, it was by accident.

Broz went AWOL the entire trip. We landed and I didn't see him again. During training, Zygmunt asked me "where's your coach Pat?" and I didn't know how to respond, just shrugged in embarrassment while I boiled inside. Broz and Linoy stayed in Paris, saw sights every day, and he texted me occasionally to check in. Even on the day of the meet, I didn't see him until after I lifted, didn't even know he was in the building. Apparently, he showed up late.

After weigh-ins, I warmed up in the back by myself (with Zygmunt coaching) and when I walked out for my first attempt, I thought "what the fuck?" In Mexico, 2,000 people packed the stands, cheering every lift like a touchdown at the Super Bowl. But at Worlds? I lifted in the "C" session, and let me tell you, it stands for "crickets" cause that's all I heard.

Broz hyped up Worlds like the most amazing sport spectacle on the planet. How the most weight gets lifted, the most competitors from the most nations. Between the three referees, five judges and the timekeeper, they outnumbered the spectators that day.

I didn't even get to lift on the same day as the Superheavyweight A-session competitors. The C session lifted the day before them. When I viewed the results, I could see everyone outlifted me. The girls out totaled me. They all had mustaches; shit all the girls at international meets had mustaches. And I was like "why am I here?" What am I even doing here?

Rage boiled inside me. At the event, at my opening attempts, and at Broz. I couldn't get past him not being there, not supporting me when I needed him. I made one snatch, my opener at 172kg, then missed 177kg twice. In the clean and jerk, I couldn't even hit 205kg. Three times in a row I cleaned a weight less than my best-ever snatch and I failed to put it overhead in the jerk.

The next day, Donnie, Zach Schulender and I took the train into Paris. We toured the Louvre, saw the Eiffel Tower and drank a few bottles of wine. I don't remember any of it. The greatest art ever created in the world's most beautiful city and it passed by in a blur of anger and frustration.

At the end of the competition week, the IWF hosted a huge banquet. Open bar with free beer and wine and French rappers performing. The party raged into the early morning, and a DJ spun tracks while everyone got hammered. I remember Klokov, shit-faced, dancing with this Ecuadorian girl and stripping off his shirt. Half the team hooked up that night; Donnie described one encounter by saying he was "on her like butter on hot toast."[113]

My flight left at six the next morning, and I stumbled out of the party with a weightlifter I hung out with all night. We kissed when I got outside my room. I felt like she wanted more, but I just wanted to pass out and forget the entire week.

As I lay in my bed, the room spinning around me, I tried to block out the humiliation—not only of bombing out, but of finishing so poorly. Two thoughts turned circles through my mind:

I could never hang with these athletes if I competed clean.

And,

Where was Broz?

Over the next eight years, many of the competitors from the 2011 Worlds tested positive for doping violations. Medalists Valentin Hristov (Azerbaijan via Bulgaria), Oleg Chen (Russia), Tigran Martirosyan (Armenia), Adrian Zielinski (Poland), Ilya Ilyin (Kazakhstan), and non-medalists Sardar Hasanov (Azerbaijan), Hysen Pulaku (Albania), Ruslan Nurudinov (Uzbekistan), among many others. Some won medals at the 2012 and 2016 Olympics. If WADA re-tested the B samples from 2005-2015 Worlds, the IWF would have to disband in shame.

I talked to Donnie Shankle after the meet. He finished third in the Pan Am Games but 21st at Worlds. And it pissed him off. Anger heightened his naturally deep voice and his Cajun drawl slurred into a growl. He hated that he could never take drugs and compete against the world's best on equal terms. I sensed that he wanted to try steroids; I don't think he ever used. How could he? USADA tested him with the same aggressiveness and frequency that hounded me.

It upset him just to talk about doping. He trained in Abu Dhabi with the Bulgarian team and they talked openly about their drug use. They said to him "why do you even lift? This is how it is in the world. You don't take drugs, why are you here?"

"Why do you even lift?" echoed in my mind for weeks.

At the next year's Pan Am Championships, Donnie took all three clean and jerk attempts with a broken neck just to secure one spot for Team USA at the 2012 Olympics—a spot he knew would go to Kendrick. And yet Donnie wouldn't touch steroids so that he could compete evenly against the rest of the world[114].

A rumor has long floated around the weightlifting community about the 2006 Arnold Weightlifting Championships. That past fall, Russia's Dmitri Klokov followed his father's footsteps by winning the 2005 World Championships in the 105kg weight class. Klokov vacationed and rehabbed an injury in the months after, then competed at the Arnold as an exhibition. Donnie tied him in the snatch at 165kg and beat him in the C&J (201 to 200kg) and total (366kg to 365kg). It is still the only time that an American lifter has defeated the reigning World Champion in competition.

Legend holds that Klokov's coach watched Donnie lift and after hearing that Donnie competed clean and still beat Klokov, he exclaimed "If that athlete used steroids, he would be world champion and not Dmitri!"

That's a big If.

I didn't have any more time or patience for "ifs." My humiliation at Worlds forced another decision. In March 2012, USAW would hold the Olympic Trials at the Arnold. I had four months left after spending the last four years trying to get to the Olympic Games. The US could only earn one men's spot, and I stood in third place, points away from Shankle but a mile behind Kendrick.

I needed to go back on something, I needed an edge. At the time, Human Growth Hormone was all the rage among bodybuilders. We heard that USADA didn't have a legit test for HGH, and that no Olympic athlete had ever tested positive for it

I thought it was undetectable. I was wrong.

Twelve:
Testing Positive, Part I

Las Vegas and Columbus: December 2011 to April 2012

I returned from Paris to another Christmas at Virginia's house. At this point, I didn't even visit my mom and Ken, but popped in to see my younger brother, who now lived with friends.

Each year, Virginia hosted "Swedish Christmas," a holiday celebration for her family and any of her sons' friends. On the 24th, she laid out a huge luncheon spread, and 20 of us—mostly my and Jason's friends from high school—sat around and feasted. Their joking and laughing distracted me from my bomb out at Worlds, and they mostly asked questions about Paris.

As we shared stories, I started to feel settled, like I had a home now, with a chosen family to be sure, but a group of people that didn't piss away their lives on drugs or addictive behavior. Instead of dreading the holidays, an inkling of looking forward stirred in me for the first time since childhood.

Virginia didn't care that I missed all my clean and jerks. All she wondered was: "can you still qualify for the 2012 Olympic Games?" I answered a "very slim yes" and told her about the qualification process: the US earned two women's spots for London 2012, but had yet to secure a men's spot. The Olympic Trials would take place in March, and USAW could theoretically secure a men's spot at the Pan Am Championships that June.

The truth, which I didn't tell her until much later, explained the colossal failure of the US Men's team in Paris. Chad Vaughn finished 16th, the highest placement of any American male. Most of the men finished below 20th place. Even on the women's side, Rizelyx Rivera set an American record in the snatch and still only finished 20th in the total (Sarah Robles earned the highest US finish at 10th place).

The other nations—the drug using nations—dominated, with 15 countries taking all 45 medals in the total and top drug-abusers Russia, Kazakhstan and China scoring 60 of the 135 overall medals.

While Virginia remained optimistic, Broz barely spoke to me. He was pissed that I bombed out and angry at my attitude before and after the competition.

Broz never treated performance like a team effort, or as something partially under his control. He never stepped back and asked, "How can we approach this differently, what could we change in training, how can I get you to a better place mentally?" And to offer, "What did I do wrong?" never occurred to him. When I bombed out—and more big misses were yet to come—it was 100% "Pat's fault." Bombing out always felt like something I did to him.

Despite feeling depressed over my failures in Paris, I didn't hide my anger. I told him that during team training, people asked me where my coach was. I peppered the conversation with outbursts of "what the fuck?" and "where the fuck were you?" My wife would later remind me how gentle the conversation really sounded. Even when I had every right, I could barely raise my voice at someone who was still my coach. But I needed to know where he was all week!

He pinned it on Linoy, his young wife that wanted to see Paris and chafed at him when he mentioned the weightlifting venue. No matter what occurred, Broz acted the consummate salesman, always quick with an answer, never owning anything, just pushing the product, even when that product smelled like total bullshit. No "I'm sorry I let you down," because he would never step up to the plate that way.

It's easy to suggest that drugs—or lack of them—played a significant role in my failure at worlds. I know that everyone in USAW and the greater weightlifting community viewed me as this super-drugged up lifter, who only totaled big when on the sauce. But by worlds, I could say I was clean for a full year.

Outsiders will never understand the loss in confidence that coincided with these major competitions. Whenever I traveled to a meet, I exhausted myself with stress. Not letting Broz down, not disappointing Virginia or Poliquin or anyone else that invested in me. The night before competing, torrents of doubt rained through my mind, eroding my self-worth. Not having Broz to help took away one of the only anchors that could restore me to an emotional even keel.

When I took steroids, I at least felt powerful and stronger than everyone else. And if I could train like the other competitors at Worlds—taking orals like Turinabol right up until a few weeks out—then I could have mitigated that stress. What people outside the sport (and even within USAW) don't realize, and which we now know to be true, is that most of the medalists dope until the last possible minute. Then their federation's doctors screen them to ensure they will pass a drug test. Want to know what a "clean Ilya" lifts like? He just did 160kg snatch, 185kg C&J at the 2019 Asian Championships. Numbers less than he hit as a 17-year-old 85kg lifter.

If I could compete at Worlds with the confidence of an athlete who knows he's walking onto a level playing field, then no problem. But every meet in 2011 pitted me as the clean guy against an army of doped lifters.

Despite staying clean for a year, USADA still hounded me. When I travelled to Paris for Worlds, they showed up at Virginia's house to drug test me. Their reasoning? I didn't enter the competition in the Whereabouts system, and they pounced on the chance to pop me. USA Weightlifting announced the team on its website, it's public information. USADA knew I wouldn't be home. When I didn't answer the door and pee in their cup, they registered a "failure to find" against me.

I filed an appeal, but USADA didn't accept it, citing "procedural violations." They wanted to fill in the slots, take away one of my "get out of jail free" cards. Now they got two against me. One more and they could boot me out of the sport.

No one needs to sympathize with me to understand that USADA taped a target to my back in 2010 and then took every procedural potshot and dirty trick in their quest to ban me. Like Javert in *Les Mis*, their moral crusader's attitude delighted in hounding even wounded prey, patting themselves on the back with every positive sanction their aggressive tactics achieved.

Months remained until the Olympic trials. I needed to take some drug to stand a chance at the international level. I fell into desperation mode, researched what I could on the Internet and thought "fuck it, I'm gonna take growth" and see if that helps.

I started with HGH, taking a pharmaceutical grade product called Nutropin. The kit included a pen, and I injected it into a fold of skin at my abdomen. After getting used to the HGH, I also cycled insulin. Each HGH injection included two IU's per day, and I took the insulin at five to ten IU's, using that right after I finished working out.

But I chickened out on insulin after about a month. Not because of its questionable legality (I bought it from a Walmart), but because of side effects I read about online: possible heart palpitations, liver damage, not to mention giving myself diabetes or going into a coma. I also had no proof that it benefited my recovery or training.

I certainly don't think the HGH conferred a performance or recovery advantage. The only study I found, showed that *when paired with testosterone*, HGH produced a significant increase in leg power and sprinting time.[115] But I was fucked in that regard. Testosterone suspension acted on a short timeline, but as far as I knew, USADA could detect the dosages I thought I needed to take. In 2011, the concept of micro-dosing had yet to filter into Internet consciousness, even though swimmers, cyclists and athletes in other sports (like MLB) already began applying regular, barely detectable doses to their training regimen.

HGH with insulin certainly didn't make me feel any more recovered from Broz's training regimen. Nothing changed from his end. Each day, snatch, clean and jerk, squat, then power snatch, power clean, squat again. Twelve to fourteen sessions per week. Two-a-days Monday to Friday.

I couldn't handle the training frequency or the volume. Broz gave no other structure, no periodization, no regular tapering. Any time I questioned his method, Broz answered, with total confidence and calmness, this is how world champions train, and I needed to train this way if I wanted to achieve the same results.

But nothing worked and I didn't get stronger. My back squat didn't budge above 300kg the entire training period. An incredible amount of pain shot through my hip, radiating into my low back and running down my leg into my knee. The pain fucked me up mentally and inhibited my ability to produce force. During the final six weeks before 2012 Nationals, I clean and jerked 170kg one time. In the final two weeks before the meet, I clean and jerked no more than 70kg. I couldn't. Heavier cleans doubled me over in pain.

Part of me started to freak out, knowing that I needed to increase my clean and jerk to pass Kendrick in the ranking. But then USAW changed their trials procedure again.[116] Now Nationals only formed one part of the Olympic selection, with the results from the 2012 Pan Am Championships (in June) counting as the rest. I held onto a thin thread of hope, kept training, and kept injecting HGH, hoping for a miracle to happen.

What did happen was a knock at the door a few weeks out from Nationals. I took HGH daily at this point and knew it took 48 hours to bleed out of my system. However, I still thought USADA couldn't detect it.[117] When lab techs showed up to take my blood and urine, I didn't panic, and with two finding failures, I couldn't hide. When they appeared on my doorstep two weeks later, I shrugged, more annoyed at the regularity of their visits than the threat of being caught.

Broz and I arrived at nationals a couple days before I lifted. USA Weightlifting held that year's championships as part of the Arnold, hoping that the added spectacle of the Olympic Trials would draw a bigger crowd and bring more athletes into the sport. I traveled early to hear professional strongman Mikhail Koklyaev speak. Koklyaev had won Russian nationals in weightlifting and competed in both powerlifting and pro strongman (he would finish fifth at the Arnold that year). His feats of strength have inspired legends. At one exhibition, he muscle-snatched 150kg, clean and jerked 240kg, deadlifted 400kg and front squatted 260kg for a triple![118]

Koklyaev gave a speech in one of the training halls. In his broken English, he bellowed, "the secret to Russian weightlifting, is the oil." And he's laughing, knocking the floor with his fist saying, "the oil in the ground, the oil that's in there, it acts." He gave this talk in front of 200 people, USAW athletes and coaches, board members and executives. What he said as a joke that everyone didn't want to get, signaled much darker thoughts for me. It's just fucking obvious, I thought, I'm never going to be a senior world champion, or senior world record holder, not if I have to compete clean, in a clean federation (one of the only clean sports in the USA to boot). And Koklyaev, perhaps pissed that the Russian Federation wouldn't let him compete for them at Worlds or the Olympics, gave the game away as an aside, with a smile on his face.

At Nationals, Shankle easily won the 105's with a 370kg total (to a 334kg second place) and Kendrick similarly blew away the competition in the 85kg class, with a 355kg total (to Travis Cooper's second place finish with 328kg).

The superheavyweights competed on Sunday, and I don't know how, but I won with a 380kg total, hitting all three snatches (165kg, 172kg and 176kg) and missing my jerks at 195kg and 200kg before finally putting together a successful clean and jerk at 204kg. Cameron Swart finished second with a 374kg total and Shane Maier took third with 370kg. After my session, USADA took more of my blood and urine, the third time in about a month. I didn't sweat it; I hadn't injected anything for days; and besides, I thought USADA lacked a test for HGH.

After the competition, the Olympic rankings stayed the same. Broz and I returned to Vegas knowing we had to improve my total at June's Pan Am Championships if I wanted to go to the Olympics that August.

A few days later, a slim, ominous looking letter arrived from USADA. I knew on sight the message it contained. Just holding it struck a chord of doom that trembled from my spine to my fingers.

Virginia picked up the mail that morning and left it for me on the kitchen table. When I got home, she sat on the living room sofa, knitting. I opened the letter and read it, once, then twice then a third time. I walked into the living room, my mouth hanging. She saw me and stood up, like she knew already the message it conveyed. Tears streamed down my face; yeah, I cried like a baby when I read that I tested positive for HGH in two of the out-of-competition drug tests.

She immediately addressed the practical issues for me. Always the mother I never had, knowing her kid fucked up, but launching into mitigation mode to deal with the aftermath. We'll need to get a lawyer, she told me.

Broz recommended Howard Jacobs. Newspapers and his own PR machine still refer to Jacobs as "the athlete's lawyer." He defended Barry Bonds and Marion Jones and many of the high-profile athletes related to the BALCO scandal. His retainer alone cost \$7,000. Virginia didn't hesitate to lend me the money.

She didn't even ask if I took the drugs. I think my crying alone answered that question, but to her massive credit, she wanted to help me—not even her own son—still fight to achieve his Olympic goals.

Jacobs, in my opinion, did little for that money. He talked about his relationships with USADA, and executed a legal back and forth with them, first getting the "B" samples tested but ultimately laying out USADA's offer for me to rat on everyone I knew that took steroids in exchange for a lighter sentence.[119]

They set their sights on Broz; in the first round of proposals USADA said that if I testified against Broz that I'd get a nine-month suspension. When I refused, they bartered a similar deal against the sport in general: tell us everyone you know that takes drugs. If we can get someone else to test positive, we'll shorten your sentence. But if your information doesn't help us nab anyone else, then you're just a big rat and you're fucked anyway.

In both scenarios, Jacobs recommended that I fess up and take the shortest suspension possible. Which meant *admitting that I had taken HGH*, which led to the positive results on both tests (*this is important*). Broz agreed with that strategy and in a bunch of late-night talks, we worked out a plan: I would admit to the charges and take a two-year suspension, the then-average ban for a first-time doping offence.

From my perspective, it wasn't a bad plan. I just turned 22, had won nationals twice, competed for Team USA at the Pan Am Games and World Championships at age 21. No part of me wanted to pack it in on the sport or my dreams of going to Worlds again, setting world records and competing in the Olympics. "It's just two years" I kept telling myself. I never thought about my reputation, I never thought about fighting the charges head on.

I never entertained these options because I could barely afford Jacobs' retainer, and absolutely didn't have enough money to pursue long-term legal action. Shit, I didn't even understand the options and never heard of the Court of Arbitration for Sport (CAS). USAW offered ZERO legal, logistical or financial support for my defense. Overnight, I went from celebrated national champion and world team member to pariah, stripped of all results. If I was a millionaire, I would have fought it. But if I had that kind of money, I wouldn't have been in this situation in the first place.

I also thought I was alone, the first athlete in an Olympic sport to test positive for HGH.

Again, I was wrong.

The year before I tested positive for HGH, Estonian cross-country skier Andrus Veerpalu abruptly retired on the eve of the International Ski Federation's (FIS) 2011 World Championships (Feb. 23, 2011). WADA-accredited laboratories had conducted tests on both the A and B sample of Veerpalu's urine and charged the skier of doping with HGH.

But Veerpalu—an Estonia national hero that won the Olympics and Worlds twice—could afford lawyers and attack the secret process guarded by WADA regarding their tests. Almost immediately, a PR campaign mounted in his defense. Prominent Estonian scientists publicly defended Veerpalu, insisting that WADA did not possess a *credible* test for exogenous HGH use.

WADA first announced intentions to test athletes for HGH at the 2004 Olympics. According to *Outside Magazine*'s Brian Alexander, WADA "basically lied" about having a valid test ready, as they wouldn't publish *scientifically validated* laboratory guidelines for an HGH test until 2010.[120]

One of the world's leading experts on HGH, Martin Bidlingmaier, developed a chemical test for all forms of HGH.[121] This method used antibodies laced with acridinium ester. These antibodies bind with isotopes of HGH in an athlete's blood sample; the ester part of the molecule luminesces (lights up) when the antibody binds to a specific isotope of HGH. The amount of luminescence indicates the use of artificial forms of HGH by an athlete.[122] Bidlingmaier and his colleagues developed this test before 2009 and WADA used it in early 2011 to accuse Veerpalu of doping with HGH.[123]

The updated 2010 manual for WADA laboratories specified the methodology for a new test, one that compared ratios of the naturally occurring form of HGH isotopes. In a doped athlete, these guidelines suggested that the percentage of the predominantly naturally occurring isotope plummeted, indicating the use of exogenous recombinant HGH. In the manual, WADA specified "decision limits" (or ratios between the different isotopes) that indicated a true positive from a false positive.

In August of 2011, FIS handed down Veerpalu's suspension, banning him for three years (rather than the customary two for a first offence).[124] His ban conveniently ran right until the closing ceremonies of the 2014 Sochi Olympics, denying him a chance at a third Olympic title.

Veerpalu's legal team challenged the FIS decision in the Court of Arbitration for Sport, a Swiss-headquartered agency that mediates disputes between athletes, their respective sporting federations, WADA, and the IOC. His legal team included two biostatisticians: Krista Fischer,[125] who worked for the Estonian Genome Center, and Donald Berry, a world-leading biostatistics expert then employed by the University of Texas M.D. Anderson Cancer Center (his statistical work for UT developed innovative approaches to running clinical trials for cancer treatments).

Calling WADA's use of statistics "Medieval science," Berry and Fischer poked holes in the process WADA employed to set the decision limits. Their critique constitutes far more than just a technicality. Yes, the CAS agreed that evidence indicated that Veerpalu doped with HGH. But they accepted Fischer and Berry's argument that the statistical modeling that WADA used to set the ratios that distinguished a positive from a negative was "unreliable" (CAS' exact term).

Veerpalu's defense team also took issue with WADA excluding outliers (of naturally high or low HGH) from the data set that WADA used to statistically determine the "natural" ratios of the various isotopes of HGH. Because WADA excluded these outliers, Veerpalu's experts argued, the data set could yield false positives for athletes whose natural levels occurred outside of the "normal" range. Moreover, Veerpalu's team of statisticians claimed that the outliers themselves showed the invalidity of the statistical modeling used.

So ultimately, CAS decided that Bidlingmaier's ester-luminescence test worked to *detect* HGH doping, but that the statistical analysis WADA employed to determine natural HGH levels from artificial levels failed. This faulty analysis kept the CAS panel from "excluding to its comfortable satisfaction that the decision limits (ratios) are overinclusive and could lead to an excessive amount of false positive results."

In plain English: the CAS concluded that WADA's test couldn't exclude false positives to a reasonable standard of doubt. That is a huge vote of no-confidence for an anti-doping test that WADA and FIS wielded in its attempt to take down a two-time Olympic Champion.

USADA popped me with the same test. And they bullied me into admitting that I took HGH.[126] Again, I'm not splitting hairs on this matter or citing technicalities. Judges invalidate confessions obtained under coercion or duress. I confessed, thinking it was my only option to avoid a lengthy ban from my sport. No one told me about any other ongoing cases challenging the validity of the test. And more importantly, FIS punished Veerpalu with an extra year's ban (their initial ruling called for two years) *simply because he didn't cooperate with and challenged their investigation.*

In their ruling, the CAS not only cleared Veerpalu's record, but ordered FIS to pay Veerpalu's legal costs. After the trial, Berry and Fischer co-authored a paper that crucified WADA. They titled it "Statisticians Introduce Science to International Doping Agency." In their article, the pair of PhD's demolished the methodological flaws in WADA's process. The shortcomings they pointed out included not conducting studies with a sufficient number of test subjects, not submitting the data to an independent panel of experts with no conflict of interest, and not analyzing the results and forming conclusions with the proper statistical modeling needed. In short, they argued that "doping tests should not be used in practice until they have been shown to be scientifically valid, and that has not yet occurred in HGH testing."

This counters WADA's general self-promotion (and public perception) of its testing and science as foolproof and of its procedures and arbitration methods as impartial and just. But Fischer and Berry argue that WADA's methods fall far short of even the scientific standard of medical diagnostics (i.e., a doctor telling a patient what exactly is wrong). Furthermore, the pair stipulated that "standards in doping testing should be higher" than that of medical diagnostics, especially in doping cases, **because "the final decision hangs on the test result alone."** And those test results can upend sporting careers and destroy lives.

WADA and USADA continue to operate extremely high margins of success, with USADA never losing an appeal—mostly by not allowing due process in how they handle doping offences.

No one from WADA, USADA or the IWF offered to have my record expunged or my sentence reduced after Veerpalu's legal team proved invalid the very same test they used to convict me of doping with HGH. I was 22 and could come back to the sport.
But in rugby star Terry Newton's case, the poor Brit killed himself! They popped him with a methodologically flawed test and whether out of shame or despair, he committed suicide.

That blood is on WADA's head.

How many of their other tests suffer similar flaws in methodology and application? And why won't they own up when their tests fall short?

"Cui bono?" or "Who benefits?" the Roman judge Lucius Cassius wisely asked when determining the suspects and motives in a crime.

Who benefits from keeping WADA and USADA like a kangaroo court? Who benefits from depriving defendants of the same due process found in a criminal court of law (even though the penalties can run just as high as severe fines, lost income and sponsorship, not to mention the "prison time" of a ban from a sport in which an athlete has devoted her entire life)?

WADA's reputation benefits. The myth of "clean sport" benefits. TV networks benefit. And the sporting federations benefit.

How so? To paraphrase another Latin motto, "follow the money."

Thirteen:
Surgery and Selling Cars

In 1972, the International Olympic Committee (IOC) operated on assets of $2 million. Over the previous 20-years, then IOC President Avery Brundage refused all commercial and corporate sponsorships. His tenure ended in 1972. Brundage's successor Lord Killinan viewed increased television revenue as a means to unite each country's National Organizing Committees (NOC) to the Olympic movement and to increase the flow of large sums into the IOC's coffers.[127] Eight years later, the IOC's assets swelled to $45 million.

Juan Antonio Samaranch took over as head of the IOC in 1980.[128] He planned to fully commercialize the Olympics and transform it into a world-class organization (albeit one that maintained the cover of a non-profit, with headquarters in tax-friendly Switzerland). When Samaranch stepped down 21 years later, those assets reached a staggering $335 million. Over Samaranch's 21-year IOC Presidency, the organization collected $12 BILLION from broadcast rights alone, with a further revenue stream of $3.5 billion (from NBC) for TV rights to the 2000-2008 Olympics. In 2014, the IOC's assets topped $900 million and their corporate sponsorship revenues for the 2016 Olympics skyrocketed to almost $1 billion. On their 2016 tax return,[129] the IOC listed revenues of $3.5 billion from TV deals alone.[130] The IOC stated their *domestic* revenue goals for the 2028 Olympics at $2.5 billion.[131] The buy-in to become a TOP corporate sponsor? Over $100 million per company.[132]

It's worth noting that in the first year of Samaranch's tenure, the Olympic movement dropped the word "amateur" from its charter.

Toward the end of Samaranch's 21-year reign, the Festina doping scandal decimated the 1998 Tour de France and threatened its reputation.[133] That same year, a bribery scandal enveloped the bidding process for the 2002 Salt Lake Olympics.[134] Samaranch decided that a new agency was needed to restore public faith in global sports.

According to Robert Weiner, a former spokesman for WADA: "They were afraid sponsor money would dry up if the Olympics was perceived as dirty."[135]

Sport federation heads and national officials convened in Switzerland. This meeting led to the creation of WADA in 1999. Until this point, individual sports federations and NOC's oversaw all doping-related matters, including testing and punishing offenders. Later, troves of evidence revealed that officials covered up many doping offences from 1976 (when the Olympics first started testing) to 1999.[136] USADA originated in a similar scandal.[137]

Samaranch himself took a rather cavalier attitude toward doping. He gave an interview to Spanish newspaper *El Mundo* (July 27, 1998), where he called for a partial legalization of drug-use in sport, arguing that sports should permit substances that enhance performance but don't harm the athlete.[138] Initially, the IOC wanted to install Samaranch as WADA's first president.[139] No, that isn't sarcasm.

WADA didn't start as an organization designed to catch drug cheats. They intended to standardize doping rules and oversee each nation and sport's antidoping program. Even today, the organization doesn't directly test athletes in most sports and leaves doping control and punishments up to national anti-doping bodies and individual sports federations, respectively.

The organization began under criticism, notably from General Barry McCaffrey (then White House drug policy director). He criticized the IOC's influence over the newly created organization and their unwillingness to uncover scandals that might tarnish the

Olympic brand. Samaranch stepped aside and Canadian lawyer Dick Pound took the reins at WADA, serving in that position until 2007.

In a recent interview, Gen. McCaffrey claimed that the IOC still hides behind WADA and that WADA "is hiding behind a flawed structure."

That "flawed structure" was set in place from the start. Not only does WADA still draw 50% of its operating revenue from the IOC—which funded its first two years—but IOC members and government officials fill most positions at WADA.[140] That is by design.

Pound's career at the IOC is a perfect example of this cross-pollination.[141] He headed WADA from 1999-2007 and since 2014, serves as Chairman of the Board of the Olympic Broadcasting Services (run by the IOC), and as Canada's IOC representative. He also holds a post as IOC representative on WADA's board, and functions as an arbiter for the Court of Arbitration for Sport (and even did so when he ran WADA!).

To be very clear: the IOC governs the Olympics and *all* participating sports, athletes and coaches. WADA sets doping rules and through a recently established investigative arm, partly polices doping. The CAS handles all judicial challenges to WADA decisions.

Both WADA and CAS receive staffing and funds from the IOC, the very agency that created its personal enforcement and judicial arms and rakes in billions of dollars maintaining an image of "clean sport." **There is no financially or institutionally independent global body that polices doping in Olympic sport.** None.

Does the corruption continue? Ask former WADA President Craig Reedie. Ask RUSADA.[142]

Las Vegas and Brazil: 2012-2013

"It's only two years." I said into my hands at night when the stress overwhelmed me. I just turned 22 and everyone on the Internet who once knew me as "The World's Strongest Teenager" now saw me as a drug cheat in the same category as Ben Johnson, Barry Bonds and Marion Jones.

Broz and I spent a lot of nights commiserating that April. Railing against USADA, concocting mad schemes to clear my name, crying over the "bullshit" test we didn't know USADA possessed. Eventually we formulated a plan: I would drop 30kg, get healthy and compete as a 105kg athlete going forward. In the meantime, I would find a job that let me pay back Virginia and save money for after my ban expired. I owed Virginia $7,000 for Jacobs' retainer. At 22, I had never seen that much money in my life and couldn't wrap my head around how to repay her.

Before Nationals that Spring, I drove to northern California and dropped in on Cal Strength to talk with Dave Spitz. While there, I also saw Kelly Starrett about my hip. After describing my symptoms, Spitz told me I probably tore my hip labrum and needed to get it cleaned out and repaired. At the time, I had no health insurance and thought that someone like Starrett could provide short term relief and a long-range plan with physical therapy. Anything to avoid surgery.

Having to find a job with health benefits took me out of the gym, and me not lifting at Broz' hurt him the most. Once USADA announced my positive test, most lifters at ABG scurried away like cockroaches in the sunlight.[143] Billy left to open his own weightlifting club. Tyler stopped coming around. Only Jared Enderton remained. I think he couldn't afford to move and struggled to launch his seminar-business.

Broz hooked me up with an old friend at a local Dodge Chrysler Jeep dealership. John makes lasting impressions on people. When he called in favors, whoever he asked knows that John doesn't tolerate bullshit or send bullshit their way. The dealership hired me on the spot even though until then, I played sports year-round and never held a real job.

I showed up to the dealership in a pair of blue jeans and a white button-down shirt. Broz told me when to go and didn't say they would interview me that day. Some of the older salesmen ragged on me for wearing jeans. The guy interviewing me gave me an application and told me to come back for a drug test tomorrow.

Right away I thought "fuck." When I first lifted with Broz, he told me to quit smoking weed and I complied. But after USADA popped me, I hung out with some friends and we rolled some blunts. Now this dealership wanted to test me for pot and other recreational drugs.

So NBD, I bleached my hair that night. Then dyed it back to its normal color with a $10 Just for Men kit. When I arrived the next day, I didn't know what to expect. The collectors from USADA always watched me pee. But here, I smiled as the HR guy handed me a collection kit and pointed toward the bathroom. That morning I duct taped a travel-size shampoo bottle full of bleach under my nuts. After I peed in the container, I poured the bleach in to kill any marijuana by-products.

Old habits die hard.

Two days later, I stood on the car lot and shadowed a sales rep. If a customer drove in, I initiated conversation and showed her some vehicles. The sales rep then closed the deal. As I watched him work, I realized how much money I could earn.

I knew my mom's salary, so I understood what a decent income looked like. But I never earned cash like this myself. My first month on the lot, I sold eight cars, earning $8,000 in commission. My second and third month I sold 15 and 16 vehicles and got a $1,000 bonus each month for winning salesperson of the month.

Each of those months, I gave Virginia $500. I still lived with her and couldn't go anywhere else. Money rolled in hand over fist at this point. In my mind, I decided to pay her $500/month toward the seven grand I owed her. But that was me being a stupid kid. She saw the $500 as rent. And I never argued with her. When she referred to it as rent money, I thought "aw fuck." So I gave her all the money I earned those first three months and had nothing. But it was great. Training weightlifting taught me that I could kill myself for nothing and still be happy.

And then I thought, well, earning money is also like being a weightlifter. And getting more money is just like getting stronger. I would earn more.

That attitude marked the big difference between me and most of the salesforce. I developed consistent work habits. For each customer, I took the same approach. Most of the other reps sat inside and enjoyed the air conditioning, took breaks, lost focus. I stood in the 100-degree heat all day, 10 to 12 hours at a time. At first, I didn't know shit about sales, or cars, or the options offered. But I studied it and became lethal.

It helped that the other reps suffered from their vices. They smoked, or drank, or gambled. The car industry teems with degenerates. And they were my competition! All the capable salespeople like me, the guys with good heads on their shoulders? The dealership promoted them to finance or desk managers. They earned the real money, upwards of 20k a month.

During those months selling cars, I overhauled my diet as part of Broz' plan for me to move down to 105kg. Broz wanted me to drop the weight quick. We heard that Spencer Moorman and Caleb Ward were trying to go down a category, taking the gradual, slow route. But Broz believed in this theory that you need to walk around at a certain weight for a long time for your body to stay there. So I planned to lose it as fast as possible.

Step one: No carbs. Step two: I didn't drink and cut out ice cream. Step three: I followed the Poliquin "meat and nuts" breakfast.

Each morning I ate a-half pound of ground beef with some almonds. Then I'd down a massive salad with chicken for lunch. At work, I kept trail mix in my pockets. After work, I ate steak or fish, always with a pound of vegetables. I probably ate three pounds of meat a day.

I dropped 60 pounds in three months.

I trained once a week and didn't do any cardio. For the rest of 2013, I stayed low-carb to no-carb and my bodyweight didn't budge over 104-105kg the entire year.

At the dealership I earned more money than I'd ever seen, banking most of it for my next phase of training. In total, I sold cars for 10 months, and won "salesman of the month" five times. Most of the sales staff hated me, giving me unflattering nicknames (like "spoon boy").[144] And I'm a hard person to hate. I didn't gloat, or strut around the dealership rubbing my paychecks in the older guys' faces. Just like any other endeavor in my life, I showed up, put in the work, learned what I needed to know and applied it methodically.

In February 2013, I scheduled surgery to fix my torn hip labrum and saved more than enough to take off all of March to recover from it. During my recovery, I reconnected with some high school friends, who made a killing selling home alarms for Vivint. They recruited new salespeople and reached out to me. I was skeptical at first, but they invited me to a weekend retreat at the company's headquarters in Salt Lake City.

Vivint hosted the recruits in a suite at a Utah Jazz game. I couldn't believe the money these young guys earned. One—just a little older than me—raked in nearly half a million, two of his *junior* associates banked just under that. Then I saw my friend's check, and thought "dude, this is the Young Millionaires of America Club." All of them sported Breitling watches on their wrists. Earning $10,000 a month selling cars was peanuts.

Virginia balked at first. Neither of us knew what alarm sales netted. In the car industry, only the managers earned $20,000 a month. The average loser salesguy pulled $41,000 a year. And if you're only average, you're not going to be successful doing a shitty job. But at Vivint, the *lowest* performers netted $6,000 a month. It came down to ceiling.

My friends told me I only needed to put in the hours to succeed. I trusted these people. Virginia wanted me to play it safe—I already brought home a ton of cash selling cars. But I thought "I can earn more."

I can put more weight on the bar.

In 2013, Vivint deployed its salesforce from April to August. They picked a city, divided it into regions and set us loose. My first week in El Paso, Texas, I shadowed my manager and watched him sign up four customers in a day (those contracts netted $3,000). I thought, cool, now I know the process, how to onboard a customer and finish a contract. I'll figure out the rest.

I hit the streets with the goal to earn "Rookie of the Year." Vivint put us up for 20 weeks, and I worked 10-12 hours every day. Didn't drink (they're Mormon-owned), didn't hook up with any girls—although plenty of lonely army housewives offered. I get it, it's hard to reconcile the kid who "cheated" at weightlifting holding moral qualms about adultery. But I locked in with this insane focus, with one goal to achieve and I wouldn't let anything distract me. And yeah, it's pretty fucked up to bang another man's wife, especially a serviceman.

That summer I closed on 199 sales in 20 weeks, after getting inside under 1,000 homes. In four months, I grossed $97,000 in revenue, took home $72,000 and earned Top Rookie in the company. That honor snagged me an $11,000 Breitling watch. Not bad for a shy kid from hicktown Massachusetts.

In Texas, I started squatting again. I hit this globo gym, sometimes with guys from Vivint, often by myself. We worked long days in the Texas heat and I lifted whenever possible. Eight weeks post-surgery, I back squatted 184kg for a quick single. Then power clean and jerked 143kg. We couldn't drop the iron weights at that gym, so I had to dump the bar into my lap to avoid getting yelled at by the skinny high school kid at the front desk. In July I added full cleans and front squats. My lifts looked rusty, but my hip felt great and I trusted the movements again.

At the end of August, I returned to Vegas for the next stage of my plan. A girl was waiting there for me. I had no idea she would become my future wife. And at first, I wanted nothing to do with her.

That September, Broz and I intended to stay in Brazil for a few months (I honestly don't know where he got the money). We wanted to scope out places for me to live and train as part of my plan to compete for Brazil.

But then I walked into Broz' gym and saw Taylor Lumpp. Right away, I thought "that girl is fucking hot." I don't remember much about our first meeting, but I sensed that she had a crush on me. She later mentioned seeing the 207kg snatch video but didn't realize it was me because I lost so much weight. There was definitely a spark.

Her story intrigued me. Broz met her at a local Crossfit where he taught classes for extra cash. She only snatched 39kg and C&J 60kg at the time, but he told her she could excel in weightlifting. Typical Broz, I thought, selling the sky to anyone gaping at it, and even more so to a pretty girl that he was probably hitting on.

Taylor immediately switched from Crossfit to full-time weightlifting. Broz can inspire confidence in anyone and gave her the same lines that sold me: "I can teach you all the secrets," "coach you like world champions train." From one conversation, Taylor started training eight to ten sessions a week. She worked for the FBI, doing ten days on, four days off. On those off-days she did double-sessions at Broz', which impressed the hell out of me.

Her job sparked my interest even more. Taylor ran surveillance for the Bureau. Las Vegas hosts some of the biggest conventions in the world, and its firearm laws are lax, even by American standards. Black Hat and CES held their annual conferences there, drawing in technology firms and the cyber intelligence and security communities. High-profile foreign targets attend these meetings, and the FBI tracked and kept tabs on them.

Taylor operated with teams of six to eight people, surveilling terror suspects and anyone with known connections to terror groups. She told stories about sneaking into hotel rooms, and basically stopping operations that led to arrests and aborted or failed terror attacks. When she arrived in Vegas, she didn't know anyone and joined a local Crossfit to meet people.

And met me instead. But I didn't want to get pinned down, not before my trip and return to full-time training. So I ignored her, packed my bags and flew down to Brazil.

Most Brazilian weightlifters trained with one of two clubs and I needed one of them to represent me in Brazil's weightlifting federation. After a few days with my dad's family in a small town called Monte Claras,[145] Broz and I headed down to Sao Paulo, where Fernando Reis competed for the Pinheiros Club. I emailed Fernando before the trip; he replied enthusiastically, hyping up the trip to his teammates, telling them how big it would be if "they got Mendes on the Brazilian team." His family arranged everything, setting Broz and I up in a hotel in Pinheiros, one of the city's wealthiest residential districts.

Imagine if a posh gym like Equinox offered training and coaching in every Olympic sport and you get a sense of where and how Fernando and his teammates trained. Pristine locker rooms, all Eleiko everything, multiple saunas and spas, massages whenever they asked, and access to high quality food round the clock. Now picture a space about three times the size of USA's OTC sitting right in the middle of Manhattan. Wealthy clients could easily afford the $10,000 initiation fee and subsequent $10,000 yearly dues and get coached in golf or tennis or the bougie sport of their choice.

But the weightlifters paid zero. The government and the club's private sponsors footed the bill, even subsidizing their nearby apartments and giving them a monthly stipend—with the best lifters "double-dipping" by receiving funding from the club and the government. They earned anywhere from 3,000 to 5,000 reais a month ($800 to $1300 USD), and all sported the latest Nike and Adidas gear and flashed the newest iPhones (which run twice the price in Brazil). Ten weightlifters trained there: Fernando and four men and five women, some of Brazil's best lifters, with Luis López (an ex-Cuban lifter) as head coach.

I lifted with them for a week, surprising myself by working up easily to a 165kg snatch, a weight I hadn't hit since 2012 Nationals. In the squat, I hit a strong 250kg, again a post-surgery maximum. But I didn't need to touch those numbers. My stay was clearly a recruiting trip. The coach knew my background and best lifts and put one adamant restriction on my membership: I had to follow his program to the letter and only he could coach me.

Problem number one.

After a few days of sightseeing, Broz and I headed north to Rio, the Brazilian Weightlifting Federation's other centralized training location. While technically in the same country, the clubs in Sao Paulo and Rio existed in separate universes. We needed to take a car to find the training center. The cabbie—I swear I thought he was kidnapping us—drove out of the city and turned onto a dirt road heading into the jungle. A few miles later we pull up in front of this open-air building with a soccer field out front, and people herding goats and barbecuing food in pits. I would've never found this place and pinned it on Google Maps so I could get there again.

Inside, no air conditioning, just slats in the walls like concrete venetian blinds. Head coach Dragos Doru Stanica (an ex-Romanian lifter) stocked the place with his own equipment. All Eleiko bars and plates, but most of these in need of maintenance.

The walls dripped with water in the humidity; everything metal rusted, like trying to keep a car at the Jersey Shore

Still, Dragos produced some beast lifters there, mostly women, including 2012 Olympian Jaqueline Ferreira. Dragos first coached weightlifting in Rio in 2002 and became the country's head women's coach because of his success. Most of the top athletes there received stipends—also from the government—and the youngest ones attended school in the mornings.

Dragos didn't care if Broz still programmed for me or wanted to help in the back at international competitions, which definitely counted in his favor.

Finally, Broz and I traveled to Belo, a regional capital and where my dad's sister lived. She let us stay in one of her apartments while we trained at Junior's gym, owned by coach Marcio Junior. He trained Luana Oliveira Madeira, who medaled at the 2017 Junior Worlds (against a stacked field of likely-doped Thai athletes). His facility offered Crossfit, Weightlifting and Jiu Jitsu. I don't think I met a more welcoming person during our trip; from the first handshake, Junior handed us a key and said we could train whenever we liked. I lifted there for a week before Broz needed to return to Vegas.

Before we left, Broz and I had to decide who to work with going forward. If I was going to stay there and train full-time, I preferred for Broz to move there with me, which we had discussed as a possible option. I didn't require much; just a place to live, a gym to lift and enough seclusion that I could take drugs and prepare for the 2016 Olympics.

Otherwise, we needed a Brazilian coach to represent us within the Federation and to function as my coach of record for International meets. I planned to go back on steroids and openly discussed doping with athletes and coaches from all three gyms. In Sao Paulo, everyone danced around the subject; I got a sense that it happened, they knew it happened, and that the preferred strategy for evading out-of-competition tests involved bribery.

Coaches and competitors in the US or Western Europe might struggle to grasp the frequency with which corporate and government officials dispense and accept bribes in other nations. After staying in Brazil, I suspect it's how many federations evade detection.[146] WADA only directly tests a few sports; in most events, the individual sporting federations handle anti-doping for their members. The guys sent out to collect urine in places like Vietnam, Brazil, Armenia, and other second or third world countries don't earn much money. To them, a bribe represents a significant financial incentive to let someone else give a sample, or say they got lost that day and couldn't find the athlete.

Some lifters got popped competing for Brazil, but it didn't happen often and with far less frequency than a heavily monitored country like the US. At the 2015 Youth Worlds, Aline De Souza Facciolla Ferreira took silver in the total, and then tested positive for boldenone (a steroid I stupidly took in my first run).[147] South American champion Alexsandra De Aguiar Goncalves got popped for the same drug, putting Brazil on WADA's "watch list" in 2015. Fernando served six months for methylhexanamine, as did another Brazilian lifter (Joellison Gomez) in 2012. But those positives didn't occur out of competition, a major incentive for me to move and train there.

I couldn't afford Sao Paulo as rents there exceeded those in Manhattan. The Brazilian Federation refused to offer me a stipend until I qualified for an international team (and even then it was not a given). The money I saved from selling alarms would dry up in months in South America's wealthiest city.

As a coach, Dragos seemed the best choice; he qualified lifters for the Olympics and grew up in a system (Romania) that understood what it took to get there. I could live cheaper in Rio and rent free in Belo. But during the week that Broz and I stayed in Belo, he received an offer from some investors to open his own facility in Vegas, an actual gym dedicated only to weightlifting. That opportunity ruled out him moving to Brazil.

We sat across from each other at a table, drank a few beers and discussed our options. Unlike when the OTC offered me residence, I now leaned on Broz more. If I lived in Rio, I could train with Dragos but might get popped. If I stayed in Belo, I wouldn't have access to a coach I trusted. No matter what option I chose, I needed to do everything on my own in Brazil.

Broz sold me a different scenario. Compete for Brazil, under Dragos. Train in Vegas. At the time, USADA didn't possess the power to randomly test a member of a different federation out of competition.[148] Under Broz' plan, I would move in with him and live rent free. If I wanted extra cash, I could coach classes at a local Crossfit.

Sometimes you trust the devil when he's all you know.

I stayed in Belo a few more weeks to mull it over and relax. In the end, I traveled back to Vegas, gambling on a plan to qualify for the 2016 Olympics.

This time for Brazil.

Fourteen
Changing Countries:
A Cat and Mouse Game,
Part II

If you believe the whistleblowers, they alerted WADA to Russia's state-sponsored doping program as early as 2010. Vitaly Stepanov worked in a RUSADA lab, and from 2010-onward, he sent 400 emails to WADA that detailed numerous instances of bribery, advance notice of testing and illicit procedures and cover-ups at that laboratory. His wife, middle-distance runner Yuliya Stepanova, videoed coaches and athletes discussing doping methods. In 2012, Russian silver medal discus-thrower Darya Pishchalnikova emailed WADA, informing them of the drugs she took and her eagerness to submit information about systematic doping in her country.[149]

Officials at WADA certainly didn't act like they believed them. Instead, WADA forwarded some of the emails to Russian sporting officials.[150] Stepanov met several times with Jack Robertson, a former DEA special agent who joined WADA as director of investigations in 2011.

In 2014, Craig Reedie took the helm at WADA. That year, RUSADA's lab fired Vitaly and he and his wife fled Russia in fear.[151] Robertson's WADA's investigation into Russia stalled; WADA denied Robertson the funds and personnel he needed. Meanwhile, Russia donated additional funds to WADA, some

1.14 million over their previous annual contributions to that organization's budget.[152]

Robertson leaked information to ARD journalist Hajo Seppelt, which set up Seppelt's 2014 documentary "The Secrets of Doping: How Russia Makes Its Winners."[153] Widespread public uproar finally forced WADA to respond to the half-decade of information the Stepanov's and others supplied. In response, WADA commissioned an independent investigation into Russian state-sponsored doping at the Sochi Olympics.

In April 2015, Reedie emailed Natalya Zhelanova, an anti-doping adviser to Russian sports minister Vitaly Mutko. Reedie's email told Mutko not to worry about the independent commission and assured him that WADA was taking "no action" against Russia.[154]

And why wouldn't he send that email? The entire time Reedie helmed WADA, he served as a Vice-President at the IOC![155] His position required him to uphold the IOC's primary mission: promote Olympism and the Olympic movement.[156] That goal requires sponsor money. Which necessitates not tarnishing the IOC's reputation or the public perception of the sports it oversees.

Dick Pound, Robertson and Canadian lawyer Richard McLaren led the independent commission investigating Russia. They published their findings in July 2016 as the McLaren Report.[157] The report concluded "beyond a reasonable doubt" that Russia's Ministry of Sport, Federal Security Service and the Moscow RUSADA lab enabled doping in Russia from 2011 to 2015. This doping benefited hundreds of athletes in 29 Olympic sports. The McLaren Report showed that Russian agents used a special tool at the Sochi Olympics to open otherwise tamper-proof urine containers and swap out doped urine for clean samples.

In response, WADA recommended that the IOC ban Russia as a nation from the Games. The IOC instead passed responsibility off to each sporting federation.[158] These organizations allowed 282 Russian athletes to compete in Rio, the seventh largest team by nation.[159] The IOC imposed one stipulation: any Russian athlete that previously failed a drug test could not participate in the 2016 Games, which eliminated Yuliya Stepanova from the event even though she served her full suspension and did not ask for a reduction—one she was entitled to as a whistleblower.[160]

As of this writing, Russia has not satisfied the conditions set forth by the IOC and WADA for participation in the 2020/2021 Games.[161] In 2016, Robertson quit WADA. His publicized resignation letter accused WADA of betraying clean athletes and forever tarnishing its own reputation. He further alleged that then-President Reedie delayed or hindered the Russian investigation so that Russian athletes could compete in Rio.[162]

Reedie said he was "disappointed" by the IOC's response regarding Russian athletes.[163] But what sounds like saving face betrays a deeper issue. The IOC staffs WADA with IOC members and supplies half their annual budget. Whether intentional or not, these built-in conflicts of interest facilitate delayed investigations, allow for appeals and deadlines to pass without incident and protect the IOC's mission while letting representatives of both agencies stare unashamedly into TV-cameras, promising that this time they're taking everything seriously.[164]

Meanwhile, it's business as usual for the IOC, collecting national fees and billions in sponsor monies. It's not ethical. But it's smart. Self-protection always is.

That's how even now, after multiple documentaries and an independent investigation, RUSADA regained accreditation, Russian athletes competed in Brazil, in the 2018 Winter Olympics[165] and will likely compete in Tokyo as well.[166]

Las Vegas: January to November 2014

"You gonna learn today!" I yelled across the platform after Taylor threw another snatch behind her head. I knew I had pissed her off but found it too funny to stop. Broz asked her to max out her snatch that session—typical, right?—and every time she missed, I grunted out that line from Kevin Hart's stand-up "you gonna learn today!"

It started when Taylor gave me shit that morning. I hesitated when loading a heavy back squat. The previous rep felt off and I grabbed a pair of 15kg plates, but then second guessed myself and put on 10kg instead. She noticed and called me a little bitch.

That afternoon, I got payback…

When Broz and I returned from Brazil, I promised myself three things:

I would never work a normal job again.
The gym environment would reflect what I needed to train at a high level.
Nothing would interfere with my preparation for the 2014 World Championships.

Then I run into Taylor and she looked *different*. Still really fucking hot, but damn. I visit Brazil for three months and she goes from snatching 40kg and C&J 60kg to snatching 60-65kg regularly and C&J'ing high 80s. Her back muscles bulged out from her sports bra, and her squat skyrocketed. Before she intrigued me with her smile and her cool job at the FBI. Now I wanted to know what else she was doing.

Plus, Broz told me that Taylor made a bet with one of girls at the gym that she could hook up with me. The girl replied, "I think Pat's gay." You can laugh, but I get it. My high school football coach thought I was gay, my younger brother is gay, and growing up, I focused way too much on sports and little on dating. And I'm a fairly good looking, put-together kind of dude, so I can see people making assumptions.

But I wasn't going to let anything fuck up my training. If I walked in and someone lifted on my platform, I kicked them off. Someone used my plates? I stripped their bar. Yeah, I acted like a prima donna, but none of the new members built Average Broz Gym, none of them donated plasma every week to train there. I had sweat equity. And I defended it.

Another snatch sailed behind Taylor's head, followed by me bellowing Kevin Hart's catchphrase. Anger boiled in her eyes, her cheeks flushed, and I danced right up to that line where she might lose her cool. Then I thought about her calling me a little bitch and kept pushing. "You gonna learn today!" I cackled, laughing through the words as she spiked another missed snatch and stormed out, crying.

A minute later, my phone blew up with texts from Broz. "I'm training" I wrote back. "Pat, you gotta be nicer to the people at the gym." He replied.

She told on me! "We can talk later," I answered, then switched to airplane mode before finishing my session. I moved into Broz' house a month earlier. He offered free rent, and we grew closer, our old wounds forgotten like missed lifts in the gym. We still bickered; I insisted he write me a long-range program and threatened to ask Dragos for one if he didn't.

His taking Taylor's side surprised me. I knew he considered her his "new project." Angelo Bianco trained there but didn't yet show the promise that turned him into a Pan Am medalist in 2017. Part of me wondered if Broz was fucking Taylor since she ran right to him. Anything was possible in that gym.[167]

Broz just signed papers on his second divorce, and I stayed in one of the spare bedrooms of his 3,000 square foot house. I hadn't lived in my own room for over five years. His house featured four bedrooms, a theater room, a stone staircase, custom Brazilian wood floors, and a 20-foot tall wrought iron door from an Italian castle. John put over fifteen years of work into that place, and I felt privileged to live there.

Free rent, free gym to train in, now I only needed a small, steady income to pay for expenses.

I never saw John as just my coach. We didn't hang out all the time, socialize with other lifters or get wasted at nationals like they do at some gyms.[168] But he bridged the gap between my fucked-up childhood and the years living in Virginia's basement. Now I helped him survive his second divorce and let him rant as we scouted locations for a new facility. During those long drives, we traded ideas that led to my online supplement business.

Broz' Internet fame brought some powerful industry leaders into the gym. The president of Muscle Pharm dropped in a few times and gave me advice on marketing, Internet sales and how to leverage suppliers. Nat Arem (the founder of Hookgrip), convinced me I could live on just online revenue.

Back in the mid-2000's, Nat lived in Vegas. Weightlifters know him for posters, t-shirts and slow-motion snatch videos. But he originally earned fame in online gaming. Nat worked as an accountant, moonlighted in poker, and launched a few poker-related websites. He gained notoriety for helping expose a massive cheating scandal covered by The Washington Post.[169] After moving to Vegas, Nat attended one of Broz' seminars.

I've watched dozens of people switch from general fitness to weightlifting after taking one of Broz' classes. Broz teaches the sport well, but he has mastered the art of selling it. People finish a class with him and believe that weightlifting is the pinnacle of athleticism, that weightlifter's achievements dwarf those of all other sports and that with just enough work and the right coaching, you too could scale those summits.

So Nat—who dabbled in Crossfit at the time—hired Broz for a private training session. When Broz offered me $100 to "go coach this crossfitter," I leapt at the quick money. Nat and I stayed in touch. He built a garage weightlifting gym at his Vegas condo and periodically dropped by ABG2 to watch and learn.

I never coached Nat again, but a few years later, I visited him in Philadelphia, where he ran this fledgling company called Hookgrip out of his tenth-floor apartment. Stacks of boxes reached the ceiling, bins full of posters and t-shirts littered the room. Plastic tubs full of mailing envelopes indicated the level of business. "What else do you do for work?" I asked. "Nothing much," he replied, telling me that in a short time, Hookgrip enabled him to train every day, travel the world to film weightlifting competitions and live in a luxury high-rise in one of Philadelphia's toniest neighborhoods. Seriously. The building sported a full-sized rooftop pool.

If I could earn a quarter of what Nat took in, I could train full time and never work again. Screw stipends and catering to the rules and demands of a federation. With the right product and some agile marketing, I could finance myself and take on the state-sponsored doping programs.

This time, I could beat them.

Early in 2014, I reconnected with Mike, who owned the supplement store near my high school. He offered access to his supplier network—at cost—which saved a ton of upfront charges. I bought a few digital scales, some bulk packing containers, a printer to spit out labels, and boom! I created a passive income stream. Now I needed to name my company, create a few Instagram posts and leverage sales off my fame in weightlifting.

While I built my online business, my ban from USAW expired. I immediately reached out and asked USAW to take the Whereabouts leash off my neck. No way would I return to full time training knowing that some lab tech could show up and hound me out of the sport. I also resigned from USAW membership and said I didn't intend to compete again.
A few email exchanges later, and I got my freedom.[170]

That Spring, the separate threads of my business, training and personal life wove together at once. I felt unstoppable and named my company: Comeback Supplements. We didn't need a tagline. During my ban, Instagram's popularity exploded and provided the perfect platform for weightlifting. No lift takes longer than 30s, and you could post one highlight after the next, all shot and uploaded from the same device.

Through Instagram, I linked to the first blog post on the Comeback Supplements website. That post detailed a "squat every day" template and received over 10,000 hits the first month. Sales rolled in. I initially sold a few products: a pre-workout, a recovery formula/sleep-aid and a protein, marketed with catchy names like "Dream Big" and "World Record Whey."[171] Every Sunday, I packed that week's orders from the bulk supplies. My income grew, and as planned, I supported myself on a six-hour workweek.

Late in February, one of my high school buddies threw a massive house party in the Vegas suburbs. I chilled there for about an hour when Rob Addell walked in with Taylor in tow. Inside, I chuckled, but played it cool, watching her reaction and nodding slyly when she saw me.

That winter, Taylor and I trained together often, or at least ran into each other. She worked ten to twelve-hour shifts at the Bureau. I lifted twice a day and kept my distance. Not unfriendly, but not eager. She intrigued me. Lots of athletes dabble in the Olympic lifts, especially at an Instafamous gym like Broz', where people pretend at weightlifting just to post about it online.

Not Taylor. She strode in and went to work. Waved hello, then stretched, set out her plates and barbell and warmed up. Taylor attacked the bar on every rep from empty bar to PR (fiercely enough that I could make her cry over some missed lifts). At this point, she had done a local meet, and her numbers wouldn't qualify her for Nationals. But watching her lift, I could tell she wanted it and her drive would get her there.

After a few minutes at the party, Taylor drifted over and said hello. "Came here with Rob?" I teased. "Yeah," she replied, "I wouldn't have known about this party otherwise." I smirked as she gave nothing; just stood there, blinking at me. We bullshitted for a few minutes before I added, "It's noisy. Let's find somewhere quiet."

I knew the layout of my friend's house, took her hand and led her upstairs, hoping no one was already hooking up in the bedrooms.

We took a couple beers with us and sat on my friend's bed. Moonlight streamed through an overhead window. Once you venture away from the Vegas strip, little smog or light pollution blocks out the night sky. A field of stars looked down as we talked until dawn. She told me her plans: earn a master's degree and advance through the bureau into a position in Behavioral Sciences (think *Silence of the Lambs*). I opened up about my childhood and my training. She asked about my ban from the sport and I didn't hide anything from her.

We kissed—Taylor is way too serious a person to fuck some rando on the first encounter—and I asked her to dinner that night. She balked, replying "I don't do same day dates." Her response caught me off-guard and I fumbled a bit, saying I would take her out next weekend. We left, and then both arrived at Broz' gym around 10am. After three hours to think, I wavered. I had slept with plenty of girls, even indulged a fling down in Brazil, but nothing that could interrupt my path. Taylor seemed different though; committed like me, serious about training, intense about everything she did and always eager to achieve her goals and move on.

I didn't go to college, so I never heard the phrase "Type A" personality before. But once I understood it—100% driven, everything to the extreme—I knew that concept pretty much applied to me, and to Taylor. If I started dating her, it would turn serious and potentially enhance my life rather than detract from it. But I had never dated anyone, so the choice was a gamble.

When I saw her at the gym that morning, I defaulted back to ignoring her. "I'll Facebook message you," I replied when she offered her phone number. And then I put my head down and attacked the barbell. I talked to Broz about it; he didn't forbid gym relationships but didn't encourage them either. When I mentioned Taylor's name, he blurted out "Don't do it!"

Taylor and I trained together six times that week, mostly in silence. Finally, she messaged me on Facebook: "Are you going to ask me out or not." Push, meet shove. We went to dinner that Sunday, fell into the same deep conversation, and stayed together since.

People can hear about our relationship and chuckle over a pair of early 20-somethings settling down so quickly (or similarly scoff at a talent like Kate Vibert marrying early). But there was no settling or sacrifice in the decision.

Yeah, we were young. But the flipside haunts the internet: Instagram teems with posts of wannabe athletes sharing the personal drama that derails their training. It kills me to read posts indulging in self-congratulation, bragging about self-inflicted hardships or worse, taking pride of place in the "struggle" to overcome something careless. Those who pretend at weightlifting and "bravely" post about leaving their spouse—which really means wrecking someone else's hard-fought expectations and commitments—or how a boyfriend or girlfriend ruined their important meet…well, these people don't get very far in sport or life.

Goals matter. You can collect kilos or you can collect lovers. If you're under 25, you can get away with both for a while, but the sluttier side of the drama will drag you down.

Serious athletes stay focused, avoid costly personal decisions, and root out sources of negativity that sap motivation and drain away valuable time, thought and energy. Yeah, I've only had one girlfriend in my life. I'm also the only American to ever snatch 200kg. #priorities

Once Taylor and I became serious, Broz adjusted. He could see that nothing changed. We wiped the feet of our personal lives at the gym door each day and worked.

It was already March; I intended to compete at Worlds in November and needed to check off three boxes along the way:

One, post a total at a local meet in Rio to qualify for Brazilian Nationals, then two, earn a spot on their World team. A 165kg snatch and 190kg C&J wouldn't cut it.

Three, I had to change country affiliation, and fast. Today, IWF rules vary by country with each national federation enacting its own process. In 2014, it was a little less straightforward and often got dirty; nations could effectively block an athlete from joining another country's team. The IWF told me I needed USAW to release me before I could lift for Brazil.

As soon as USAW removed me from Whereabouts, I began taking Oral Turinabol and injectable testosterone again. No crazy dosages like before; and nothing with a long half-life (like trenbolone). My numbers shot right back up. The 160 and 165kg snatches turned into regular 175 and 180kg snatches and my clean felt solid again. My squat crept back up to 290kg and slowly, my confidence returned.

Then the summer heat wave hit. The Crossfit that hosted Broz' gym lacked air conditioning. We threw open the big garage doors, moved fans near the platforms. Even then, we could barely tolerate the morning sessions when temperatures rose into the 90s. Most afternoons, the heat index soared over 110. Post-training, we drug in big bags of ice, laid them on each other's backs and quads, and huddled on the floor, panting and exhausted.

No one PR'ed in June and July. Then one afternoon, I dropped in at a Crossfit that offered AC and indoor temperatures of 70-degrees. That day I snatched 190kg for the first time in two years. The lift felt good and fast and I knew I could hit it again under the right conditions.

Broz and I bickered regularly. He still hadn't given me a real program. I'd ask for a full macrocycle; he outlined one week. Most days repeated the same progressions: power snatch, power clean, squat in the morning, then full lifts plus squat in the afternoon. On Saturday's I totaled (with some variations like reverse total). Tensions flared with the spiking temperatures. Comeback supplements slowly provided an income to support my training, but John left me to extricate myself from USAW and plan my trips to Brazil. All the details a full-time, professional coach should have handled fell on my shoulders.

That spring and summer, I emailed back and forth with Phil Andrews and anyone I could get in touch with at USAW. Initially, I played it coy, letting them know I wanted to retire and not weightlift anymore. Then I casually implied that I might switch countries. Phil wrote back, outlining the steps to take, and I shot back a quick thanks, still trying to disguise my intentions. That same month, I enrolled in Brazil's Federation and registered for a meet there in September.

Around mid-summer, I contacted USAW again. I knew that if I made Brazil's team, the IWF required me to enlist in ADAMS (Athlete Anti-Doping Management System, their version of Whereabouts). The current guidelines called for a minimum of two months in ADAMS prior to an International event. But I heard they planned to raise that to six months and I panicked because USAW hadn't released me.

Once I stated my intentions clearly, no one returned my emails anymore. Like complete radio silence from USAW's end.

"Hey, I'm going to lift for Brazil now, can you approve of the country transfer?"
Nothing.

"Getting ready for a local meet in Brazil and plan to compete at their nationals. Can you sign off on this please?"
No response.

Dragos scheduled a meet at his gym, and I booked a flight. Broz and I discussed attempts and I tapered off drugs. I assumed I had to clean out three times that year: once for the local meet, again for Brazilian Nationals and finally for Worlds. The websites I read generally agreed on the same basic information: WADA could test for ratios of testosterone[172] to epitestosterone and Oral Turinabol took five to seven days to leave the body.

As the meet approached, I switched from testosterone suspension to the cream, knowing the latter contained lower dosages and minimized detectability. I stopped Turinabol on the recommended guidelines of two weeks out. Each time I paid a fee to the testing company to ensure I cleaned out properly. And each time, my urine showed acceptable ratios and no traces of steroids.

Taylor and I flew to Rio for the meet. Dragos received us warmly, excited to coach me in competition. I crushed an easy 180kg snatch and 200kg C&J to qualify for Brazilian nationals two months later. After my last C&J, I nervously scanned the warm-up room for anyone holding a clipboard. I hesitated to ask if I needed to wait for an antidoping official to release me. Dragos' lifters began to put away barbells and plates. Ten minutes passed and then twenty.

Taylor came back and found me in a daze. "What are you doing?" she wondered. "Nothing," I stammered, "I just got a little dizzy." I packed up my gear, we had dinner that night with Dragos, spent a few more days in Rio and flew home. No one got tested at that local competition.

I cleaned out for nothing.

Back home, I prepared for Brazilian Nationals. My total at Dragos' meet showed promise; he emailed saying that if I could replicate those numbers at Nationals, and beat Brazil's current best 105kg athlete, they would have to put me on their World team. If I had continued doping, and only tapered off for nationals, my total could have surged even higher.

No one from USAW wrote back to me about the country transfer. Three months from Worlds and I had to re-enroll in ADAMS. But if I did under USAW, USADA could test me at any time, and I might become ineligible for Brazil. I reached out to a lawyer at the IWF.[173] She replied quickly, offering to investigate my options.

After Dragos' competition, I declared my intentions with USAW and started seeing USADA agents everywhere. They couldn't ask me to update my location through whereabouts, but a new rule now enabled them to show up randomly at Broz's and ask me to piss in a cup anytime they wanted.[172]

If someone sat in a car outside of Broz' gym, I waited inside until they left. Driving home, I imagined someone following me. At a restaurant with Taylor, I hid in the bathroom for ten minutes because I mistook some dude at the bar for a USADA rep. I spun around if I heard footsteps and shot my head nervously toward sudden noises.

"What's wrong with you?" Taylor demanded. Eventually I told her, and she laughed. "Pat, I follow people around for the FBI. I'd know if someone was tailing you." Although Taylor said she wouldn't turn me in, she also made it clear that she wouldn't fuck up her job at the Bureau by lying for me or helping me hide.

My training suffered as I tried programming for myself. One day I could snatch right up to 180kg. The next heavy session I missed 175kg four times in a row. My trust in Broz deteriorated, my squat didn't budge upward, and I couldn't go back on testosterone suspension or Oral Turinabol before I had to taper off again.

I didn't need to post a super high total. Brazil's Nationals would pit me against Mateus Gregório, who competed for Brazil at Junior and Senior Worlds but consistently hovered around a 160kg snatch and 190 C&J. He was younger than me and continued to improve over the next five years. My plan at Nationals involved out-snatching him and then staying even in the C&J because I had no idea what I could hit. Once we got into the session, I crushed a 180kg snatch and took a shot at 206kg, the Brazilian record in the C&J.

Brazil's national championships took two days. Despite the sport's success in that country, few clubs fielded athletes at the senior national level. After my session, Dragos hugged me, the President of the Brazilian Federation shook my hand and then embraced me. I had outpaced Gregório, locked up my spot and hit a number that could place me in the A session at Worlds.

The temporary excitement of winning masked my nervousness. Once again, I completely tapered off drugs, sent my urine anonymously to the testing agency, and gotten back clean results. But even at Nationals, I didn't see any anti-doping officials. The other competitors had packed up their bags and filed out of the competition hall.

Ten minutes passed. One of the marshals waved at me. "OK, this is it," I thought, "time to prove I'm clean." But she just directed me toward the medal ceremony. Later that night, having drinks with the team, I casually brought up the lack of anti-doping control at the meet, pointing out the difference between their national championships and those in the US. Everyone I asked sounded the same refrain: "Why would we be tested?"

Not a single competitor got drug-tested that weekend. At their national fucking championships. Where Brazil selected its 2014 World Team.

Again, I cleaned out for nothing.

I flew back to America with six weeks to prepare for Worlds. Before I left, officials from the Brazilian Federation informed me that they would field me on Team Brazil, but only after I worked out my country affiliation. Because of that hold-up, I counted as a late entry, and needed to pay my own way to the competition.

Every time I checked off one box, three more took its place. The trips to Brazil drained my savings. Comeback Supplements grew slowly, providing just enough income to live on. Now I had to find $3,500 to cover my flight, entry fees and hotels to Kazakhstan, while training and pestering USAW to release me.

Although I performed well at Brazilian Nationals, cleaning out multiple times in a few months destroyed me physically and mentally. Taylor noticed, telling me that overnight it looked like my back transformed from a chiseled, muscular physique to resembling one of the bowls of ice cream I scarfed down every evening. Some nights I sobbed uncontrollably while watching a movie. The testing company indicated that my testosterone levels had plummeted to 200 ng/dL. During foreplay, my dick randomly went soft.

My relationship with Broz fell apart. I wrote my own program after the local meet in Rio and ignored his suggestions. "I got this!" I screamed at him one day when he tried to cue me, barely holding back my frustration that he didn't help at all with USAW or raising money for Worlds. Most nights, I crashed at Taylor's apartment, but those times when I fell asleep in my bedroom at his house, I thought angrily about everything I owed him. He didn't charge rent, I trained at his gym for free, cooked in his kitchen on his utensils and ate off his plates. But the clock kept ticking and my temper ran short.

I posted a GoFundMe for my trip to Worlds on Facebook and Instagram. I asked for $6,000 to cover airfare, hotel and registration fees for Broz and me. Donations poured in from around the world. Guys younger than me, probably earning minimum wage, would pledge $20 with a note saying, "You got me into weightlifting." I almost cried reading them.
Their collective kindness buoyed my spirits. I slowly figured out a program that worked and began to regularly snatch 170kg, then 175kg. My squat didn't budge, but I knew I could do a 370-375kg total on my openers if really pushed.

We received over $3,000—enough to book two flights and pay for the venue hotel. Brazil listed me on their team entry even though USAW still hadn't released me. The IWF lawyer gave no confirmation, just a vague promise to reply "as soon as it gets straightened out."

Broz and I boarded a plane from Vegas to New York. I hit refresh on my phone as soon as we landed. No word from the IWF. I sent another email, panicking. Our connecting flights would take us to London, then Kazakhstan.

In about 20 hours I would land in Almaty for my second World Championships. I did all this work to prepare, and I still didn't know if I could compete.

Fifteen: The Roar of the A Session

The best way to avoid a positive drug test? Get your federation—or even better, your entire sport—to cover your tracks so you can dope year-round, even in competition.

Think it doesn't happen?

Pretend for a moment that USAW CEO Phil Andrews sat down with IWF President Tamas Ajan and had the following conversation:

Phil Andrews: Doping still plagues our sport and we must do more to combat it.

Tamas Ajan: I know that in the past we have not cracked down enough on the doping and doping nations

Phil Andrews: You've been head of the IWF for almost two decades! How do you explain that lapse?

Tamas Ajan: You have to understand. The IOC, they come to us, they say "we must see world records set in the Olympics."

Phil Andrews: And?

Tamas Ajan: So what am I to do? (picture a resigned shrug of one shoulder) Many world records are set at World Championships, at Asian Championships, etc., and these are doped records. But I must get athletes to set world records at the Olympics too…

Now imagine a version of that conversation actually took place.[175]

Weightlifting doesn't occupy a marquee position in the IOC hierarchy like Track and Field, Swimming,[176] Cycling[177] and Gymnastics. Those sports play to huge fan bases and for TV ratings across dozens of events with top-tier companies like Nike and Speedo shelling out millions for sponsorships and coverage. Whatever mandates weightlifting receives from the IOC carries far greater weight for those premier events. Do we have evidence to support that claim? You bet.

As of this writing (June 2020), Lamine Diack has stood trial in France for crimes he allegedly committed as the former President of World Athletics (previously known as the IAAF, Track and Field's governing body). According to prosecutors, Diack solicited millions in bribes to cover up test results from athletes suspected of doping. These cover-ups enabled athletes to compete at the 2012 London Olympics and the 2013 Moscow World Championships.[178]

The French Court will deliver its verdict in September 2020. But Part II of WADA's Independent Commission Report[179] already concluded that "Diack was responsible for organizing and enabling the conspiracy and corruption that took place at the IAAF," including sanctioning the "extortion of athletes."[180] The IAAF has since levied a lifetime ban against Valentin Balakhnichev, (former head of Russian Track and Field) for his role in the bribery scandal.[181]

We know this corruption transcends one or two rogue IAAF executives that took bribes to alter or expunge doping records.

We know this because a whistleblower dropped a bombshell on the eve of the 2015 IAAF World Championships. This whistleblower released the results of 12,000 longitudinal blood tests from 5,000 track and field athletes spanning the 2001 to 2011 World Championships and the 2012 London Olympics. The file came internally from the IAAF, not from WADA.

That blood result data revealed that from 2001-2012, 146 total medals, including 55 Golds in events from the 800m to the marathon, were captured by athletes who recorded suspicious doping results (10 medals at the London Games showed "dubious test results"). Russia and Kenya were both implicated as being beneficiaries of this coverup. On average, one of every six tests had a "highly suspicious" value that indicates an athlete who had doped at some point.[182]

Australian antidoping scientist Michael Ashenden[183] analyzed the leaked data and said:
"There's no question that the Athletics World Championships and Olympic distances have been contaminated by blood doping. I feel deeply sorry for the genuine athletes who were cheated out of medals, because it would have been damn near impossible to have competed against some of the blood values listed. Some of the results were simply grotesque., quite easily the worst I've ever seen."[184]

Why didn't the IAAF pursue any of these suspicious values?[185] Australian antidoping scientist Robin Parisotto concluded: "Someone has seen these results and decided not to take any action." Jack Robertson, the former FBI Investigator who spearheaded the McLaren Report said, "The report showed that all the way up to the President, people from IAAF were involved with reaching out to athletes, extorting monies from those athletes in exchange for allowing them to compete."[186]

After Lamine Diack retired, British two-time Olympic Gold medalist Sebastian Coe took over the Presidency, after serving as Diack's Vice-President. Many argued that Sebastian Coe could not have "not known" about the scandal. Indeed, email evidence suggests that he was aware as early as 2014,[187] long before the BBC released their coverage of the leaked data.

Corruption at the IAAF trickled down from the top.[188] But the distances of the races—800m and up—might be what really matters.

As a sport, World Athletics builds on a history of doping, tainted through the 1980s by the East Germans and Soviets, continued into the 1990's and beyond by doped Americans and Jamaicans.[189] Some records—in the short distances and power events—have stood since 1983.[190] What drugs did athletes use then? Derivatives of testosterone like Turinabol. But they didn't have EPO and sophisticated peptides that enabled greater red blood cell production and greater oxygen carrying capacity.

Those newer classes of drugs enable Athletics to push for new world records (and exciting television coverage) in distances at and over 800m.[191] It's no coincidence that the pursuit of world records goes hand in hand with developments in doping, even though the measures Athletics used to cover it up might still surprise some idealistic believers in clean sport.[192]

Almaty, Kazakhstan: November 2014

The minute we touched down in Almaty, Broz and I scrambled to find an ATM. We needed cash, and it had to be American.

Broz elbowed me when our plane landed. I startled, then panicked, flicked on my phone, and hit the email refresh button about 30 times, waiting for a cellular signal. Finally, it popped up, an email from the IWF lawyer.

"You're cleared to lift," her message read. A flood of relief washed over me. All around, people stood in the cabin, stretching or pulling luggage from the overhead compartments. I was pinned to my seat; my shoulders sagged, my legs heavy with expectation and happiness that I could compete a few days from now in my second World Championships.

A taxi ride later and Broz and I arrived at the venue hotel to discover that we couldn't check in until we paid our bill to the IWF. In cash, American dollars only. We hailed down another cab, who drove us to four different banks before finding an ATM that spit out US currency. We each needed $275; to cover my athlete registration fee, Broz' coaching credentials, and then more money to cover the mandatory four-night minimum at the venue (jacked up to IWF prices).

Back at the hotel, an IWF volunteer directed us to a room on the sixth floor. We knocked; no one stood guard outside and my jaw dropped when the door opened on a room littered with cash. Actual piles of money, and a current of IWF workers and volunteers running stacks through counting machines, with a safe in the corner open to reveal bundles of American dollars inside. Later, after traveling officially with the Brazil to the 2015 Pan Am Games, I realized that their coaches always carried about $15,000—in American money—with them to any IWF international competition. Why? The entry fee for each country cost ten grand. Cash only.[193]

No one offered a receipt and I didn't ask for one. A volunteer took our money and checked our names off a list. Another volunteer handed me my athlete badge and Broz his coaching ID. Now we could pick up our room keys.

I hit the pillow and passed out. Broz left to meet with the Brazilian coaches. When he came back, he delivered some good news: I would lift in the A-session of the 105kg class, competing directly against the titans of the sport. Olympic Champion Ilya Ilyin squaring off against Russia's C&J World Record holder David Bedzhanyan, both fighting against the past-year's World Champion Ruslan Nurudinov. Add into the mix China's 2010 Asian Champion Yang Zhe and this 17-year old kid Simon Martirosyan who set Youth World Records when he won the 2014 Youth Olympic Games a few months earlier.

Our session was the most stacked A-group in 105kg history. Arguably the most competitive session ever at a World Championships.

That good news came at a cost. In order to put me in the A-session, the Brazilian coaches declared my entry total at 406kg, six kilograms more than I ever totaled in competition or training.

They gambled on that number. Over 50 athletes registered in the 105kg class and they wanted me in the A-session. The IWF's 20kg-rule dictated that I couldn't open with less than a 386kg total, and Broz insisted I declare a 180kg snatch opener at weigh-ins.[194]

That number gnawed at me all week. "John, I don't think I can open at 180kg."

"You're smoking that number all the time in training." He replied.

"Yeah, and sometimes I still miss it."

Those misses stuck in my mind. Broz brought up the 190kg snatch—from six weeks earlier. Yeah, I snatched 190kg during the training cycle, but only once. During some other sessions, I hit 185kg, which realistically put 180kg as 95-98% of my current max. No one opens that high. No lifter or coach risks that.

"What about 176kg?" I offered at dinner the next day. "I could definitely open there."

"And then you've gotta C&J 210 on your first attempt." Broz shot back.

True. But I felt way more confident giving all three attempts to a 210 C&J than starting with a 180kg snatch. Even today I can't tell you why. It stuck in my head that 180kg was too high. And I think as a coach, when you know an athlete is in his head, no matter how great of a coach you think you are, or how much influence you have over them, just let the athlete make that call. But Broz didn't budge. He always looked ahead, from the opening attempt to what lift put an athlete on the podium. To him, a 180kg opener set us up for 185kg and then 190kg, which—by the past three year's results—medaled in the snatch.

In my head, I thought, "I'm 24 years old, at my second worlds. I don't need to medal now when I can compete at this level for the next six to eight years." Thoughts of my last Worlds—where I bombed in the snatch—consumed my confidence.

The next day in training, I snatched 185kg after missing it six times in a row.

When I finally locked it out overhead, Broz leapt up from his chair, and shot his hands into the air. "See!" He exclaimed, "you can hit these big numbers."

I shook my head, internally noting that lifters get three attempts, not seven. To Broz, those misses factored into his theory of how the snatch works, that mentality where he tells and retells the story of snatching 150kg after missing it on 30 straight attempts beforehand. To him, an athlete has to learn how to move a certain weight and that process might include a ton of misses.

Only that approach doesn't reflect how world-class weightlifters train. Yeah, everyone watches that Iron Mind video where the great Bulgarian 77kg lifter Zlaten Vanev takes an unofficial world record 210kg C&J for five straight misses in the training hall at the 1998 World Championships. Coaches and lifters tout him as an example of grit and fight. But in the snatch, it's sheer stupidity to miss that often. Looking around the training hall that week, I didn't see any competitors missing six snatches in a row at weights they wanted to hit in competition. That method might work early in an athlete's career when he's chasing a milestone PR's. Then they can bang their head against a wall on failed attempt after failed attempt.[195]

But when you're heading into a world championship (or any big meet), you need to learn how to fight with heavy weights you can successfully execute. And then you need to make those weights, over and over, six, seven, ten times a session. Only then do you teach your body how to move a true maximum. When do you see Lasha missing five or more snatches in the training hall? Or Tatiana Kashirina?

"What about 178kg?" I asked at breakfast the next day.

"C'mon Pat." Broz' tone told that he tired of my complaints. "You've got to see it in your head, like a vision," he added. "Wrap your mind around it and it will happen."

"I just think 178kg and 208kg will go better." I replied.

Broz didn't listen. I know that Broz has since changed on this point, especially after working with Angelo Bianco and achieving much more success with him. But in 2014, he couldn't separate out that it wasn't him lifting the weights. He didn't—and maybe couldn't—see it from my perspective, understand what I was trying to deal with, especially my bombout in 2011.

And it's easy to say, "Pat's being a head case." But the 2014 World Championships marked my twelfth meet. *Ever.* USADA had drug tested me almost twice as often. Not learning how to compete—at any level—meant I never learned how to trust myself or to understand what I should think or feel a week out from competition. And even after snatching 185kg in the training hall at Worlds, I doubted my ability to hit 5kg less on my opener.

Coming off drugs increased that doubt even more. Testosterone fuels ambition and risk-taking and confidence. That hormonal plunge clouded my judgment, sapped my self-confidence and eroded my strength. I was convinced that I was weaker than the weights I wanted to hit.

After that last conversation, I shut up about my opener and buried my emotions. The rest of the week passed slowly. Unlike my first worlds for the USA, the Brazilian team trained together, ate together, followed a set schedule. Which left a ton of down time to spend, mostly with Broz, whiling away hours in the hotel room or the lounge downstairs.

Hanging out in the training hall broke up the boredom, letting me enjoy some of the week's real jockeying. Russia's Aleksei Lovchev and Ruslan Albegov swaggered around their platforms while Iran's Bedhad Salimi set up for a heavy lift. The Iranians whooped and cheered whenever Salimi lifted anything, and

Hossein Rezah Zadeh's presence electrified the room. Seeing the two-time Olympic Gold medalist coach what looked like a version of his younger self felt like watching Eric Clapton give guitar lessons to Eddie Vedder.

The super heavyweights presided over their training sessions like professors giving clinics. Every lift cut through the air, and the way they approached the bar, intense and casual all at once, smirked "watch and learn little man, watch and learn."

I had a lot of learning left to do.

The night before my session, Broz and I sat out on the hotel's terrace. We had spent too much time in our room and needed some air. A cool breeze blew over the sound of taxi's and smell of smog.

"I just want you to know Pat," he began. "You're going to do great tomorrow."

I nodded and swallowed hard. No matter the sport, from little league baseball to high school football, I always choked up at these talks.

"Even if you don't, I want you to know that I'm proud of you, of what you've achieved."

Looking up, I saw a tear in the corner of his eyes.

"Just think," he continued, "last summer you were selling alarms in the 110-degree heat. None of these other guys have even worked a day in the last five years. For you to come back from your ban, from hip surgery, supporting yourself this entire time and get to the A-session of the World Championships! No one here has achieved that, and no one can take it away from you."

We shook hands, did one of those half-hearted bro-hugs you see grown men perform in locker rooms and called it a night.

My competition started tomorrow.

The alarm sounded at 9am. I don't remember anything about that morning, couldn't tell you if it rained or if the sun shone over the mountainous landscape surrounding Almaty. Everything was luminous and blurry at once. I woke feeling fresh, clear-headed and ready, and sat on the edge of the bed, trying to visualize my lifting without getting too excited. My weight was on point, so I could eat breakfast; during the past months I never weighed more than 106-107kg and my cut took little effort.

Around three PM, Broz and I caught up with Dragos and rode the shuttle bus to the venue for weigh-ins. The rest of the Brazilian coaching staff headed over earlier. While I weighed in, Mateus Gregorio competed in the 105kg B-session and totaled 370kg on two lifts. He missed 170kg twice before securing it on his third snatch, then C&J'ed 200kg on his opener before missing the Brazilian National Record at 207kg and 210kg.

The weigh-ins took place in a locker room of the Baluan Sholak Sports Palace, an indoor stadium that sat 5,000. International weigh-ins stink, literally. Picture a cramped space—usually a locker room or bathroom—crammed with 12 to 15 already sweating heavyweight men. Add in a few coaches and personal entourage each, and multiply that by a nervous, quiet intensity, like the kind that rustles through a prison yard moments before a fight.

No one wears deodorant either.

Once the meet organizers finalized the start list, they assigned random lot numbers to each competitor, which determined order of weigh-in. I drew a low lot number and weighed in right before Ilya Ilyin. The scale read 103.66; a little light, but nothing to cause worry. While I dressed back into my warm-ups, I watched Ilya escorted out of the weigh-in room with his coach and what looked like a doctor carrying a satchel. The rest of the athletes had to go find a quiet place to eat and rehydrate, but Ilya's group immediately disappeared into another room at the venue— benefits of home field advantage, I suppose.

Did they go off and use intravenous methods to rehydrate the defending Olympic champion? The WADA rules forbid it, but it happens. A 105kg man carries about 60% of that weight in water, or 15 gallons worth. Some athletes cut five kilograms or more through various methods of water manipulation—legal or otherwise. Weightlifters receive a one-hour window from the end of weigh-ins to the start of competition. Not getting that water back into muscle cells absolutely affects performance. Intravenous methods ensure the quickest hydration.

An hour later, Broz, Dragos and I filed into the warm-up area. We found our assigned platform and I began some light stretching. The remainder of the competitors trickled in, a slow-moving caravan of athletes, trainers and coaches. Quiet, expectant chattering turned into a symphony of rumbling grunts and the crashing of plates on platforms.

The electronic scoreboard lit up with everyone's declared attempts and the coaches swarmed over to calculate attempts. Broz and Dragos pointed at the board, discussing their strategy.

"Your 180 puts you as low as seventh." Broz told me. "But you could go as high as tenth, depending on what these other guys do." As I put my lifting shoes on, he and Dragos discussed the two Iranian lifters in the session, Kia Ghadami and Mohsen Bahramzadeh, both my age or younger, who might finish all their attempts before I opened. "Yeah, maybe as high as twelfth," Broz muttered. I needed to start warming up.

I swallowed my relief at not having to go first. My shoes on, I paced around the platform, then did a few air squats and picked up the barbell. It spun freely in my hands and sat like a broomstick in my fingers—usually a good sign. Broz and Dragos loaded 50kg onto my bar, I powered it then full snatched it, then repeated that process at 80kg, then 100kg and 120kg.

The marshals lined us up for introductions. In the back, I didn't sense the energy growing on the other side of the curtain. But I walked out with the other 10 competitors to a cheering crowd of

5,000. We formed a semi-circle behind the platform; when the announcer called Ilya's name, thousands rose to their feet, stomping the stands and screaming his name.

People in Kazakhstan love sport, and they revere Ilya, their two-time Olympic Champion and national hero. He still appears in TV and print ads for major companies. At the 2012 London Olympics, Kazakh athletes won 13 medals (their most ever), with weightlifters taking home four of Kazakhstan's seven Gold medal winning performances.[196]

The Iranian fans whistled and blew through horns as they announced Ghadami and Bahramzadeh. In Iran, weightlifting ranks just behind soccer; in 2003, 15,000 spectators packed a stadium for two-time Olympic Gold Medalist Reza Zadeh's wedding. Millions who couldn't attend watched a live broadcast. When he retired, his hometown of Ardabil built and named a stadium in his honor.

After they announced me, I tried to process my stage fright. It didn't take much; the surge of energy I got from the crowd, combined with the roster of names called next to mine fired me up and crushed my nervousness. I strode into the back pumping my fists.

My remaining warmups felt smooth. I powered 120kg, then smoked reps at 140kg, 150kg and 160kg. The ten-minute clock ticked down to zero. I trembled a bit as they called the first competitor, Ghadami at 171kg. Three-warmups to go. Ghadami smoked 171kg and jumped up, bringing Latvian Artūrs Plēsnieks out for his opener at 174kg, which he managed easily. Arkadiusz Michalski of Poland opened at 175kg and missed it. A few competitors in the B-session snatched 180kg, so no one took medal-contending lifts yet.

Broz slowed down my warm-ups. Dragos hovered near the scoreboard, letting Broz how many attempts I should wait until I snatched 175kg. Out on the competition platform, Michalski made 175kg, Bahramzadeh opened at 178kg and missed. Then

Armenia's Simon Martirosyan crushed that same weight on his first attempt. Ghadami snatched 178kg on the next lift before Bahramzadeh came back to hit it on his second.

Dragos signaled for me to take my last warm-up at 175kg. I chalked my hands and stepped to the bar. Off the floor it felt even—not too heavy, but not light either—and I locked it out solidly over my head. Standing up, it sank in my hands, a little heavy. Not walk-it-forward-to-save-it heavy, but heavy enough. I dropped the bar, breathed in and thought "Ok." No misses warming up.

At the pre-staging area, I sat next to Russia's David Bedzhanyan, the C&J world record holder. I felt strangely comforted and scared that he opened at the same weight as me. The announcer called my name for 180kg. I walked up the short flight of steps to the raised platform, stopped at the chalk bucket and glanced once more at the packed stadium. Five thousand raving fans, no big deal, I told myself as I zoned them out.

As I approached the platform and locked out, a hundred and eighty kilograms stared back at me. I marched up to it, then bent down and felt each hand grip the barbell. I relaxed my arms and upper back, sat into a squat position, visualized the lift one last time.

The last thing I remember thinking as I pulled it off the ground was "wow, this feels really light!" I straightened out and drove hard through the floor. The bar careened into my hips and sailed upward. I punched hard with my fists, and then oh shit, felt that I over-pulled it, then gritted and buckled down right before it dropped behind my head.

I shook my head as Broz and Dragos escorted me into the back. "It looked so light," Broz told me. "You're gonna go out and murder the next one."

He conferred with Dragos. "Please don't go up," I thought in my head. But in all the meets I've done with Broz or seen him coach, he always jumps up in weight if the athlete misses behind. It's stupid, really; he holds onto this attitude of "well, you basically made it." A pit formed in my stomach as I watched Broz walk to the table.

As I waited, Bedzhanyan man-handled 180kg on his opener. After that lift, Ilya bumped to 183kg. I glimpsed the scoreboard; Broz moved me to 182kg, leaving two attempts at 180kg: Jorge Arroyo of Ecuador on his first, and Michalski on his third, plus Ghadami's second attempt at 181kg. Three lifts, I said, calming my nerves.

Arroyo opened with no shot of making that weight and now a two-minute clock appeared on the screen. Any change in athlete re-starts the clock, causing longer breaks between attempts for anyone that's already taken lifts. Ghadami's second attempt at 181kg stretched that wait even more. Now I've been sitting for three attempts, getting colder by the second.

"C'mon," Broz motioned toward my warm-up platform. Dragos stripped my barbell to 140kg. "Just power the fucking thing," Broz commanded. I re-chalked my hands, swallowed a big breath of anger and grabbed the bar. After not moving for five minutes, the bar felt light, but the movement—bar to knees, knees to hip and then overhead—played like staccato notes on a piano.

Dragos signaled from the scoreboard. "Still a few more attempts," Broz relayed. Arroyo missed 180kg again, bringing Michalski up for his third. No movement from the Ecuadorian coaches; Arroyo stayed at 180kg, meaning that three more attempts—and about five minutes of time—needed to pass before my second lift.
Michalski missed 180kg. Arroyo bombed at the same weight. Out of the corner of my eye, I watched Ilya stride toward the pre-staging area for his opener at 183kg. Ghadami left 181kg out front. Finally, "182kg, second attempt, Patrick Mendes," sounded over the loudspeakers.

On my way to the platform, I passed by Ilya. He looked completely composed, relaxed even as he conferred momentarily with his coach. The crowd settled down; some notes of encouragement rang out from my teammates. I chalked my hands and looked out. You can do this.

I gripped the bar hard and pushed with my feet. Too much time had passed since my opener and 182kg now weighed a ton. My feet drove into the floor and I ripped hard toward my chin, but not enough acceleration or pull followed. My torso dropped forward. The bar remained in front of me and I watched it drift through my line of sight, picking up speed as gravity towed it downward.

"Fuck!" I muttered under my breath as I stepped off the platform. Broz delivered a few instructions, to push harder and pull more aggressively. The clock ticked down from two minutes. No breaks now, do or die on my third attempt.

In the chair next to mine, Ilya stared straight ahead, cool and confident. I breathed deep, my torso rocking as I amped myself back up for the next lift. One-minute left on the clock.

"Big pull up!" Broz screamed as I walked up the stairs. The crowd cheered their support—knowing I needed this lift to stay in the competition. Hearing them, I smiled, probably the first time that day.

The barbell waited for me at the center of the platform. In these moments, I've often wondered whether it's my enemy or friend. It's 20kg of cold steel that I've spent more hours with alone than with my wife or any friend or family. I felt the familiar touch of its knurling, squeezed my thumb against its rough surface. My feet gripped into the floor and I could sense how fast it moved as I shot upward and ripped down with all my might.

One-hundred-eight two kilograms whipped by my eyes in a silvery blur. I punched out aggressively. Chomped my jaw so hard my teeth hurt.

An eternity compressed into those few seconds, as I gripped the bar and tried to will it back into a place where it stabilized overhead. My toes clawed through the rubber of my shoes; my arms pleaded with their sockets for leverage. For a few moments, the bar and I formed an inverted Atlas, pushing through the world rather than hoisting it aloft on his shoulders. Years of practice concentrated into a single effort to defy gravity and momentum and the anguish I knew would result as I felt the bar slip from my grasp and crash to the unforgiving earth below.

My life to that point crashed behind me as well. The sound of a buzzer and three red lights ended my last snatch attempt at Worlds, and I shuffled, head-down off the platform.

Broz slung his arm around my shoulder. I heard him mumble some words of encouragement, but the roaring crowd drowned them out as Ilya smoked his 183kg opener. Martirosyan hit the same number on his third attempt, then Bedzhanyan crushed 185kg on his second.

The game was on and I watched the scoreboard light up with attempts I only snatched in training: Nurudinov opened at 185kg, Zhe Yang one-upped him with a 186kg first attempt, Ilya bested the same weight on his second, and Bedzhanyan finished with 187kg on his third—a lifetime best for him and a number he never lifted again in international competition.

Two attempts remained for both Nurudinov and Yang, with Ilya yet to take his third. Every successful lift now locked up a medal, and the coaches shifted around their three changes like pawns on a chessboard. Nurudinov was forced to take 190kg on his second. He dangled his tongue defiantly from his mouth while chalking his hands, then stomped toward that bar. It flew overhead, Nurudinov screaming as he stood it up. He quickly bowed to the crowd with a smile before three white lights lit up the scoreboard.

On his third attempt, Ilya ripped the same weight off the floor, a slight wobble of his elbows and shoulders giving his face a quick worry. But no matter! Three white lights on that lift moved him into gold medal position and secured a podium spot regardless of Yang and Nurudinov's last lifts. Yang bumped to 191kg and snatched it with the ease of a warm-up—a number that at 23 years old, he never equaled again in international competition.

Nurudinov roared back onto the stage and silenced the crowd with a 193kg third attempt (and three-kilogram personal best) which handed him the snatch gold medal.

In the back, I had already begun warming up my clean and jerks, knowing that I took the first lift at 206kg after the intermission expired in ten minutes. "You can still make this good!" Broz barked at me as I finished my last warmup at 195kg.

Bahramzadeh dropped his opener down to 206kg and went out first to take it. The event organizers lined the warm-up platforms in a single row, stretching out over 100 ft from front to end. My platform sat at the farthest end of the room—Ilya's team snagging the closest spot to the board, the marshal's table and the competition platform, naturally—so I had to walk somewhat shamefully past all the other competitors on my way to the stage.

My opening clean felt light, even when I pulled too quick off the floor. On 206kg, I stood up so easily that I didn't think and rushed the jerk, positioning it a little out front. I tried to drop under and squat jerk it but couldn't wrestle it back overhead and lost it forward. Ecuador's Arroyo scratched all three of his C&J's, leaving me a two-minute clock before my second attempt.

I stepped back out, confident that I could smoke it on my second. Again, the clean flew to my shoulders, but this time, I mentally worked through my setup and easily locked out the jerk. That lift set a Brazilian record in the C&J; finally, a highlight to feel proud of.

On my third, Dragos bumped me up to 214kg; not an odd choice as it gave me some rest between attempts and because I didn't want to see blue plates on the bar (a barbell loaded to 215kg included three red 25kg and one blue 20kg plate on each end). Dragos yelled from the edge of the platform to "be strong." "No problem," I thought, I've spent my whole life doing just that. I picked up 214kg with ease, racking it the fastest of all my cleans that day. But again, I failed to set up properly for the jerk and pushed it forward.

A one-for-six day and another bomb-out at my second World Championships. On a perfect day, I could have opened at 175kg and maybe snatched 185kg, then C&J'ed 215kg to match my best training total. The 406kg entry was a stretch by a wide margin. Broz correctly called 190kg as a medal-winning snatch, but I needed a miracle to lift it.

Even a 400kg total would have only placed me fifth in arguably the greatest weightlifting session of all time. I fumbled my 214kg jerk after Martirosyan opened at 213kg then sat in the back as the 17-year old took two cracks at Youth World Records in the C&J at 220kg and then 221kg, missing the jerk on both attempts. Nurudinov's coaches calculated that a 220kg opener guaranteed a podium spot, so Ruslan swaggered out to what should've been his last warm-up and crushed it, his tongue wagging like a wolf's during the entire lift.

Bedzhanyan's coaches opted for the same approach; he snatched 187kg and an opener at 225kg (an easy lift for the C&J world record holder) solidified a podium spot in the total after Yang only totaled 411kg. I watched as Bedzhanyan walked out coolly, like a CEO approaching a board meeting, and put in a place-setting first lift with a power jerk that he barely bent his knees to dip into. Both he and Nurudinov faced a long wait—Ruslan over 10 minutes—until their second attempts. The crowd roared in anticipation each time the announcer called Ilya's name before his coaches bumped up his opener, first to 231kg, and finally to 233kg—the same weight he lifted to win the 2012 Olympics at 94kg.

Five-thousand fans stomped their heels into the bleachers as if Achilles and Hector battled before them. The announcer begged them to remain silent, but Ilya called to them for more noise, more rage to fuel him. He barely set his hands on the bar before he ripped it off the ground like Hercules pulling the head off a lion, then launched it overhead without a thought.

The crowd leapt to their collective feet. Ilya bent over the barbell and kissed the plates—on his opener!—as if he had won the day already. His 413kg total moved him right into gold medal position (on lighter bodyweight), and Bedzhanyan called for 235kg to move back into the silver medal spot. On his second lift, the Russian under-extended on the clean and ran out of power for his jerk, bobbling it in his hands briefly before it crashed to the floor.

On his final lift, Nurudinov moved the bar up to 239kg for a world record attempt! Ilya retained two attempts and Bedzhanyan one, meaning that any of the final four lifts could set a world record clean and jerk! No session in history had seen this many world record attempts in a row! Ilya moved up to match him at the same weight, meaning the two-time Olympic champion would take the weight first, attempting to set a world record with one attempt in his back pocket!

Ilya ran up the stairs to the platform, chalked his hands and bowed to the bar. The crowd again defied the announcer's pleas for silence. He yanked the barbell off the floor with the same aggression, but this time drove the jerk forward. Despite Ilya's best efforts to stabilize it, his elbows buckled, and the bar fell to the ground. No lift! He still held onto first place in the C&J and total and this time patted the bar like an old friend.

His miss gave Nurudinov an edge. With a 3kg lead in the snatch, a successful lift at 239kg gave the Uzbekistani a 9kg advantage in the total. Nurudinov's tongue wagged the least on his final C&J, like he had finally settled down and gotten serious. Two years later he would win the Olympics with a 2kg-lighter lift in a contest where he wouldn't face either Ilya or Bedzhanyan.

But in 2014 he wrestled with giants and a giant weight awaited him. He screamed before setting his fists around the bar, racked it easily and then drove it over head in the strongest of his three lockouts that day! His 432kg total lagged only four kilos behind Andrei Aramnau's World Record and set an impossible bar for Bedzhanyan to pass.

Nonetheless, the big Russian moved up one kilo, unwilling yet to yield his title of C&J world record holder. The day would not deny him. Two-hundred and forty kilograms flew to his shoulders, and a stronger jerk followed that impressively strong world record clean. Too-eager judges—perhaps in awe of watching two world records in a row—gave him an early down signal, but no matter. Bedzhanyan recaptured his crown.

And then Ilya called for 242kg on his final attempt—asking for not only the fourth world record lift of the session, but a number that—if successful—catapulted him into first place in the total. He hadn't competed internationally since the 2012 Olympics, almost 18 months prior. In interviews, he claimed to take long periods off between meets, and his bodyweight fluctuated wildly in those interims. At the 2012 Olympics, he competed as a 94kg athlete. When he helped teach the "Super Seminar" at Sean Waxman's gym in November of 2013, his arms hung pencil-thin from his sides and he struggled to snatch 120kg.

Now, his arms and legs drove like massive pistons at 105kg bodyweight—25lbs heavier than when he won gold in London. I watched him nearly power clean his last warm-up attempt at 220kg before opening eight kilos above his nearest competitor. In the back, he alternated between periods of calm and mania, sometimes following his coaches' commands to sit with a towel draped over his shoulders, and at others, buzzing from one platform to the next, chit-chatting and smiling with a schoolboy's enthusiasm and energy.

When he pulled the bar off the floor on any lift, he drew from a deep, concentrated well of rage that no one else exhibited. On his final C&J, he tore 242kg from the earth as if gravity held no sway, then drove it overhead with an ease that mocked his miss three kilograms earlier. After the successful lift, he wandered around the platform for a few moments, dazed, as if he didn't realize what had happened, that he won his fourth world title and destroyed a world record by four kilos.

My mouth hung open, watching the screen in the back. I might have stood there indefinitely, but a short man with a clipboard tapped my elbow and said, "we need you at doping control." "Are you kidding me?" I wanted to ask, amazed that WADA drug-tested me after a bomb out, when they should've rounded up the lifters that just set back-to-back-to-back world records.

I complied and grabbed my gear. Twenty minutes later, I sat right next to Ilya in doping control as a technician drew blood from my arm. Then I watched in disbelief and horror as the world champion underwent the same procedure.

Doping control follows a very formalized protocol. A technician taking urine asks you to select a kit; verify its contents, then sign for it. Then that same tech escorts you to a bathroom and watches you pee. With blood draws, the phlebotomist ties a cord around your arm, finds a vein and inserts a syringe to remove two vials (an A and a B sample).

But they only took Ilya's blood. He didn't get urine tested at all!

The tech boxed up Ilya's vials—blood draws that contained zero evidence of any amounts of steroids he might have used to set a four-kilogram world record.[197] Testing methods in 2014 could detect EPO and HGH in the blood but no anabolics. Ilya held the band-aid on his elbow, then smiled and waved to everyone as if to say "hey, thanks for securing my world record for me."

And I just sat there, trying to do exactly what Ilya did, without the hundreds of thousands of dollars for bribe money, without even being in the same conversation to pay off whoever decided he would only get blood tested, without access to state-sponsored doping support and medical care. I'm doing what he's doing, training 12-15 times per week, trying to take the same steroids he used and—the results of our actual lifting aside—not even coming close to the same results in terms of fair and equal treatment by WADA, by the IWF, by my own country's federation. There's no amount of money I could raise on a GoFundMe to achieve that level of corruption.

Earlier in the week, the Kazakh Federation didn't even try to hide their abuse. In the women's 53kg class, Zulifaya Chinshanlo smoked a 134kg C&J, breaking her own world record in that lift and thrashing the second-place finisher by 15kg in the total. Just two years later, the IOC would strip away her 2012 gold medal after re-tests of her B-sample showed steroid use. But her and Ilya's world records from the 2014 Worlds still stand.[198] In 2015, a bitter fight between the IWF and USADA over which organization conducted drug tests led to 24 positive tests from the competitors at the 2015 World Championships in Houston (which ESPN called the "public bottoming out" for weightlifting).[199]

But not this year, the twilight of Turinabol.

I didn't speak to anyone for the next 20 minutes, just drifted around, dumbfounded. When I finally caught up with Broz outside the training area, he had packed up all my stuff. My head must have hung low because he asked how I was holding up at least two or three times before I even recognized his face and responded.

What could I tell him? In that small, makeshift medical room in Kazakhstan, my heart broke. Not because of my second bombout at worlds, but because I could never achieve in competition the results reached by athletes in a state-sponsored system. My energies, my attempts, my sheer *chances* at totals would never match theirs. And I had to give up. Not on my dream of going to the Rio Olympics (which I could still accomplish for Brazil), but my dream of being an actual contender on that—or any—international stage.

What was the point of taking moderate amounts of drugs, at scattershot times of the year, hiding from USADA, feeling paralyzed and stressed every moment I'm outside the safety of my own home? What's the point when I can never show up with the full measure of performance enhancing benefits experienced by athletes of nations with the resources and political will to pay the money that enables their lifters to win gold medals and set world records?

I had to go clean. From now on I would compete as a journeyman weightlifter. No drugs, no shot at A-sessions or records or medals at the World level. I hung my head because it broke my heart to feel that way.

But even after I cleaned out, they got me. Just like they got everyone else.

Sixteen
Testing Positive, Part II:
The Dream Killer

Is USADA clean as a whistle? Or bought and paid for just as badly as RUSADA?

In a 2013 interview with *60 Minutes*, USADA CEO Travis Tygart gave himself a public pat on the back for turning down a near-$250,000 donation from Lance Armstrong.[200]

Flash forward to 2015, when USADA added *several million* to its annual revenues by partnering with The Ultimate Fighting Championship (UFC). In its 2015 annual report, USADA referred to the partnership as the "first independently administered anti-doping program in professional sport."[201] USADA's revenues swelled over 20-percent in the first full year of this relationship, an increase of almost $3.7 million from 2014 (the year before the UFC agreement).[202]

That kind of money makes Armstrong's donation look like chump change.[203]

USADA began testing professional boxing fights around the same time.[204] The anti-doping agency contracted directly with promoters for specific fights, rather than with the boxing federation overseeing the fights. A lengthy article at SB Nation[205] detailed a litany of conflicts of interests and scandals that occurred from 2012 to 2015, including exorbitant fees, ($150,000 to test one fight), retroactive Therapeutic Use Exemption's (one granted

18 days after a fight), the same procedure guaranteed in a boxing contract, and in Erik Morales' case, he was allowed to fight despite three separate "A" samples and one "B" sample indicating the presence of the banned substance clenbuterol (several of those positives from doping tests weeks before the event).[206] Athletes in an Olympic sport would not be given the same treatment. For instance, when swimmer Jessica Hardy tested positive for clenbuterol, USADA didn't grant her permission to compete in the 2008 Olympics while she contested the results of her drug test.[207]

In Olympic sport, USADA can credibly call itself an "independent testing agency." It receives funds from the federal government and the USOC for this purpose; neither of those funders are directly tied to or subservient to *any* particular USA sports federation. By comparison, the relationship between USADA and professional boxing (as depicted by the SB Nation article) violates any clear conception of an "independent testing agency." A boxing promoter contracts boxers for a fight, pays USADA; and fights go on despite the results of illegal procedures observed or adverse analytical findings uncovered. Sorry, but anyone getting paid directly to conduct a service is not a third party or independent entity.

Now say USADA contracts with an organization such as The UFC, that is both the sports federation, event organizer and its promotional arm, and also *employs* and pays all the athletes.[208] Will USADA get to function like an independent testing agency, where the demands of the client (and the results experienced) do not or cannot affect USADA's actions and integrity, such as upholding the WADA Code?[209]

Let's see…

"When we first started testing UFC, everyone came back positive." That's a statement from a USADA doping control officer (DCO) given to this author personally in March 2020. "The organization (UFC) started freaking out." According to this DCO, USADA met with them and said, "we're not gonna deal with this.

We're going to give you guys three and a half months to clean your act up and then we'll start the testing again."[210]

Since 2016, dozens of UFC fighters have received doping-policy-related suspensions, including card-headliners, former and current champions and fan favorites Anderson Silva, Nick and Nate Diaz, Junior Dos Santos, Frank Mir, Brock Lesnar, Lyoto Machida, BJ Penn, Mirko Filipovic and Jon Jones.[211] All these fighters tested positive for substances, that if detected in an Olympic athlete, would result in immediate suspension.

In late October 2019, Nate Diaz allegedly tested positive for a SARM (LGD-4033). The UFC scheduled him to fight Jorge Masvidal on November 2. Rather than go forward with the fight and deal with the arbitration process later (USADA allows this for UFC), Diaz challenged the result publicly (in a tweet on October 24), threatening to withdraw from the event. Less than a day later, the UFC and USADA cleared him.[212] Jeff Novitzky, UFC's Vice-President for Athlete Health and Performance, said that USADA scientists confirmed that the 50-picograms of LGD-4033 detected in Diaz' urine conferred "unequivocally no performance enhancing benefit."[213]

That November, USADA unveiled significant changes to their UFC anti-doping policy.[214]
These revisions included:[215]

Letting athletes use intravenous hydration methods deemed "medically necessary."

<u>Setting decision concentration thresholds</u>[216] for the following substances:
Clomiphene: a *women's* fertility drug that has been shown to *double* testosterone levels in men.[217]
Hydrochlorothiazide: a diuretic and masking agent banned by WADA.[218]
Selective Androgen Receptor Modulators (SARMS)[219]
Trenbolone metabolites![220]

Zilpaterol, a substance like trenbolone, used primarily to improve the growth of beef in cattle![221]

And the biggest change: the new guidelines have set detection concentration thresholds for M3, a specific and by this point, notorious long-term metabolite of Oral Turinabol, which the IOC used to "catch" and punish dozens of track and weightlifting athletes in the Olympic re-tests.

None of these detection thresholds comply with guidelines specified by the WADA Code, to which USADA is a signatory. Why then does the UFC get a different set of testing standards and protocols from USADA, a supposed independent testing agency?

Could it be the money involved?

Las Vegas and Montreal: December 2014 to July 2015

I knew I recognized this guy's face in the crowd.

In front of me, Jon North riled up the spectators that attended the inaugural expo of the American Weightlifting Federation. We battled head-to-head in the snatch at Vegas' Crossfit Sin City; about 40 people watched while a pulsing beat blasted from speakers flanking the platform.

Jon worked the crowd into a frenzy, writing "S H A N K L E" in giant letters across the floor, screaming after every successful lift and calling me out to put more weight on the bar. We each snatched 150kg and Jon asked the crowd who wanted to see 160kg go down!

In moments like these, I retreated into that shy kid from my childhood. While I earned all-state honors, dominated local sports, and competed internationally for two nations, I let others play the showman. Even at the Pan Am Games, I never hollered after a big lift, never spiked my bar.

But the AWF expected that kind of behavior. Jon created this competitor federation because USAW wouldn't let him slam bars at national meets. At least that's his stated reason.[222] Over the past five years, Jon won National Championships and competed at the 2011 Pan Am Games and 2013 Pan Am Championships.

During that time, he built a brand that, along with the Cal Strength videos in which he starred, singlehandedly popularized weightlifting in America more than any other factor except Crossfit. Jon crisscrossed the country hosting seminars that blended PT Barnum antics with basic weightlifting drills. Crossfit brought the masses to weightlifting, but Jon taught them to drink deep from a rage and hunger that fueled big lifts.

As Jon ranted and raved, I studied the crowd. When we finished snatching, I followed the guy I recognized into the bathroom. I stood next to him at the sinks and studied his face in the mirror but couldn't place him in my memory.

Back on stage, Jon and I threw down again. I hit a 190kg C&J to beat him, then bowed to the crowd. After a brief Q&A, we mingled with the crowd and this mystery guy approached me.

"Hey Pat, I'm so-and-so from USADA, and this is my phlebotomist." Now it clicked. This motherfucker tried to pop me at Virginia's house a couple years ago.

My heart rate spiked momentarily before I reminded myself that the testing company in California cleared me before Worlds. I caught Taylor's eye across the room and chuckled. She always mocked my paranoia of seeing USADA agents everywhere, and here they were.[223] Worlds ended that past Sunday, November 16th. I arrived home on the 18th and now USADA tested me a few days later on the 22nd. Did they really think I would dive right back into doping?

I hadn't yet come to terms with going clean and fortune sends a sign that I chose wisely. Cleaning out wrecked my body. Since returning home, I ate a half-gallon of ice cream for dinner every night, my legs ached for no reason; depression kept me in a dark bedroom until noon every day.

For the past six years, I lifted 12 to 15 sessions per week, setting unofficial world records in the process, and using drugs—just like every other world-record holder—to achieve them. Then, at Worlds, I realize I'm not going to get anything that I originally signed up for. Weightlifting was my full-time job. When I took steroids, I got paid double for the same amount of work. Seeing firsthand how the doping nations cheated without consequence stole that bonus from me. But here I was, sticking with the sport, like that factory worker that stays at their job because they don't know anything else and feel too scared to change.

That was the future I had to wrap my head around as two grown men stared at my dick in a dirty Vegas bathroom stall.

As the holiday season approached, some rays of hope and optimism shone through. Taylor and I visited her family for Thanksgiving—my first real family dinner in two years. We moved in together after the FBI vetted me and approved our cohabitation (yeah, that's a thing). My supplement business took off. Despite the bombout, competing for Brazil at Worlds increased my Instagram following 25%.

Broz didn't care that I moved in with Taylor. He knew she took weightlifting seriously, and by this point, I spent five nights out of seven at her place. Taylor and I rented a house with a garage, which gave me more space and time to focus on growing Comeback Supplements.

But my trust in Broz deteriorated further. The first month after Worlds, I trudged into his gym every day. I would squat, then give Taylor some cues on her lifting. After the expo, Jon North asked me to promote the AWF's first competition that January, but I did little to prepare for it.

North hosted the meet at Vegas' Monte Carlo casino and invited a few high-profile lifters to participate. He offered cash prizes, a full set of plates and a barbell to the winner of each gender's session. Entry cost $75, and he secured sponsor booths outside the competition area. Caffeine and Kilos showed up (their co-owner Charlie Zamora lifted), Jared Enderton and Ian Droze competed, and Kendrick Farris spoke before the event, calling it a significant step forward in the growth of weightlifting in America.

That day, I hustled from the competition hall to Comeback Supplement booth. We sold over $500 in product that afternoon; a big windfall since I only paid Taylor $300 a month for our shared rent. I competed—and won—snatching 166kg and C&J'ing 190kg. On my final lift, I put 173kg on the bar. The AWF abided all IWF standards, including weight classes. At the time, 173kg would've set an unofficial US record in the snatch for the 105kg category.

But I got too amped up and threw it behind my head. The crowd erupted in cheers, excited to see even an unofficial record attempt. Afterwards, we sold more product, people wanted to shake my hand and I felt a surge of joy from weightlifting that I hadn't expected to experience again.

Lying in bed with Taylor later that night, I thought "I didn't even train for this meet and almost snatched an American record. And I cleaned out over three months ago."

The part of me that wanted to go back on steroids knew that USADA could now test a member of any nation's federation anywhere they found them. I didn't want to live my life peering around corners or looking through car mirrors. And I couldn't risk my life with Taylor or cause her trouble with the FBI.

I turned 25 that year and saw myself competing internationally for another eight to ten years. Taylor began nutritional coaching on the side for this upstart company Working Against Gravity, earning part time money working in her car while on stakeouts. We both bought into the Tim Ferris-Gary Vaynerchuk lifestyle and mentality. With a stipend and my growing supplement sales, I could earn a solid living and continue to train full time.

The Brazilian Federation laid out an aggressive competition schedule for 2015. Starting with the Manuel Suarez meet in Cuba, they expected me to compete at their National Championships, then the Pan Am Games in Toronto and finally at Worlds in Houston. All North American travel, which facilitated long periods of training. All easy on the wallet too, since Brazil picked up the tab. Despite my bomb-out at Worlds, Dragos said that Brazil penciled me on their team for the 2016 Rio Olympics.

My decision to go clean provided clarity and a new path forward. I would never again attempt or set a world record. But I could live a good life. As a weightlifter.

That March, I competed for Brazil in the 34th annual Manuel Suárez In Memoriam International Weightlifting Tournament. Cuba founded this competition to commemorate the tragic passing (in a motorcycle accident) of Suárez, their first weightlifting coach to produce an Olympic champion (Daniel Núñez Aguiar, 56kg, 1980 Moscow Olympics). Most of the Pan Am member federations sent competitors, including the USA. For South and Central Americans in particular, it gave us an annual celebration of Latino weightlifting and a year of bragging rights for the winner.

Brazil flew me to Rio for a two-week training camp before the Suárez competition. I prepared consistently through February—but on Broz' old system—and couldn't regularly hit any numbers above 160kg and 190kg. My lifts moved sluggishly; my squat plateaued, the bar path lacked speed and crisp execution. Those numbers wouldn't cut it. Brazil used the Suarez meet to test our competition shape before the Pan Am Games and I needed a bigger total.

That year, Cuba hosted the meet in Cienfuegos—literally the town of 100 fires—and the heat and lack of amenities lived up to that name. Cienfuegos sits about 160 miles inland from Havana and some of my teammates nearly puked on the rickety bus ride from the airport. We stepped out to a place where time stopped 50 years ago; every building like 1950's main street USA and cars to match. Worse, no cell signals or Wi-Fi, and only half the hotel rooms provided air conditioning. Luckily, mine did, which gave everyone an excuse to crowd my room.

The competition took place March 10-14; I lifted Saturday the 14th and won gold across the board snatching into the 160s and C&J'ing in the mid-190s (again beating Mateus Gregorio, Brazil's second 105kg athlete). Fernando lifted in the session after mine; I thought he was going to murder the officials. The heat sweltered that afternoon, swelling the wooden planks in the platform so much that it broke apart three times, including on one of his last C&J's. As he lunged into the jerk, the planks separated, nearly ripping apart the knee of his front leg. He finished the lift, but then spiked the bar and screamed something untranslatable in Portuguese.

I got piss-tested, but no record of that event's doping control exists in WADA's online database. I doubt the samples ever left Cuba.[224] You can't even find the meet results on the IWF website—even though the US sent a team that included Youth athletes. I still own my medals, but otherwise, it's just one more example of the shade under which the sport conducted business back then.

After the Suárez meet, Dragos told me that I officially earned a place on Brazil's Pan Am Games roster. Now I wanted to train. Now I was hungry for the first time since my bombout at Worlds. I had something to prove and knew I could do it my way.

Dragos told me to apply for a Brazilian social security number so the Federation could disburse a stipend of up to $3,000 a month. I felt even greater pressure to prove my worth, and let Broz know that I would program for myself until the Pan Am Games that July.

At first he balked, but now I argued. I told him that during these trips, I learned how Dragos programmed, how Reis and Mateus lifted day in and day out. I knew I couldn't handle Broz' mock Bulgarian system anymore. From now on, I would roll the dice on my own abilities.

In addition to programming for myself, I started helping athletes online. I posted my coaching services on the Comeback Supplements Instagram, offering to take on ten weightlifters at $150/month. My inbox filled overnight, and I selected athletes from around the world to coach. I discovered what worked for them by testing it on myself first. Sales for Comeback Supplements spiked that Spring. The AWF meet increased my following and I posted giveaways, promotions and challenges in response. Comments on my videos turned mostly positive again.

Taylor and I planned our life together. Over the past year, WAG grew from a small company where Taylor advised just a few dozen clients to one where she now managed 200. She considered resigning from the FBI, seeing greater opportunities with an Internet startup. Knowing WAG's online model brought in five-figure monthly revenues drove my ambition to achieve the same. A medal at the Pan Am Games would cement my reputation as an international lifter and draw more clients to my product line and coaching.

I had three months to put it all together. During my Pan Am Games preparation, I kept my schedule simple. Every Sunday, I rested. On Monday's, Wednesday's and Friday's, I trained twice. Mornings, I back squatted to a max over no more than six or seven sets. A few easy doubles or triples to warm up, then right to heavy singles. I started to hit 270kg regularly, then 280kg and finally put 290kg on my back. One single and done, just to keep my legs primed.

After the squats, I worked quickly to snatches at 140kg and then to a C&J around 180kg. One or two singles and out. No more than 70 minutes training time. Monday afternoon kept me hungry all week. Snatch to maximum. I allowed myself two misses (during the rest of the week, I wouldn't go up in weight on a sloppy rep). This big change in mindset—not missing anymore or rarely—shot my confidence up. Wednesday afternoons I snatched from blocks, power cleaned and sometimes front squatted. Tuesdays I did both lifts, to moderately heavy singles, and Thursdays I treated as a light day, working to a heavy back squat before calling it.

Every Friday I maxed out both lifts in the afternoon. In the morning, I still trained heavy squats, but only to prime the afternoon's bigger attempts. The big numbers came back quick.

On Saturday's I squatted heavy singles and performed technical work on the jerk. I rarely front squatted. High school football left me with a ton of upper body mass to support heavy cleans; but I still needed to figure out the jerk and got a breakthrough when I attended one of Billy Bybee's seminars. Bybee told the participants to push their shoulders up in the jerk and I thought about it and was like "oh, that sounds stupid." But then I watched a few Oleksiy Torokhtiy videos on YouTube and tried it myself. It felt incredible; suddenly the bar didn't crush my chest. A few weeks of practice and I jerked 220kg for the first time since I cut to 105kg (and almost hit a lifetime PR!).

Not doing two sessions every day helped the most. It freed up a lot of head space, prevented me from obsessing about training, relaxed my CNS and tempered my anxiety. Instead of driving to the gym 15 or more trips a week, I traveled nine. Not strapping on my shoes and taping up so often let me declutter and unwind from all the superstition and routine.

By the time Pan Ams rolled around, I snatched 180kg in multiple training sessions. Without drugs. And hit 210kg in the C&J. At Brazil's National Championships, I clean and jerked 208kg for another Brazilian national record. My back squat peaked out at 290kg, but mostly because I still squatted fast and refused to grind out a heavy rep. I understood the jerk more and more with each heavy session and saw bigger lifts on the horizon.

Staying on a consistent, manageable program for 12 weeks let me lift off-drugs what I could only lift with drugs before. And I had truly cleaned out. I passed the USADA test in December, I passed the Cuba test, my blood draw from Worlds came back clean. I can say with absolute certainty and conviction that **I did not take a single drop or pill of steroids since October 2014.**

But WADA had other plans. Pushed by Germany, Japan and the United States, they dropped a bomb that year, revealing one of the biggest doping scandals in Olympic history and destroying the reputations and achievements of hundreds of athletes.

In weightlifting circles, we called it "the dream killer."

Back in 2011, RUSADA head Grigory Rodchenkov—the "hero"[225] of the documentary *Icarus*—developed a test to detect long-term metabolites of Oral Turinabol. In February 2012, he and his assistant Tim Sobolevsky published their findings in *The Journal of Steroid Biochemistry and Molecular Biology*.[226]

In 2014, the current WADA test for Oral Turinabol could only detect the presence of that steroid in urine for seven to ten days (and by some reports, only as few as three). The old detection method enabled dopers to ingest Turinabol right until a competition. If their national federations didn't test them out of competition—and all indicators suggest that many nations never engaged in that IWF and IOC mandated process[227]—then athletes could essentially take Turinabol in long cycles, building strength, developing lean muscle mass, lowering body fat, and recovering from punishing training sessions.

By his own paper's calculations, Rodchenkov's new method extended that detection window to sixty days. It would later prove to catch cheaters months and months after the fact. Maybe years— if you believe the claims of athletes like UFC fighter Jon Jones, whose defenders[228] argue that the body stores these long-term metabolites in adipose tissue,[229] and that an athlete will then inadvertently release them while cutting weight.[230]

Since the publication of Rodchenkov's paper on long-term metabolite detection, several WADA-accredited labs confirmed the detectability of these Turinabol byproducts and refined the testing protocols (although perhaps not to the satisfaction of scientific rigor—see Appendix One). At the 2015 World Weightlifting Championships, dozens of lifters returned positives.

But in 2016, the IOC used the dream killer to re-test the urine samples of hundreds of weightlifters from the 2008 and 2012 Olympics. The tsunami of positive results shook the sport to its core. This scandal led the IOC to threaten weightlifting, one of the original Olympic sports, with expulsion from future Games.

A long list of medalists and world champions woke up to find their titles and medals stripped away overnight, most without any form of due process. Dozens of weightlifters from more than 20 nations forfeited their medals, and the arbitration of test results continues to this day (as recently as December 2019, Ukrainian Oleksiy Torokhtiy received news of his disqualified Gold medal finish from the 2012 Olympics for those long-term metabolites).

But I was one of this new test's first victims. At first, I thought someone was prank calling me.

I didn't travel with the Brazilian team to Toronto. They convened in Rio and flew from there; I booked a flight from Vegas so that I could train a few more days at Broz' gym. The night the Brazilian Federation arrived, Fernando Reis called me (I roomed with him during the Games).

"Pat, Canada's doping officers are looking for you." Fernando told me from our dormitory's hallway. "They're in the room, tearing the place apart." The doping agents upended the bed, inspected the bathrooms, and demanded to know why I hadn't landed in Toronto yet. I talked to them, explained the situation, said that if they had checked my ADAMS (Whereabouts data), they would see that I arrived in Canada a few days later.

As soon as I checked into my dorm, officials from CADP (Canadian Anti-Doping Program) knocked on my door. "Pat, we're here to drug test you." I shrugged at the now familiar routine. The officers took blood and urine; I didn't think much of it, just told them, "I'll see you again after I compete." Their visit marked my fourth drug test since worlds, I passed the first three and cleaned out eight months ago. After they left, this surreal, yet calming feeling washed over me: I was at the second biggest sports festival in the world, and I couldn't believe my life brought me here.

In my childhood and experience, I didn't expect to be part of a story that worked out.

I unpacked my clothes for the Opening Ceremonies. Brazil outfitted all their athletes—from sports as diverse as soccer and Tae Kwon Do—with suits for the Games. Not a tracksuit, but a sharp, dark green three-piece suit with blue and yellow accents, (Brazil's colors!), and a sick green fedora to top it off.

Broz still hadn't landed, and problems started when he did. He never filled out any of the forms for the competition! Brazil needed to register him so that he could stay in an event hotel and coach my warmups. To my knowledge, he didn't even book a room until the week before. I don't know if he thought Brazil would fix it or it wouldn't cause an issue, but as a result, Broz couldn't attend training sessions or enter the athlete village.

The weightlifting competition kicked off the day after opening ceremonies, with multiple weight classes competing each day over five days (July 11-15). I left Broz to deal with getting a pass and tried to ignore it. Fernando, Mateus and I lifted on the same day (the 15th), and we trained together that week. I never felt so pumped for a meet in my life! The excitement of seeing so many athletes living and training together, running into some former USA teammates in the cafeterias, catching up with old friends and meeting new ones. Broz, Dragos and I sat down the night before my session and discussed our strategy. Everyone spoke confidently about my chances. Based on the entry totals, I could definitely medal. Maybe even win the damn thing.

I weighed in at 104.95kg, with no stress during the cut. Broz devised this plan that he would borrow the ID badge from another coach and just wave it at the guard as we walked into the back. But the volunteer that checked at the door recognized Broz and held us up, saying "That's not your badge." (we later sleuthed around on the Internet and found out he posted some nasty anti-

Broz comments). We tried to argue that Broz lost his ID and had to borrow one, but the prick held fast and wouldn't let Broz in. Dragos assured me he would help with my attempts, and I tried to block this drama from my mind.

My warm-ups felt sharp and fast. I opened at 170kg, 3kg ahead of Mateus, and with two attempts left, we jumped to 175kg for a second attempt. Mateus smoked a competition best at 172kg, leaving him, Venezuela's Jesus Barrios, Ecuador's Arroyo and I with attempts remaining. Arroyo smoked 175kg on his second; I left the same weight out front, then watched as Barrios missed it on his second. Mateus came out and crushed 175kg, another competition personal best!

Without Broz in the back, I paced my own warm-ups and called my numbers on the platform. Dragos popped by every so often and told me how many attempts until my next lift. Because he also coached Mateus, I mostly sat alone to prepare. The Pan Am Games didn't award separate medals for snatch and C&J (only total). A good lift at 175kg would keep me in position with the leaders, and I called for it on my third attempt.

The bar sailed up, but I couldn't secure it and it fell to the floor. No problem, I thought, I came here to crush the clean and jerks, and could chip away at the difference on that lift. I opened at 200kg, and solidly locked it out over head. A 370kg total, with two more attempts to build. Mateus hit 202kg on his second attempt, stretching his lead over me to seven kilograms and tying the total of Barrios, who opened at the same weight. Arroyo missed 200kg, then made it, then missed the jerk at 204kg! I only needed 206kg to move into a medal position and we put it on the bar for my second attempt.

No dice! I cleaned it easy but pushed the jerk out front. Venezuela's Barrios succeeded with the same weight and extended his lead over the group further. Cuba's Alejandro Cisnero made 206kg after missing a kilo less, but his relatively poor showing in the snatch left him too far behind the leaders. I only needed to clean and jerk 206kg to slide into a bronze finish.

I gripped the bar and pushed hard with my feet. The clean sailed to my chest and I stood easily. I drove up and moved under but not through! I tried to run it forward but gravity beat me to the punch.

Barrios, Mateus,[231] Arroyo, me. Fourth place stung a bit, especially after leaving a medal-winning lift on the platform twice. After the session, a reporter from a Brazilian newspaper interviewed me, asked how I liked competing for Brazil and my hopes for the Rio Olympics. In the fog after the competition, I sounded more disappointed than anything.

Once I cleared my head though, I began to see my failure at this meet as part of a progression I could learn from. At the Pan Am Games, I matched my average Friday max-outs from the training cycle: 170kg snatch and 200kg C&J. Some Friday's I hit 180kg and 210kg, which meant I could total more in competition once I understood how to better peak and taper. I saw how Fernando's coach calculated openers and attempts in the lead-up to a big event. This competition gave me one data set; now I needed to compete more and plan better.

At 25, with eight years in, I saw myself just getting started in a sport I could compete in for the next decade. Taylor worked more for WAG, whose growth skyrocketed. I believed Comeback Supplements could shoot just as high. Under Phil Andrew's leadership, USAW began paying out massive stipends and I thought, "compete for Brazil at the Olympics, then return to the states and earn a nice, long, sustainable living. As a weightlifter."

Not taking drugs and having to clean out removed a huge stressor. I didn't need to worry about getting caught and having my dreams crash down via a letter from USADA. Sure, I went from thinking "I can break world records, even if in total secrecy," to accepting that even if I broke my own country's records and stood atop their national podiums, I would only eek out average results in International meets.

But I could handle that, because I envisioned a stable future, earning money from stipends, supplement sales and coaching. I would never accept being like Donnie Shankle—dirt poor his entire weightlifting career—and having to eat dinner at his coach's house on Friday night just to get a good cut of steak once a week.

This reverie continued as I drifted off to sleep in the airplane home. The flight had just boarded; I tucked a sweatshirt behind my head and nodded off.

Then my cell phone rang.

"Hello Pat?" I recognized the voice; the Brazilian reporter who interviewed me a few days earlier.

"Tell me, Pat, what do you have to say about your positive drug test from the competition?"

I nearly dropped the phone. "What the fuck are you talking about," I shot back.

"You tested positive at the Pan Am Games. What do you have to say about it?"

Panicking, I hung up and thought how fucking weird.

A minute later he called back, "Pat, please comment on testing positive."

"I did not test positive!" I screamed into the phone, slamming it shut and scaring the passengers around me. Was it a prank? Did he get the name wrong? And who gave him the results of a positive test? Reporters shouldn't hear sensitive information before an athlete and their coach.

Back in Vegas, I ate dinner with friends, and we laughed about it over drinks. A few days later, I received an email from CADP, informing me that the initial analysis from the dorm-room urine test found long-term metabolites of Oral Turinabol.

No athlete had heard of this new procedure that could detect traces of steroids in the body long after a lifter stopped using. But after the 2015 Worlds and into the lead-up to the 2016 Olympics, a steady drum beat of articles announced scores of positive re-tests, first from the 2015 World Championships, then from the 2008 and 2012 Olympics. The IOC stripped results and medals from those two Olympics for almost a hundred weightlifters.

No federation could pay to get around this test. It caught every country off guard. The Germans, the Americans, the Japanese, everyone that played mostly fair were done losing to the doping nations and said, "no more." The IOC engaged in a massive investigation and re-tested hundreds of stored urine samples. It was revenge of the nerds in the white coats, tearing down the legacies of every enhanced athlete in the sport. All for a level playing field that to this day *does not exist*.

They started with me. The Montreal labs acquired the long-term metabolite detection methods from laboratories in Germany and Switzerland. Now I have the double-distinction of being the first weightlifter to get popped with a flawed test for HGH and the first weightlifter who had his career ended from a flawed test for Oral Turinabol. At a hearing in Houston that November, I received an eight-year suspension, killing my dreams and ending my career in the sport.

They came for Ilya too. His stored urine samples from the 2008 and 2012 Games showed the presence of long-term steroid metabolites. As punishment, the IOC stripped his Gold medals from both Olympics.

Two offences should have led to a four-year ban or greater, but via a thin legal technicality, the IWF's disciplinary panel had to treat them as one violation. The labs performing the re-tests discovered the 2008 adverse finding around the same time as they found the 2012 infraction. Because the IWF didn't notify him of the first positive before they found the second, they had to treat them as one offence. Even though those two positives occurred four years apart.

While I have long since returned to my full-time job in sales, Ilya received a two-year ban, most of it absorbed by months of legal wrangling and arbitration. Now, going into the final period of the 2020 Olympic quad, he still gets to train, and compete in Olympic-qualifying meets in England, in Qatar, in Japan. Wherever he wants to lift he can lift, and even shoot for a spot in the 2020 Olympics.

Someone protects him; someone else pays for that protection.[232] I can't even be a journeyman lifter, attempt a national record or aim for a podium at some hemispheric meet. Meanwhile, lawyers combine Ilya's two Olympic positives into one failed test and his world record C&J still stands. He keeps all the millions he earned. The Internet, his nation and the world, still loves him.

In America, I am weightlifting's public face of doping. And there is no justice for people like me.

Epilogue

The most important change in USADA's new UFC guidelines set detection concentration thresholds for M3, a specific and now notorious long-term metabolite of Oral Turinabol. which the IOC used to "catch" and punish 100's of track and weightlifting athletes in the Olympic re-tests.

In many regards, these detection thresholds exclusively benefited one fighter: Jon Jones.[233]

Jones received his first *drug-related* suspension[234] after testing positive for Clomiphene and Letrozole in June 2016.[235] (Recall that USADA's new policy also set allowable detection concentration limits for Clomiphene).[236] Strike One.

In August 2017, USADA announced that Jones' urine showed M3 metabolites of Oral Turinabol from a sample taken at the weigh-in of his title fight against Daniel Cormier (July 28, 2017).[237] The UFC stripped him of his title and gave him a four-year suspension. USADA reduced that sentence by 30 months, and an arbitrator reduced it by a further 3 months, enabling Jones to fight again in the fall of 2018.[238] Strike Two.

That arbitrator was none other than Richard McLaren, of the McLaren Report that investigated state-sponsored doping in Russia.[239] McLaren's arbitration decision concluded that Jones' positive test resulted from a contaminated supplement.[240]

In writing his decision, McLaren basically took Jones at his word,[241] that the M3 must have resulted from a contaminated supplement or contaminated nutritional product, despite USADA having tested all 14 of the supplements Jones claims he took at the time (including, I imagine, the cocaine,[242] because everyone knows that drug dealers cut their blow[243] with Oral Turinabol).[244]

McLaren's arbitration decision concluded by stating "that a third anti-doping policy violation will result in a minimum period of ineligibility of double the period of ineligibility for a second violation and up to lifetime ineligibility."[245]

Meaning: *Jones would serve real time if he tested positive again.*

And then things got really interesting for Jones. In 2018, USADA tested Jones multiple times; sometimes he returned positive levels of M3, at others, negative results for that metabolite of Oral Turinabol.[246] They tested him again on December 9, 2018 and returned a positive finding for M3 metabolites. As a result, the Nevada State Athletic Commission refused to let Jones fight on December 29 against Alexander Gustafsson for the light heavyweight title, a card-headlining bout.[247]

How did The UFC respond?[248] First, they moved the fight to California on a few days' notice.[249] Second, UFC Vice-President of Athlete Health Jeff Novitzky announced that Jones' positive test result for M3 metabolites was not a violation stemming from a **new ingestion** of Oral Turinabol, but the result of a "pulsing effect," where the body releases metabolites over long periods of time, far longer than the 50-60 days estimated by Rodchenkov's original, peer-reviewed and published scientific paper.[250]

Third, the UFC got USADA and WADA scientists to give statements to the California State Athletic Commission (CSAC) supporting this pulsing theory. USADA's Chief Science Officer, Dr. Matt Fedoruk, attested to a review of more than 20 studies as sufficient evidence favoring the pulsing theory.[251] Dr. Daniel Eichner, the director at Sports Medicine Research and Testing Laboratory (SMRTL), the WADA-accredited lab in Salt Lake City[252] submitted a letter on Jones' behalf.

Eichner's letter stated "There is no evidence that DHCMT (Oral Turinabol) has been re-administered" and that the presence of long-term metabolites was most likely caused by "residual levels from a previous exposure."[253] Jeff Cook, the results management and investigations senior director for USADA also wrote "the presence of the metabolite is not consistent with re-administration of a prohibited substance, and this very low level *would not result in any performance enhancement* in relation to Mr. Jones' upcoming bout."[254]

Finally, Novitzky told Joe Rogan (on his podcast) about the abnormalities in Jones' doping records, citing low-picogram levels of M3 in August and September (2018), but no positive findings in October.[255] According to Novitzky, USADA reached out to experts worldwide to validate the pulsing theory, ensured the CSAC that residual levels conferred no performance-enhancing benefits and that **these metabolites could potentially "last forever" in Jones' system.**[256]

No wonder the UFC got Turinabol detection concentration thresholds[257] as part of its updated agreement with USADA, that "independent testing agency" they hired to look after their athletes.

And why wouldn't they? Jones' net worth is nearly $10 million, and he is sponsored by $40 billion company Nike. He headlines fights for an organization worth billions, so when his career is on the line, USADA gets the top anti-doping scientists in the USA to clear him of any re-administration of Oral Turinabol (based on laboratory data).[258] Their testimony enabled him to fight after testing positive repeatedly for M3 metabolites (which cropped up well into 2019).[259]

But poor Oleksiy Torokhtiy, who competes in a low-revenue Olympic sport for no major company, loses his Olympic Gold medal for trace amounts of the same substance. Who's greasing who?

Does this situation call USADA's integrity into question?

Setting detection concentration thresholds for Turinabol (and the other substances) falls outside the WADA Code, which operates on a concept of strict liability (and does not acknowledge pulsing effects for Prohibited Substances). Again, USADA is a signatory to the WADA Code.[260]

Instead of acting as an "independent testing agency," it sounds like USADA has established two anti-doping protocols: one for Olympic sport and one for big money sports like boxing and the UFC.

Why does the UFC receive a different set of rules from athletes in Olympic and amateur sport? Is it because professional sports like boxing and UFC have:

Athletes with real pull and vocal fan bases willing to boycott events?
Athletes that can afford lawyers to negotiate contracts and conduct drawn out litigation?
An organization willing to protect its athletes with financial and legal backing?

Or the flipside: that USADA—with its meager $20mil/year budget (most of that devoted to testing expenses and overhead)—knows that it cannot afford litigation, due process, a public loss of face, or the loss of a client that now accounts for 20% of its yearly budget?

It's not easy to take Tygart at his word when he calls the new UFC rules and detection thresholds, "changes...we're all really excited about," and a "great evolution of the program" that will help other sports interested in protecting clean athletes create fairer systems. To his credit, he publicly hoped that WADA would adopt the same rules.[261]

And if they do, then where does that leave all the athletes punished under the concept of strict liability, like Ilya, and Torokhtiy and hundreds of others stripped of their success and medals over what USADA now attests is a flawed approach and detection method (for M3) that cannot differentiate repeating yet inc. "pulses" of picogram levels of a long-term metabolite from actua. administration of Oral Turinabol and genuine cheating?

Where is their re-instatement and return to the field of play?

Houston: 2015 World Weightlifting Championships

The supposedly clean countries aggressively targeted the doped nations at the 2015 World Weightlifting Championships. USADA and the IWF fought a rancorous and publicized[262] battle over who would test athletes at this event.[263] USADA won. Which means that Germany, Japan, and the USA won.

The self-appointed doping police even used the hotel staff against athletes that trusted in the sanctity of a private room at the venue. They asked cleaning crews to turn in any syringes or pill bottles they discovered, then knew who to target for testing. Stasi tactics for East German steroids sounds a poetic ring, albeit one that USADA and USAW shouldn't feel proud to admit.

And what did their methods achieve? Did they reform the sport? They shook it to its core, gave it a public black eye, but what changed?

Only now (June 2020) have the crusaders forced out long-serving President Tamas Ajan. But what might work well for weightlifting doesn't necessarily suit Track and Field, Swimming, Cycling or combat sports. All of which fill the roster of doping sanctions while trying to hide their scandal-filled attempts to keep the *public* number of positives as low as possible.

As a result of the re-tests, the IOC put weightlifting—one of its original sports[264]—on provisional status. A probation of sorts, that might lead to us getting kicked out of the Olympics after Paris 2024, even if we clean up Ajan's mess of cheating and corruption.

In most other sports, it's business as usual.

NBC shelled out $775 million for the 2014 Winter Olympics, another 1.23 billion for broadcasting rights to the 2016 Summer Olympics, and then close to $2.5 billion for 2018 in South Korea and 2020 in Tokyo. In 2014, NBC inked a deal to pay 7.75 *billion* for the Olympics until 2032.[265] The notion of "clean sport" matters in the USA, Europe and Japan, precisely those huge, *wealthy* markets where NBC expects to profit from its coverage of the next four Olympiads. "Look what we're doing to those cheaters in weightlifting" they and the IOC can boast, while swimmers and cyclists and sprinters receive advance notice of out-of-competition testing. Why shouldn't they? In those prestige sports, there's billions of dollars on the line.

And the IOC and the viewers want to see world records fall.[266]

What was set by doping can only be beaten by doping. Other sports don't face the same scrutiny as weightlifting. Where are all the re-tests of stored samples for the 30-percent of those 5,000 track athletes that admitted to using a banned substance in the 12 months before the 2011 T&F World Championships?

Those re-tests will never happen. Federations with power—such as USA Track and Field or USA Swimming—protect their image and the ability of their athletes to compete on the world stage against the obviously doping nations like China and Russia. The IOC protects its image even more fiercely. Cycling in Britain,[267] which claimed to clean up, undergoes the same sort of scandals that have plagued that sport in every other race and country.[268] Are you telling me that the US can field Olympic gold medalists in Swimming, Track and Field and Cycling, but not weightlifting? That's absurd. There's a money line between those sports and ours. And where there's a difference in money, there's always a difference in policy.

Speedo takes in over 110 million pounds a year and sponsors swimmers across the globe. Nike's revenue topped 39 BILLION in 2019. Sportswear also-ran Puma earned over four billion.

Puma-sponsored athlete Usain Bolt earned 32 million in 2016 alone. That kind of investment demands protection. And gets it. In 2009 five Jamaican sprinters tested positive for banned stimulants, costing Jamaica a relay medal from the 2008 Olympics.[269] Later, Nesta Carter and 100m World-Record holder Asafa Powell[270] tested positive for different substances, but Bolt competed clean the entire time, right?[271]

Worldwide, the sporting-entertainment industry accounts for up to 3.5-percent of a nation's GDP![272] Scandals tarnish that image and lower revenues.[273]

It's clear to me now that **weightlifting is the low-revenue patsy that protects other Olympic events while enabling the IOC to continue to uphold a false notion of "clean sport."** The doping police can always point at weightlifters and say:

"Look what we did to those cheating bastards in weightlifting."

They sure enough did it to me.

I attended the 2015 World Championships as an athlete, but not to compete. The IWF held its disciplinary board hearings concurrent with Worlds, and a few dozen lifters showed up for our trials. They held these sessions at a banquet hall in the venue. Before I flew down to Houston, I bought a new suit, for my weightlifting funeral. I was the one getting buried.

The IWF scheduled me in a time slot, 11:00 to 11:30. I recognized a few other weightlifters standing in the hallway outside the conference room. They chatted quietly with their lawyers and coaches. Broz didn't attend and I didn't hire counsel; I think in our heads we imagined that if I defended myself, pleaded to being this impoverished weightlifter with no resources, that it would look pitiful and invite sympathy.

I'm pretty sure the opposite happened.

Five officials from the IWF sat at a table across from me as I stood and pleaded my case. The lawyer that helped clear up my country affiliation was there. One official read the results of my initial test and asked if I understood the charges. Then he informed me that the "B" sample also tested positive, for metabolites of Oral Turinabol.

"How do you think this drug got in your system" one asked me.

I mentioned the possibility of a tainted supplement. But I couldn't present any evidence; I explained that I couldn't afford a lawyer, and in turn, couldn't pay for testing on any products I ingested.[274] "I'm just a poor weightlifter. How was I going to take steroids," I pleaded.

One thing I did know: If I admitted guilt, they could have banned me for life.

Someone asked me if my coach or anyone else knew about the drugs. Or if I would provide additional information about people connected to me or the sport that...

I didn't cut the question off mid-sentence. But I hung my head a bit and blurted out "It's just me." Could I have gotten a reduced sentence if I ratted people out? Maybe. At this point I accepted whatever happened. I already returned to selling alarms for Vivint, and I knew that whether they gave me four years or eight years or life, I probably wouldn't compete in weightlifting again.

"OK," one of them replied, "we will take this into consideration." Someone else detailed an appeals process with the CAS and I left, avoiding the eyes of everyone lined up in the hallway, knowing they faced the same fate as me.

The IWF banned me for eight years. A practical death sentence on my weightlifting career.

If WADA treated high profile athletes in track and field and swimming and cycling with the same aggressiveness and tenacity that pursued me, you wouldn't have any debate about clean sport. You would have it. But you wouldn't see world records set at the Olympics either.

I was a nobody. A low-level player in a poor sport who won a few national championships. I wasn't a marquee athlete like Justin Gatlin or a Jamaican sprinter or a Kenyan distance runner.

Why did they hound me so hard? Why did they waste resources on me, and not expend similar tactics on the world's high-profile athletes? Why did Russia escape with minimal penalty? Why was Nike's project Oregon allowed to go on for so long?

It's not because they want clean sport. I don't believe the IOC truly cares about that. They care about highlight reels, promotional events, international superstars, huge advertising contracts and billion-dollar TV deals. It took documentaries from a smalltime German broadcaster to show the whole world how other sports— especially track and field—were doping out of their minds.

But I'm the criminal worth targeting, the poster boy, the deterrent. You want to know why they wasted tens of thousands of dollars testing a non-international medalist like me? The answer is always the money involved. I couldn't have earned them much revenue. But I sure as shit played into their bogus narrative about fighting doping.

In 2015, USA Weightlifting tacked the American Open onto the back end of Worlds. Since the IWF hadn't officially sanctioned me yet, I coached Taylor there. She finished 33rd in the 63kg class, making only her openers.

On Christmas, a few weeks later, I proposed. She cried as she accepted, and we planned our lives together. Taylor still wanted to compete in weightlifting, and I programmed for her while she lifted at Broz'. My career in sales kicked into high gear, and I only went to the gym to squat, if at all.

A few months later, Broz asked me to pay a gym membership. His request blindsided me; his rationale "that he thought I would stay more involved in the sport" didn't make any sense. I needed to begin my life after weightlifting and couldn't marry on a weightlifting coach's salary.

Taylor flipped out when I told her. She quit Broz' gym that day. I still owned a squat rack and a set of weights, so we built a platform in our garage. I tried to stay connected to the sport and undertook the 600lb-squat-a-day challenge, where each day, I posted Instagram videos of me squatting that weight or more.

Neither of us talked to Broz for months. Taylor competed at 2016 Nationals, where Phil Andrews kicked me out of the warmup room. She finished 8th in the 63kg class and took Bronze in the snatch with an 86kg lift! After that meet, she tried to move on to another coach, but my reputation followed her. One high-level coach said that he would assist her at meets, but she could never represent his club.

We planned our wedding. Taylor wanted three bridesmaids, requiring me to pick three groomsmen. I picked my two best friends, then waffled on the third choice. Taylor knew my hesitation and plainly stated, "We have to deal with the Broz situation." She and I only met because of Broz and I needed to work it out with him before I could move forward.

Taylor insisted that he apologize. And he did. I gave him a card, on his birthday, asking him to stand in as my third groomsman. He read it and cried like a baby.

That spring (2016), the IOC released batches of positive re-tests of the 2008 and 2012 Olympics. Medal after medal and name after name fell from their vaunted position. Ilya lost both his golds and became the most public face of a scandal that almost pushed weightlifting out of the Olympic Games.

Hearing that these lifters tested positive didn't cheer me up. But it lessened the sense that I was the only one penalized by the new test. "Superman doesn't exist" Taylor used to tell me in my darkest moments when I doubted myself and why I bombed or why I lost so poorly in the A-sessions at Worlds. Now we had proof.

That December, Taylor competed at the 2016 American Open, medaling again in the snatch, this time taking silver with an 89kg lift. She finished fifth overall in the 63kg class, after making her 102kg opener in the C&J. I stayed far away from the back room.

We married on January 17, 2017 and moved to Philadelphia. Taylor resumed training. I popped into Philadelphia Barbell once a week to squat and talk shop. At a local meet that fall, I stood silently in a corner of the room while Taylor shone, easily earning best lifter award. I didn't feel any guilt; people there knew my story. That sense of being ostracized didn't bother me. But not being able to help Taylor left me empty and ashamed.

At the 2017 American Open, I sat in the stands, frantically texting Taylor's coach in the back, sending in comments about attempts and how the other lifters performed. Taylor medaled in the C&J and total for the first time at a senior National meet, winning Bronze in both.

I cheered from the audience as she received her medals. In weightlifting, I had become a face in the crowd, a footnote to an era of rampant, state-sponsored doping, facilitated by sports federations, possibly encouraged by the IOC. My attempts to go it alone left me defenseless when the hammer finally dropped and fate presented me with the bill.

My name is Patrick Earth Mendes. This is my story.

Appendix One: WADA's Flawed Test for Oral Turinabol Metabolites

Just to recap: In 2012, Rodchenkov and Sobolevsky published a new method for detecting long-term metabolites of Oral Turinabol. Over the next few years, scientists at WADA-accredited laboratories confirmed that this method worked to detect *those metabolites*. At the 2015 Weightlifting World Championships, USADA applied this test and caught dozens. A few months later, the IOC conducted re-tests of stored urine samples from the 2008 and 2012 Olympics.

If a stored sample from those Games contained the presence of long-term metabolites of Oral Turinabol, the IOC stripped away medals and results, and through the governing bodies of the athlete's sport, levied bans of up to four-years.

For weightlifting athletes, the IWF process immediately suspended them and enabled a "possible appeals process."

It's clear that WADA and the IOC wanted to punish quickly and make a show of certain people and certain sports.[275] The bulk of the athletes punished consisted of weightlifters from over a dozen nations[276] and track and field athletes from Russia.[277]

The federations and the IOC punished all of these athletes under WADA's concept of **strict liability**.[278] Under this blanket doctrine, the mere presence of long-term metabolites constituted a per se violation or an Adverse Analytical Finding (AAF, or positive test result); the positive test result automatically met the WADA Code's requirement for "comfortable satisfaction" of proof or evidence that an Anti-doping Rule Violation (ADRV) had occurred.

As a doctrine, **strict liability** asserts that athletes are 100% responsible for the presence and consequences of what they put into their bodies. If a drug test returns an AAF for a Prohibited Substance, its Metabolites or Markers, the athlete is strictly liable and is considered to have committed an ADRV (except in rare, exceptional circumstances).

If an athlete took a contaminated supplement, he is still guilty of an ADRV. A competitor ingests a medicine at the advice of her doctor? She is still responsible, and the response from WADA is "choose better medical practitioners." An athlete's boyfriend (or now husband) spikes her drink with a banned substance? Strict Liability says that an athlete is responsible for who she surrounds herself with and allows to handle her food, drinks and supplements.[279]

Under the WADA Code, Oral Turinabol is listed as a Prohibited Substance, and thus falls under the doctrine of strict liability. As a metabolite of a Prohibited Substance, the prominently detectable long-term metabolites M3 and M4 (hereafter referred to as "**long-term metabolites**") also fall under strict liability and therefore are per se violations of the WADA Code.

Is Strict Liability the Right Method for Oral Turinabol?

Anti-doping scientists have learned much about the behavior of Oral Turinabol long-term metabolites since the IOC conducted the 2008/2012 re-tests in 2016. Much of that important work has been done by USADA when testing fighters in The UFC.

For instance, USADA and Dr. Daniel Eichner (the head of the WADA-accredited SMRTL lab in Salt Lake City) have consistently argued that these long-term metabolites pulse throughout an athlete's system over time. In layman's terms: the body stores them somewhere (the leading theory is adipose/fat tissue), and factors such as high-intensity exercise and weight loss cause these cells to release the long-term metabolites at irregular intervals over long periods of time. Years and years in some well-documented cases (such as fighters Jon Jones and Grant Dawson).

As a compound that pulses intermittently through an athlete's body and urine, the long-term metabolites of Turinabol present a very real, very practical problem for the concept of strict liability regarding both *evidence* of/for an AAF, and in terms of what constitutes an ADRV, and what, if any sanction is justified from the presence of these metabolites in an athlete's urine.

Take the case of Major League Baseball catcher Cody Stanley.[280] The St. Louis Cardinals slugger first tested positive for the long-term metabolites of Oral Turinabol on July 18, 2015, after being called up to the majors. He was tested again on July 25 and tested positive again. Major League Baseball combined the two positives into one offence and gave him an 80-game suspension on September 12, 2015.[281]

During that suspension from July 18, 2015 to May 26, 2016, MLB tested Stanley multiple times. He tested *negative* for metabolites on February 10, 2016, but positive on May 4 and May 26, 2016. Baseball again combined the two positives into one and issued him a 162-game ban (a full season).[282]

As part of his defense, Stanley submitted samples of all the supplements he took at the time, none of which showed traces of Oral Turinabol or its metabolites. He again appealed, but lost again, which effectively ended his MLB career.[283] Stanley maintains his innocence, says he doesn't know why he tested positive for long-term metabolites.[284]

How could Stanley test positive for a certain substance so many times in a six month and not test positive for it on other occasions if he wasn't, in fact, re-ingesting it?[285]

A Brief History of Oral Turinabol

Understanding the answer to that question requires a quick explanation of the pharmacokinetics of Oral Turinabol and its metabolites. Oral Turinabol—also referred to as DHCMT—is a chlorine-substituted version of Dianabol that combines Dianabol with clostebol.[286] Both Dianabol and clostebol are modifications of testosterone; the chlorination of testosterone in clostebol prevents it (and Turinabol) from being converted to DHT or estrogen, thereby eliminating some of the unfavorable side-effects of doping (such as gynecomastia). The chlorinated nature of Turinabol is also important; few pharmaceutical steroid hormones include a chlorine atom and that chlorine makes Turinabol's signature recognizable (and easily detectable) in modern drug tests. **All six of the identified long-term metabolites of Oral Turinabol contain a chlorine atom.**

After the athlete ingests Turinabol, the liver processes it (called a "first pass"). The liver breaks *some* of it down, leaving the parent compound (Turinabol) and short-term metabolites present in the athlete's system. The parent compound has a short half-life before excretion in urine; modern drug tests can only detect it *for a few days* as it is quickly broken down and excreted by the body. This fact explains why athletes ingest Turinabol daily as part of a doping regimen.

The short-term metabolites of Turinabol also possess a short half-life. Consequently, detection time ranges from two weeks to twenty days.[287] Until Rodchenkov and Sobolevsky's research, athletes could take Turinabol very close to a competition without having their cheating detected. Rodchenkov discovered long-term metabolites—biological byproducts and waste-products of the parent and short-term metabolites. He and Sobolevsky detected six such long-term metabolites (naming them M1 to M6), the "most important" being M3, which Rodchenkov *speculated* could be detected 50-60 days after the initial ingestion of Turinabol.[288]

This new method is how the IOC and WADA caught dozens of athletes for alleged use of Turinabol when those organizations conducted the re-tests of stored urine samples from the 2008 and 2012 Olympics. In the lead-up to those Olympic Games, athletes *could* have taken Turinabol, and ceased usage around three weeks out from the Games, knowing that the then-available detection methods wouldn't flag their urine for an AAF. They didn't know that **for years later**, some then-undetectable long-term metabolites remained in their systems.

But is the test for long term metabolites valid?[289]

Meaning, does it A) meet the standard of "comfortable satisfaction" set out by the WADA Code to indicate an AAF and does it B) uphold the notion of strict liability needed to consider that AAF actionable (and punishable) as an Anti-doping Rule Violation, and C) is the test able to distinguish false positives from actual cheating?

The remainder of this essay will prove that the answer to all three of those questions is a resounding "No."

What Does the Science Tell Us?

Since the re-tests of the stored samples in 2016, USADA and WADA scientists have learned much about the behavior and appearance of Oral Turinabol long-term metabolites.

In December 2018, USADA dismissed a potential doping violation against UFC fighter Grant Dawson, who tested positive for picogram levels of long-term metabolites of Oral Turinabol (but no parent compound). USADA said it was likely that his positive test for those long-term metabolites stemmed from ingestion of Turinabol *prior to Dawson coming under the UFC Anti-Doping Program*. Dawson's first positive test occurred in

November, 2018, and he fought in the UFC's contender series in Summer, 2017.[290] UFC's Vice-President of Athlete Health and Performance Jeff Novitzky[291] said it was determined that he did not take Turinabol recently, but the findings showed the long-term metabolites had lingered in his system, perhaps for years, long before he was in the UFC.[292]

Dawson continued to test positive for picogram-levels of Turinabol as recently as January 2020. A picogram is one-trillionth of a gram, or as Novitzky put it "Take a grain of salt. Cut it 55 million times. One of those pieces is a picogram."[293] Or one drop of water in a swimming pool.

Again, USADA cleared Dawson, and the Virginia state athletic commission licensed him to fight. USADA similarly cleared Russian fighter Muslim Salikhov after he tested positive in June 2018. In Salikhov's case, USADA said that his pulsing levels of long-term metabolites did not show parent compound and they could not determine *when he ingested Turinabol* (**if ever**), stating that it is likely that he could have been exposed to Turinabol up to a year before he came under the UFC's drug testing program in November 2017. Salikhov's record of testing is similar to Dawson's and Jon Jones (see below), as Salikhov **showed seven negative and three low-picogram level positives** from November 2017 to February 2019.[294] Under USADA's logic, his positive tests in late 2018 could have stemmed from Turinabol exposure in 2016 or earlier. [295]

In August of 2017, USADA announced that Jon Jones' urine showed long-term metabolites of Oral Turinabol from a sample taken at the weigh-in of his title fight against Daniel Cormier on July, 28, 2017.[296] He received a 48 months ban as a result of that test, his *second* anti-doping rule violation.[297]

Jones appealed this 48-month suspension and an agreement with USADA brought it down to 18 months. An arbitration hearing—headed by Richard McLaren—reduced that suspension to 15 months. In his decision, McLaren affirmed that Jones initial positive test resulted from a contaminated supplement or substance. McLaren accepted Jones' explanation that he must have unwittingly ingested a contaminated product, despite USADA finding no traces of Turinabol after testing all 14 of the supplements Jones provided and claimed to have taken.

McLaren cited four CAS cases as precedent for not requiring evidence of a contaminated supplement to still accept that a positive test resulted from such (see the footnotes).[298] In the specific case of the long-term metabolites of Oral Turinabol, McLaren thereby established a precedent that we have *just as much reason* to believe that a **low picogram level** resulted from a contaminated supplement or nutritional source as it did from *intentional* ingestion of Turinabol.[299]

Jones served his 15-month suspension and the UFC scheduled him to fight Alexander Gustafsson on December 29, 2018 in Nevada (at UFC 232). But in early December, Jones tested positive again for long-term metabolites and the Nevada State Athletic Commission (NSAC) revoked his fighting license.

The UFC moved the fight to California and applied to the California State Athletic Commission (CSAC) for a license for Jones to fight Gustafsson. Four prominent antidoping scientists[300] submitted *sworn written statements* on Jones' behalf, **testifying that the mere presence of the long-term metabolites did not— by itself—indicate that Jones took Oral Turinabol.**

Jeff Cook, (JD, Pepperdine, 2006) the Results Management and Senior Investigations Director for USADA said of Jones' low-picogram and fluctuating levels of Oral Turinabol metabolites:

> "Upon careful consideration of the very low concentration of the DHCMT long-term metabolite in Mr. Jones' Sample from December 9, 2018, and taking into account the human pharmacokinetic characteristics of this particular long-term anabolic steroid metabolite based on data to which USADA has access and in consultation with scientific experts, some of whose opinions are enclosed, USADA concluded, consistent with prior residual

amounts detected in Mr. Jones' samples, that **the presence of DHCMT long-term metabolite in Mr. Jones' Sample #1618215 is consistent with residual amounts from exposure prior to July 28, 2017.**

Stated differently, the presence of the metabolite is "not consistent with re-administration of a prohibited substance, and this very low level would not result in any performance enhancement in relation to Mr. Jones' upcoming bout."[301]

Dr. Matt Fedoruk, the USADA Director of Science[302], said that "determination of the circumstances of ingestion" becomes more difficult when it's the only long-term metabolite present in the urine and the test doesn't detect any of the parent or other metabolites.[303] His testimony revealed that USADA reviewed the details of **more than 20 DHCMT metabolite cases**, similar to the one with Jones, where there were sufficient tests and investigations completed, before coming to its conclusion.

> "In this (Jones') case, the detection of the single long term M3 metabolite at the tail end of the detection window and combined with the aforementioned factors, makes detection challenging – so a pattern of detection in some samples and absence in others is not uncommon," Fedoruk wrote.[304]

Dr. Larry Bowers, the retired former USADA Director of Science, submitted a letter that said:

> "In conclusion," from the presence of the long-term metabolites in urine, "I cannot determine with any certainty when, at what dose. or what chlorinated anabolic steroid was ingested that gave rise to the July 2017 result. Based on the data provided, I conclude that no DHCMT (Oral Turinabol) exposure occurred between August 2018 and December 2018" (Jones showed negative for metabolites in August 2018, then positive in December). He finished by saying "the appearance and disappearance" of the metabolite is "not unique to M3 of

DHCMT," and "I cannot exclude the possibility that the December 9, 2018 result arose from exposure before July 2017."[305]

Dr. Daniel Eichner, the Director at Sports Medicine Research and Testing Laboratory (SMRTL) in Salt Lake City, one of three WADA-accredited laboratories in North America said of the presence of long-term metabolites in Jones' urine:

> **"There is no evidence that DHCMT has been re-administered"** and "there is no scientific or medical evidence that the athlete would have an unfair advantage leading up to the competition in December 2018."[306]
>
> Eichner's lab analyzed Jones urine and his testimony argued that the "most likely" cause of the continued presence of long-term metabolites was due to **"residual levels from a previous exposure."** In other words, Eichner asserted that Oral Turinabol long-term metabolites **"pulse"** in an athlete's system.[307]

Dr. Eichner reaffirmed these conclusions on January 29, 2019, when he again testified under oath (this time in person) for Jones, who now sought a fight license in Nevada for UFC 235.[308]

During that hearing, Commissioner Dallas Haun asked Eichner "the July 28, 2017 only showed long-term metabolites. So in your opinion, Jones has not taken this drug since before that time? Eichner replied "I see no evidence of use after that time."

Eichner added that "the parent compound has a window of detection of several days, and then its broken up into metabolites" and that the intermediate-term metabolites are detectable for *several months*. He said that Rodchenkov's previous study that put the window of detection for the M3 metabolite at 50 days **"is untrue"** and added that he has seen it detected **"at very low concentrations for well over two years."**[309]

Commission Chair Anthony A. Marnell III[310] pushed the issue further: "If we're not seeing the intermediate metabolites and we're only seeing the long-term metabolite, say for a period of six months, is it safe to say that the athlete has no performance-enhancing effect from the original ingestion."

Eichner: **I agree with that statement.**

Commissioner Staci Alonso asked: "If the picogram levels shot up to say 500 picograms, but still only showed the long-term metabolites, your expert opinion is that it is still not re-ingestion even though the picogram levels are higher?"

To which Eichner responded: "I would like to see evidence of other metabolites, that would give me the most confidence to say "absolutely no re-administration" but I think you will get to a concentration even of the M3 metabolite where I will say "this looks a little unusual and may indicate re-administration rather than residual." **In other words: without evidence of the parent compound or short or intermediate metabolites, there's no picogram level of long-term metabolites that would *by itself* indicate re-administration** (again, remember how miniscule a picogram is, compared to say a 25mg tablet of Oral Turinabol).

In the same vein, Commissioner Christopher Ault asked, "If we tested Jones today, and it showed long-term metabolites in the range of 33 to 80 picograms, would you still consider that residual effect from the previous (exposure), would you assume?"

Eichner said he would do much more than assume. "I would be stronger and say there's no evidence that he re-administered, because we know there's a short window of detection for the parent compound and the short-term metabolites. **So I would be stronger on that one there. That there's no evidence of re-administration.**"

To make this issue very clear: Eichner told the NSAC that evidence of actual administration of Oral Turinabol requires

the parent-compound or intermediate-term metabolites to be present in urine.

When Commission Chair Marnell asked him, "Pulsing or residual effects from ingestion a long time ago is a real concept. In other words, it's not BS, it's the real deal?"

Eichner responded, "**Absolutely**."

When asked under oath how long the metabolites would last, Eichner said "it would depend on the **amount of exposure and the frequency of use**."

In his January 29, 2019 testimony, Eichner also argued that the body sequesters long-term metabolites somewhere—and releases them intermittently and in inconsistent amounts over long stretches of time.

Where exactly does the body sequester it? In the Court of Arbitration for Sport Case 2018/A/5768 *Dylan Scott v. International Tennis Federation*,[311] Dr. Jonathan Dordick (the Vice-President of Biochemistry research at Rensselaer Polytechnic Institute, PhD from MIT) testified under oath that:

- The long-term metabolites of Oral Turinabol are highly lipophilic (able to dissolve in fats)
- The long-term metabolites become sequestered in fat tissue[312]
- The sequestering of these long-term metabolites in fat tissue explains why they do not show a classic drug elimination profile in urine (but instead, "pulse" residually over long periods of time).

If all the above is true, testing would show variable levels of excretion over long periods of time, with an elimination profile influenced by extrinsic factors such as exercise and weight loss and a duration of excretion contingent upon the dosages of Oral Turinabol ingested.[313]

Are there other steroid hormones that behave this way? During his testimony to the NSAC on January 29, 2019, Eichner mentioned clomiphene as a hormone that behaves similarly to the long-term metabolites of Oral Turinabol.

Eichner co-authored a study published in the October 2018 *The Journal of Clinical Endocrinology and Metabolism*. That study, entitled "HPT-Axis Effects and Urinary Detection Following Clomiphene Administration in Males"[314] gave 12 athletic males 50mg of clomiphene for 30 days (1.5 grams total). Urine analysis could still detect pulses of clomiphene metabolites up to 260 days later. These residual amounts fluctuated in concentrations and did not follow a linear excretion pattern.

It's worth noting that clomiphene also contains a chlorine ion and that the urinary detection of clomiphene relies on identifying chlorine in its metabolites.[315]

This Science is a Game-Changer

Not all WADA-scientists have yet accepted this new understanding of Turinabol long-term metabolites. In *Dylan Scott v. International Tennis Federation*, Christiane Ayotte—the head of the WADA lab in Montreal—testified against Scott for the prosecution.

Ayotte's understanding rested on the "Schänzer Study" conducted by scientists at the WADA-lab in Cologne, Germany. In that experiment, scientists gave a single subject a single-20mg dose of Oral Turinabol. Despite this single-subject, single-dose experiment, urine tests still showed long-term metabolites of Oral Turinabol in that person's urine 250 days later. Ayotte alleged that the length of detection in urine reflects Oral Turinabol's metabolism process and "because its chemical structure lends itself to detection at very low levels."

But Ayotte's explanation for why residual levels occur on such a long timeline cannot at all explain how or why Jones' urine tests show no picogram levels one week and then magically show low picogram levels two weeks or a week later without any traces of the parent compound or short-term metabolites present. And Jones is not the only athlete to exhibit this pulsing effect (Cody Stanley, Dylan Scott, Muslim Salikhov, Grant Dawson, etc.).[316]

There is reason for Ayotte's concern. By enlisting the support of Dr. Daniel Eichner and others for its "pulsing theory," USADA has called into question the notion of strict liability concerning the long-term metabolites of Oral Turinabol.

A substance with long-detectable, long-term metabolites poses a serious problem for the doctrine of strict liability, *especially* if the "pulsing theory" is correct (and the body stores long-term metabolites like M3 in adipose tissue and then releases them on an erratic timeline).

These scientists have effectively argued that the mere appearance of long-term metabolites by itself cannot *automatically* count as evidence (an AAF) for an anti-doping rule violation.

And their testimony carries weight.

Section 3.2.4 of the WADA Code asserts: "**The facts** established by a decision of a court or professional disciplinary tribunal of competent jurisdiction which is not the subject of a pending appeal shall be *irrebuttable evidence* against the athlete or other Person to whom the decision pertained of those facts unless the athlete or other Person established that the decision violated principles of natural justice."

The CSAC, NSAC, CAS cases and arbitrations undertaken by USADA (in this case, Jones' own arbitration in front of McLaren) count as "courts or professional disciplinary tribunals of competent jurisdiction." Under WADA's own Code, the two fight licenses granted to Jones based on the evidence provided about oral Turinabol metabolites establishes Eichner's and other's testimony **as facts** that now count as *irrebuttable evidence* going forward concerning the presence of Oral Turinabol metabolites in an athlete's urine.

Eichner and USADA seem to be aware of this potential problem in their actions to consistently clear Jones and Dawson whenever their urine shows pulses of long-term metabolites. And Eichner's own testimony before the NSAC on January 29, 2019 reflects this understanding.

In response to a question[317] from Commission Chair Marnell, Eichner reflected on what the long-term metabolites mean:

> "As our knowledge evolves, and we've learned a lot about oral Turinabol in the last few years, and if we just stopped at 'you know, this is the way it can only be detected for 50 days'" (per Rodchenkov's original paper), " and we just thought like that no matter what, then we wouldn't be doing a good job, because we've got new data, and its opened us up now, our knowledge has evolved on how substances like this can persist over long periods of time." And now, we need to "take it on a case by case basis…And I think that if you've identified the M3 metabolite for the first time, I don't think there's any disagreement that there's been *exposure* at some time, but as far as you only see the M3 metabolite going forward, I would probably have you do it on a case by case basis, gather longitudinal data, and then make an individual determination. Because I don't think it's easy enough to say, 'if you have a concentration below this level, then this is what happens.' *I think every case has to be taken individually, and my hope is that we don't get a lot of these (cases) going forward, (because) it's a lengthy process to weigh every individual case."*

Indeed. It's much easier for WADA, USADA and the IOC to apply the blanket of strict liability to all cases in which an athlete's urine shows long-term metabolites.

But that approach would not satisfy our standards of justice. Because the mere presence of long-term metabolites cannot offer proof of doping, at least not by WADA's own standard of evidence.

Not So Comfortable Satisfaction

Based on the *sworn testimony* given by the WADA and USADA scientists above—which according to the WADA code, counts as evidence for purposes of determining an ADRV—the presence of long-term Oral Turinabol metabolites in urine presents an extremely complicated and difficult situation for determining whether or not an athlete has committed an ADRV.

Granted, a big question remains: How did those long-term metabolites get into the athlete's system to begin with? Doesn't the mere presence of Turinabol long-term metabolites indicate that the athlete—at some point—took that steroid?

Per Eichner's testimony before the NSAC in January, 2019: if the urine sample does not reveal the presence of the parent compound or short-term metabolites of Oral Turinabol, and only shows long-term metabolites at picogram levels, the presence of long-term metabolites "do not indicate re-ingestion of Oral Turinabol," nor does the mere presence of long-term metabolites confer any "performance enhancing benefits."

It follows, logically, that if the presence of long-metabolites does not show re-ingestion of Oral Turinabol, it also does not indicate ingestion *per se*.[318] (To be very clear: it follows from the statements given by Eichner and others, that the mere presence of long-term metabolites of Oral Turinabol in urine does not indicate whether or not an athlete ever took Oral Turinabol.)[319]

If a drug test can't distinguish re-administration from a residual pulse of that drug in an athlete's system, then how can it actually prove or show *any* administration?
Only on the concept of strict liability.

The WADA Code's stipulation of strict liability implies that the presence of a banned substance, its metabolites or markers is enough to constitute an AAF, and that AAF is sufficient proof of an ADRV per WADA Code 2.1.2.[320]

But does strict liability hold true for the long-term metabolites of Oral Turinabol?

Only if an AAF (positive test) for those metabolites actually counts as proof of an ADRV.
Let's see what the WADA Code says in Section 3.1 Burdens and Standards of Proof:

> "The anti-doping organization shall have the burden of establishing that an anti-doping rule violation has occurred. **The standard of proof shall be whether the anti-doping organization has established an anti-doping rule violation to the Comfortable Satisfaction of the hearing panel**, bearing in mind the seriousness of the allegation which is made. This standard of proof in all cases **is greater than a mere balance of probability but less than proof beyond a reasonable doubt**. Where the Code places the burden of proof upon the athlete or other Person alleged to have committed an anti-doping rule violation to rebut a presumption or establish specified facts or circumstances, **the standard of proof shall be by a balance of probability**."

In most cases, WADA has asserted that evidence of an AAF—such as the presence in urine of a banned substance, its metabolites or markers—is enough to comfortably satisfy[321] that burden of proof for an ADRV. Meaning, under strict liability, if a urine test shows long-term metabolites of Oral Turinabol, then WADA asserts the athlete ingested Oral Turinabol *at some point* and is guilty of an ADRV. We've seen—through the testimony of Eichner and others—that continual re-appearance and pulsing of long-term metabolites does not constitute an ADRV.

But what about the first time those long-term metabolites show up in someone's urine?

WADA's contention throughout—especially regarding the IOC/WADA 2008/2012 Olympic retests—relies on a strict-liability driven scenario: that the presence of long-term metabolites is comfortable satisfaction of proof that an anti-doping rule violation has occurred.

But that "strict liability" situation *is only one of at least four possible scenarios* for how or why an athlete's urine would show the presence of long-term metabolites of Oral Turinabol.

Possibility One: the athlete took Oral Turinabol at a time years past, before they started competing in a sport that falls under the umbrella of WADA drug-testing. According to Eichner, Fedoruk, Bowers, and others, metabolites of Oral Turinabol pulse in an athlete's system for at least several years, and as Novitzky puts it "potentially forever."

In the case of the UFC fighters Jones, Dawson and Salikhov, USADA and WADA-lab head Eichner have consistently argued that the presence of long-term metabolites persists years after any initial ingestion of Oral Turinabol.[322] Both Jones and Dawson first showed the long-term metabolites in urine tests years ago, and in Dawson and Salikhov's cases, USADA ruled that any possible use of Oral Turinabol on their part stemmed from a time *before* USADA began testing each athlete. Long-term metabolites of Oral Turinabol still showed in Dawson's system as recently as January 2020—three years later—and USADA still cleared him to fight based on that argument.

USADA has tested Dawson and Jones dozens of times since their initial positive tests for the long-term metabolites. Despite pulsing irregularly—positive on some tests, negative on others for the long-term metabolites, **not once** has either athlete's urine shown the parent compound or short-term metabolites of Oral Turinabol (which, according to Eichner and USADA, would indicate actual administration of Oral Turinabol).

If USADA is willing to accept that Dawson potentially (it has never been proven) ingested Oral Turinabol before he was subject to USADA testing, and metabolites still pulse in his system three or more years later, then we have *no grounds to dispute* the claims of any athlete (such as Dylan Scott) alleging a similar explanation for the presence of oral Turinabol metabolites in his or her urine.

Moreover, according to three of the top doping experts in the USA, **these pulsing, picogram-levels of long-term metabolites provide no performance enhancing benefit**, and offer no grounds for consideration as an ADRV **because there is no way to distinguish a pulse from a re-administration if the parent compound or short term metabolites are not present!**

There is simply *no* evidence that an athlete took Oral Turinabol based on *only* the presence of its long-term metabolites.

The athlete should, in this scenario, remain free to compete in his or her chosen sport, and perhaps tested more frequently[323] as WADA and other agencies perform more studies to investigate the duration and potency of metabolites of Oral Turinabol in human athletes.

Possibility Two: the athlete took a contaminated supplement or nutritional product **at some point in the past** (maybe before they even started competing) that was tainted with Oral Turinabol (or a similarly chlorinated steroid) and these trace amounts led to a later presence of long-term metabolites in the athlete's urine.

Again, if one 25mg tab in the Schänzer study led to the presence of metabolites 8 to 10 months later, then why wouldn't residual amounts of Turinabol found in tainted supplements effect a similar outcome? And perhaps even pulse for longer periods—per the argument of Dylan Scott's scientific expert—if the athlete took a particular contaminated supplement for a prolonged period of time and in great quantities?

Don Catlin[324] is the founder of the WADA-accredited lab at UCLA and the father of anti-doping in sport. He has argued on his blog (and publicly) that contaminated supplements[325] offer a very strong possible cause for the presence of long-term metabolites,[326] at least as likely as the intentional ingestion of Oral Turinabol for the purposes of cheating.[327] Moreover, Richard McLaren, one of the top arbitrators for the CAS and the head of the WADA-commission into state-sponsored doping in Russia has argued—*in his own decision on the Jon Jones case*—that we can and should take the athlete at his word that the presence of long-term metabolites resulted from a contaminated supplement, ***even with no evidence whatsoever***.[328] In that regard, the athlete testimony alone should provide at least as much comfortable satisfaction to prove against an ADRV as a positive test for *only* the long-term metabolites. Especially considering McLaren's very public contribution to this debate in the Jones' decision.

To wit: Major League Baseball officials have attested[329] that over 40 supplements, including some sold at GNC, can trigger a positive test for Turinabol.

Does this type of contamination happen with other known steroid hormones regarding nutritional products? WADA used to consistently argue for strict liability in those situations. But in the past few years, multiple cases have convinced both USADA and WADA to clear athletes for contamination from clenbuterol, trenbolone and zilpaterol and WADA has begun setting picogram-level detection thresholds for clenbuterol based on potential meat contamination.[330]

Most importantly to this consideration, Eichner testified to the NSAC on January 29, 2019, that the performance enhancing benefits of even a doping level regimen of Oral Turinabol would be gone by the time the intermediate metabolites were no longer present (3 months after last ingestion). Meaning: if only the long-term metabolites are appearing in urine, Eichner has said that the athlete is no longer receiving performance-enhancing benefits from any Oral Turinabol, no matter how the athlete consumed it.

At the very least, this possibility should mitigate any potential sanction and—like the case of UFC fighters—enable the athlete to continue in his or her chosen sport. Otherwise, the case law for this situation tilts towards judicial caprice and away from equal treatment under the rules. Imagine telling a fourteen year-old female weightlifter[331] that no, we don't believe you (and will punish you harshly) when you claim a contaminated supplement caused your positive test, but in this other situation, Richard McLaren[332] will absolutely believe the similar testimony of someone like Jones who once fled the scene of a DUI hit-and-run on a pregnant woman's vehicle?

I would further argue that if the picogram levels of metabolites are so low that they could also indicate food or supplement contamination, than the burden of proof shifts to WADA to show instead how it must have been Oral Turinabol and must have been intentional ingestion for the purposes of obtaining a performance enhancement (cheating).

Possibility Three: *the athlete took Oral Turinabol with the intent to cheat* during their time as a competitor in a federation overseen by WADA. This is the situation WADA wants to believe occurs most often (if not always) and asserts that an AAF for long-term metabolites constitutes an ADRV based on this scenario alone.

However, low levels of long-term metabolites cannot tell you when an athlete intentionally ingested Oral Turinabol (by the testimony of the three USA antidoping experts, it could have been years ago), and long-term metabolites confer no performance enhancing benefit. So WADA can, under strict liability, punish an athlete for the presence of this non-beneficial metabolite. But now it seems that a punishment is unwarranted and driven simply by the desire to punish, which offers no deterrent effect whatsoever as the ruling in these cases stem entirely from the caprice of the judicial body picking this situation over any of the other three possibilities.

Possibility Four: the athlete never ingested oral Turinabol, but some other chlorinated supplement or product that leads to the formation of the long-term metabolites. Don Catlin, on his blog,[333] has mentioned that designer drugs (including steroids) could lead to this possibility but there are no studies on it. There is only the testimony of anti-doping experts, which has informed cases in both amateur/Olympic and professional sport to clear athletes of ADPV's.

In all four cases, **there is no smoking gun[334]** to determine when an AAF for long-term metabolites counts as evidence of an ADRV. A positive test result for *only the* long-term metabolites **cannot differentiate between any of the four scenarios above**. It is just as likely to be any one as any of the others. Moreover, only under one of those four scenarios did the athlete ingest Oral Turinabol with the goal of achieving a performance enhancing benefit in a drug-tested sport.

There is no understanding in which a one in four chance provides a comfortable satisfaction that rests on a "balance of probabilities" per the WADA Code (not to mention the fact that the presence of the long-term metabolites cannot distinguish a "pulse" from actual ingestion of the drug!).

In clearer terms: the long-term metabolites test (as currently implemented) is unable to determine if an athlete committed an ADRV or not (i.e., cheated or not).

But we need to punish cheaters!

But let's say that WADA still wants to be punitive and doesn't care if their punishment violates their own standard for a burden of proof or any conception of equal treatment under the rules.[335]

That leaves WADA only believing Possibility Three: an athlete using Oral Turinabol with the intent to cheat. Let's examine what the presence of long-term metabolites can tell us about how to proceed based on that assumption.

Remember, we have four clear pieces of evidence to consider:

Multiple scientists that work for USADA and/or WADA-accredited labs have said that **low levels of long-term metabolites DO NOT, by themselves, indicate ingestion of oral Turinabol.**

Multiple scientists that work for USADA and/or WADA-accredited labs have stated that low levels of those long-term metabolites confer no performance enhancing benefit.

Richard McLaren reduced Jon Jones' sentence because he believed the low levels of long-term metabolites likely stemmed from a contaminated supplement and not from intentional ingestion of a Prohibited Substance (Oral Turinabol), its Metabolites, or Markers (remember, there was no proof in any of the 14 supplements Jones provided for analysis).

A sports-governing body—the California State Athletic Commission—permitted Jones to compete in his sport on the basis of the first two pieces of evidence presented above. In other words, a de facto clearance of him from any ADRV despite the AAF from long-term metabolites. Another sports-governing body—the Nevada State Athletics Commission—heard further testimony from USADA scientists and WADA-SMRTL lab-head Eichner—and then gave Jones a one-fight license based on evidence that his still present picogram levels did not constitute a further ADRV or evidence of ingestion of Oral Turinabol. (This took place nearly two years after Jones first showed picogram levels for the first time.)

But let's assume for a second that we still want to keep the notion of strict liability when we consider the cases of athletes whose only evidence for an ADRV is a positive urine test for long-term metabolites and it happens for the first time.[336]

In those cases, we have three options:

Option One: to assert that the presence of long-term metabolites indicates strict liability of the athlete, thereby saying—in effect—that at some point in the past, the athlete in question intentionally ingested Oral Turinabol or a similarly chlorinated steroid (like clostebol). This conclusion is the one WADA and the IOC asserted when they stripped medals and positions away from athletes during the re-tests of the 2008 and 2012 samples.

A few caveats to this approach:

In January 2019, Eichner testified under oath that the intermediate metabolites of Oral Turinabol appear for several months after cessation of ingestion. Eichner also testified that the performance enhancing benefits of a doping level regimen of Oral Turinabol would be gone by the time the intermediate metabolites were no longer present (3 months after last ingestion). During the same testimony, he said they know of cases where long-term metabolites pulse through an athlete's system two years later or more.

So enforcing a strict liability approach to a positive result for only the long-term metabolites denies the comfortable satisfaction requirement and also stretches thin the concept of punishment for cheating. Imagine a similar situation in which a student created a cheat-sheet months before an exam but then forgot to bring it to school the day of the test. What crime are we punishing?[337]

Again—by the sworn testimony of Eichner and others—the continued presence of long-term metabolites does not, by itself, indicate administration of the parent compound (Oral Turinabol).

But I suppose that if WADA or the IOC wants to punish merely for the sake of being punitive, they can. Make no mistake, doping with Oral Turinabol occurred all the time from 2008-2014 and likely earlier. But I would argue that the re-tests that only discovered long-term metabolites of Oral Turinabol offer no credible evidence and no justification for punishment by WADA's own standards, especially in light of the testimony given by WADA and USADA scientists on behalf of Jones and Dawson.[338]

It also follows that any athlete once punished on the concept of strict liability for an AAF that only showed long-term metabolites of Oral Turinabol can never be punished again by the same concept,[339] unless their urine also shows the parent compound or short or intermediate metabolites.[340]

Option Two: We can punish a first-offense for picogram levels of long-term metabolites under the concept of strict liability but have to mitigate any assumption of intent to cheat with the equally likely scenario that the athlete instead took a contaminated food product or supplement.

On his blog,[341] Don Catlin wrote that Oral Turinabol "remains prevalent online and has been seen as a contaminant in dietary supplement products as well." Catlin further argued that "If the drug infiltrates the raw material supply for supplements, it could lead to trace amounts of contamination that the new urine-testing methodology would be more likely to expose" and that a quick Google search shows that supplements that contain DHCMT are "not hard to find," with at least "ten different websites" offering "the drug in pill form." He wrote that "many of these raw material providers also offer legitimate and legal supplement ingredients to the supplement marketplace, leaving open the real possibility for inadvertent contamination of benign products."

Major League Baseball officials, as I already mentioned, have identified over 40 supplements, including some sold at GNC, that can trigger a positive test for Turinabol.

If we are to treat athletes equally under the law (WADA Code), it follows that we must mitigate their punishment for a first offense under strict liability with the same or greater allowance that Richard McLaren gave to Jon Jones in reducing his sentence. Given that Jones' positive test for long-term metabolites constituted a *second offence*, we should give even greater credence and leniency to first-time offenders that only show long-term metabolites.

As such, what are we punishing? Shouldn't we, like McLaren did for Jones or USADA did for Dawson, reduce or void any punishment? And also let the athlete continue to play their sport, since Eichner, Fedoruk and others have told us that by the time their urine is only showing long-term metabolites, they are no longer receiving *any performance-enhancing benefit?*

Option Three: We must conclude that the mere presence of long-term metabolites does not justify the concept of strict liability for an ADRV at all. Rather, it calls forth the need for greater monitoring of any athlete that returns an AAF for only long-term metabolites. In these cases, WADA and USADA should treat athletes in Olympic sport the way that USADA has treated UFC fighters: allow them to continue to compete and train and then test them with even greater frequency going forward (which has the double benefit of providing more data for longitudinal studies on excretion of Oral Turinabol metabolites).

On this option, there is no grounds to punish the athlete at all. Based on the evidence presented by WADA and USADA scientists about the behavior of the long-term metabolites and the lack of performance-enhancing benefits accrued *and* given that the presence of long-term metabolites by itself fails to comfortability satisfy the evidence requirement for an ADRV, *this is the most just approach to take.*

Again, that doesn't mean it satisfies everyone's emotional desire to punish or revenge themselves on athletes or countries suspected of state-sponsored doping. It means, that given what we know about the long-term metabolites, given our adherence to concepts of natural justice (such as avoiding double jeopardy and providing equal treatment under the law), we should not punish an athlete on strict liability for the presence of long-term metabolites of oral Turinabol.

And now it becomes difficult.

Upholding Our Concepts of Justice

Regarding the 2008/2012 re-tests, I would argue that given what we now know about how little the presence of long-term metabolites can tell us about actual doping, and by WADA's own conception of comfortable satisfaction, WADA should return all of the medals and results and void all the punishments levied for *only* the presence of those metabolites on the re-tests. Athletes like Cody Stanley should absolutely be given financial restitution from Major League Baseball and be enabled to quickly return to play.

Moreover, given what we know now about the persistence of long-term metabolites, and on WADA's own conception of strict liability, any athlete that showed an AAF for long-term metabolites on the 2008 re-tests should absolutely be considered as showing residual-pulsing effects if their 2012 re-test also showed only the long-term metabolites. Otherwise we risk violating the principle of double jeopardy and punishing an athlete twice for the same first offence. A short list of these athletes affected by this violation of double jeopardy would include Ilya Ilyin, Intigam Zairov (Azerbaijan), Khadzhimurat Akkayev (Russia) and most likely also Nadezhda Evstyukhina, Svetlana Podobedova, Cristina Iovu and Dayana Dimitrova.[342]

Again, if we are serious about upholding an ethical anti-doping approach grounded in justice, fairness, treating like cases alike and punishing primarily for the sake of deterrence, we must overturn the results of the 2008/2012 re-tests if the urine only showed long-term metabolites of Oral Turinabol. Moreover, the IWF should immediately re-instate Pat Mendes and any other athlete whose AAF's from 2015-onward showed only long-term metabolites of Oral Turinabol.

I understand that many people will not like what follows when we fully analyze the implications of the long-term metabolites test for Oral Turinabol, because then it becomes more difficult to punish actual cheaters who may have used a drug of considerable potency and a legacy of abuse since the 1970s.

But that is the position we now find ourselves in thanks to WADA and the IOC's over-zealous aggression in stripping medals and suspending athletes after the 2008/2012 re-tests[343] and thanks to USADA's continuing efforts to help the UFC secure fight licenses for some of its athletes. I am not saying that the science or arguments presented by Eichner, Fedoruk and others is in error or wrong.[344]

I am saying that the argument put forth above proves that considering an AAF for long-term metabolites as an ADRV and levying punishments or sanctions has no grounding in the WADA Code and its conceptions of evidence or justice.

And if we continue to act like it does, we risk far more than returning medals to a few likely drug cheats.

WADA Risks Its Credibility, Period.

To USADA's great credit, that organization has realized the many flaws in the application of the long-term metabolites test and has changed its practices (at least regarding the UFC) by setting detection thresholds and by clearing fighters and allowing them to continue to practice and compete in their chosen sport while it conducts more analysis and longitudinal studies.

The World Anti-Doping Agency, by contrast, continues to uphold the results of the 2008/2012 re-tests. Moreover, that organization and the IOC continue to retest stored samples from those Games and other events for long-term metabolites of Oral Turinabol using what USADA now knows is a highly flawed detection method.

These actions call WADA's credibility into question.

WADA faced a similar set of circumstances in the aftermath of the Andrus Veerpalu case.[345] His fight against WADA mirrors the situation faced by Jones, Dawson, Stanley and the hundreds of athletes affected by the 2008/2012 retest results. In both cases, WADA rushed ahead with a test that could detect a substance but did not do so in a way that conclusively showed that the presence of that substance indicated an anti-doping rule violation.

In 2011, WADA used a new test for HGH to accuse Veerpalu of doping, Veerpalu appealed to the CAS, and in its decision, the

CAS panel said that "there were many factors...which tend to indicate that Andrus Veerpalu did in fact himself administer exogenous HGH." Similarly, it is likely that some of the athletes caught on the 2008/2012 re-tests for long-term metabolites of Oral Turinabol also doped intentionally with that steroid.

But the CAS—**in acquitting Veerpalu**—noted that the governing body that sanctioned him "failed to meet the applicable standard of proof with respect to the procedure followed," and that "procedural flaws have been found in the statistical side of the WADA studies." WADA now faces the same set of issues over the long-term metabolites test for Oral Turinabol.

As a result of WADA's flawed method for detecting HGH, the CAS overturned Veerpalu's ban and acquitted him of all charges. It would be nice if all that happened to the two-time Olympic Gold medalist was a lengthy court proceeding, but no, WADA and the FIS (International Skiing Association) effectively ruined the tail end of Veerpalu's professional cross-country skiing career. WADA and the FIS not only cherry picked when they dropped the hammer of his charges (on the eve of the World Championships in 2011) but they also punitively extended what should have been a two-year ban for a first offence to three years, with that suspension conveniently ending Feb. 23, 2014, the final day of the Sochi Olympics.[346] His ban was extended because he refused to simply admit that he had taken HGH, which would have given credence to WADA's flawed test. USADA similarly strong-armed Pat Mendes, saying they would come down harder on him if he didn't just sign off on the results. But they used the same flawed test that CAS ruled invalid when they exonerated Veerpalu!

Fortunately for Veerpalu, and unlike many Olympic athletes accused of doping, he enjoyed the widespread support of his country and its institutions, with even the news media defending him against the charges.

WADA's Public Embarrassment, Then and Now

WADA's reputation suffered after the CAS decision favoring Veerpalu. Don Catlin, then head of the WADA-lab at UCLA, publicly remarked on the Veerpalu case that it was "scary" and showed that WADA can make big mistakes and find innocent people guilty.[347]

In a follow-up to the Veerpalu case, biostatisticians Krista Fischer and Donald Berry[348] published "Statisticians Introduce Science to International Doping Agency: The Andrus Veerpalu Case."[349]

Fischer and Berry identified the following sources of potential error in anti-doping tests that rely on data to establish a "decision limit" (such as the amount of picograms of long-term metabolites that distinguish a false positive from genuine cheating). Among these are the **testing process** (seen to be uncertain in the case of Jones and others as it is unable to distinguish ingestion from re-ingestion), and the **"variability within each individual depending on age, gender, time of day, season, diet, exercise, etc."** not to mention **"substance used, dose and time since administration."**

WADA-scientist Eichner and others have testified under oath that the length of detection of long-term metabolites in urine is dependent on exercise, training age, length of time on Oral Turinabol and dosages taken. To date, WADA has not conducted any longitudinal studies to examine how *these factors* would affect the detection of long-term metabolites. But as we have seen in the "burden of proof" section of this essay, understanding exactly when an athlete took Oral Turinabol, when he or she stopped, and the dosages taken, **absolutely informs why long-term metabolites still pulse in their bodies and absolutely impacts future detection of those metabolites**.

We have seen these sources for error consistently in cases involving the long-term metabolites of Oral Turinabol. In Grant

Dawson's case, USADA accepted that he took Turinabol (or a similarly chlorinated steroid hormone) before he joined the UFC and USADA began testing him, and they accept that the long-term metabolites from that ingestion still shows up in his urine today. Both USADA and the athletic commissions of two states have endorsed a similar understanding regarding Jon Jones.

Tennis player Dylan Scott argued the same—that he had taken a tainted supplement well over a year before he began playing tennis professionally.

In Scott's case against the International Tennis Federation, WADA-scientist Christiane Ayotte countered with the "Schänzer study," where scientists at the WADA-lab in Cologne gave a single subject a single-20mg dose of Oral Turinabol and the subject only showed long-term metabolites 250 days later. Ayotte speculated that the length of detection in urine reflects Oral Turinabol's metabolism process and "because its chemical structure lends itself to detection at very low levels."

Using the Schänzer study as evidence, Ayotte argued that Dylan Scott's excretion of long-term metabolites should follow a similar pattern, with long-term metabolites detectable until 250 days later but not thereafter (again, how does one single-dose study lend any value to the general causal statement that Ayotte claims? One study is not science; it's barely an anecdote!).[350]

Scott's scientific expert Jonathan Dordick contended otherwise, asserting that "the excretion time" for Scott "must be substantially greater than the eight months observed in the Schänzer subject," because Scott took dosages—before starting professional tennis—"several hundred times greater than that administered to the single Schänzer athlete." Therefore "it is highly likely that the detection window" (of long-term metabolites) "would be multiples of the 250 days observed" in Schänzer.[351]

Dordick noted that hydrophobic compounds (such as the long-term metabolites) tend to accumulate in adipose tissue and that because of this propensity, fat cells would release them slowly over time. He noted that Dylan Scott lost significant weight just before his positive test in 2017, which is consistent with the pulsing theory and with a usage that took place years earlier.

Ayotte countered—again, relying on the single-dose Schänzer study—by saying that Dylan Scott's claim to have ingested high dosages of DHCMT 21-22 months earlier (before he began playing professional tennis), *seems inconsistent*[352] with the existing knowledge (Schänzer). She then argued "I am not aware of the detection"[353] of picogram levels of long-term metabolites in any athlete's sample collected 21-22 months after the last ingestion of DHCMT. (Despite this last claim, she told the CAS that she disagreed with USADA over the Jones' case, which means she is at least aware of one athlete who showed picogram levels two years after ingestion).

Ayotte speculatively concluded her argument, noting her own incomplete knowledge: "Therefore, although we cannot deduce with any certainty the timing and frequency of use from a single test result, the delay between the last administration of DHCMT in July 2017 *must be* much less than 20 months, more realistically a few months." [354]

From one single-dose study, Ayotte speculated as to what must be the case for athletes that take dosages far in excess of 25mg and over considerable periods of time (i.e., a doping regimen). Ayotte's speculation would not matter so much except that her scientifically unfounded testimony cost a young person four-years of his tennis career and tens of thousands in legal fees.

In Scott's defense, biochemistry professor Dordick testified to the lipophilic nature of Oral Turinabol metabolites and argued that an athlete's body sequesters them in fat cells, releasing them under periods of intense exercise or weight loss. Is there evidence for this claim? Ayotte argues it doesn't happen, but the head of the WADA-lab in Salt Lake City (Daniel Eichner) has testified under oath that it does. And the NSAC agreed with him when it gave Jones a fight license based on that testimony.

In Jon Jones' 2019 NSAC hearing, Commissioner Staci Alonso asked, "what is the scientific explanation for why the picogram levels can sometimes be higher on these tests and lower on others, especially after so much time?"

Eichner explained the behavior of Turinabol metabolites via an analogous scenario resulting from an athlete's use of Meldonium. That substance also possesses a short half-life but can be detected in urine for a long time. Eichner testified that "subsequent studies at WADA's Cologne laboratory showed that Meldonium is sequestered within red blood cells" which have "a lifespan of about 100 days, and then they die, and release that residual Meldonium," which can then be picked up again by other red blood cells. This process "can keep going forward, so that you have a situation where a drug with a very short half-life is detectable for an awful long time in urine."

Eichner then remarked that:
> "with Clomiphene and Oral Turinabol, those studies haven't been done. I suspect that it's sequestered somewhere in the body and it can come out later" and that the metabolites of Oral Turinabol don't "act like a lot of the other drugs we see. For instance, if you inject nandrolone, that can be detected for over 12 months, but the concentrations go down over time. It's still detectable, but in lesser and lesser amounts over time. Something like Oral Turinabol, we don't know where its sequestered. It could be in fat cells, it could be in some other tissue and once you get down to that low (picogram) level, you get a bit of fluctuation, and you see that."

Dordick's defense of Dylan Scott also referenced a model by Dr. David Cowan, head of the WADA-accredited Drug Control Center at King's College London. Cowan created a statistical model for Oral Turinabol ingestion and long-term metabolite excretion over time (any such model providing another potential source of error noted by Fischer and Berry). This model stipulated that an athlete "would need to: (1) ingest 20 grams of Methylclostebol in order to show 30 pg/mL of M4 metabolite in his/her urine 22 months later." The panel in Scott argued that Scott—even on a very generous appraisal of his consumption of a supplement—had not ingested that much of a chlorinated substance.

Again—as Fischer and Berry aptly demonstrated in the Veerpalu case—statistical models cannot replace actual studies on divergent populations. Berry further noted that these models would never count for evidence regarding other real-world problems, like whether or not the FDA approves a new drug for widespread usage.

But even if Cowan's model granted accuracy, we do have plenty of instances that can provide data for athletes that have taken near or in excess of these amounts. Gerd Bonk, the former East German weightlifter, consumed over 12 grams of Oral Turinabol over a 12-month period.[355] If we also take someone like Pat Mendes at his word—that he ingested 40mg of Oral Turinabol daily for a similar and even longer period—then we have a second athlete that now exceeds 14 grams of dosage in a single year. Presumably, Pat's results, which fall far short of his international opponents, may have stemmed from lower dosages of Oral Turinabol than what his competitors in state-sponsored systems ingested.

Knowing that athletes in this sport and others have consumed Oral Turinabol on doping regimen levels, we could then test hypotheses related to the longitudinal excretion of long-term metabolites in those populations (rather than rely on speculation over one single-dose study or a mathematical model). Nurudinov and Torokhtiy and Ilya are all retired. Have them do a few weeks of cross-training to burn their fat stores. Then give them a urine test to see if they release long term metabolites—presumably years after long-term, high-dosage doping.

If they don't show parent compound of Oral Turinabol or its short term metabolites and—in Ilya's and Nurudinov's case, they presumably stopped usage in 2016, and they still show long-term metabolites today, I think you have more of a foundation for understanding just how long these metabolites of Oral Turinabol remain in an athlete's system and can also gain greater clarity on both the lipophilic nature of these metabolites and their potential for fat sequestration.

But no one has done these studies! Just like the Veerpalu case, it's not that WADA's test can't detect long-term metabolites of Oral Turinabol, **it's that they have no scientific justification for using the appearance of long-term metabolites as evidence for an anti-doping rule violation and any consequent punishment!**

The Test Can't Be Trusted

WADA took a test developed by Rodchenkov—a RUSADA lab director that admitted to the McLaren commission that he helped Russia cheat—and then applied it uncritically to hundreds of stored urine samples. When that method—which we now know is highly flawed in terms of what it can actually show—returned positive test results for long-term metabolites, the IOC immediately began stripping away medals and results and handing out lengthy suspensions.

But now we know that the long-term metabolites—the only "proof" of oral Turinabol—hang around and pulse for a very long time in an athlete's system and we also know that WADA has not done the scientific analysis required to distinguish the false positives of lingering, pulsing long-term metabolites from genuine cheating.[356]

Just like the Veerpalu case.

Fischer and Berry criticized WADA's methods over their faulty HGH test in 2013. The pair noted that:
> "doping tests should not be used in practice until they have been shown to be scientifically valid, and that has not yet occurred in HGH testing. At minimum, doping tests should have to meet the scientific standards for medical diagnostics. Actually, standards in doping testing should be higher. Most diagnostics have follow-up tests

and procedures. Doping testing is currently in the hands of a single worldwide agency that answers to no one except CAS…This is in sharp contrast to medical product development, say, where regulators around the world ensure a high level of science before drugs and medical devices can be used in practice."

A single-subject, single-dose "study" from Schänzer falls far short of that standard.

Seven years after Veerpalu's exoneration, WADA continues to apply another flawed test under the misguided imperative of strict liability. And at what cost for justice?

Fischer and Berry noted that even with an acquittal from CAS,[357] an athlete is forever tainted by the results or accusation of a positive drug test, which is often the sole criterion for guilt.

"Doping" as Fischer and Berry argue, "can have serious implications for the athlete's health, including early death," but we must balance protecting athlete's health against unjustly ruining an athlete's career, depriving them of their livelihood and the possibility of suicide or self-harm from being banned from sport, as occurred with 31-year-old rugby star Terry Newton.

It's worth noting that Newton killed himself over a positive result from the same flawed HGH test used to wrongly convict Andrus Veerpalu and Pat Mendes.

Fischer and Berry pointed out WADA's failure to operate on scientific principles seven years ago. It's time to start viewing the entire long-term metabolites test and WADA's belief in the infallibility of its testing methods[358] with a bit more healthy suspicion and finally force them to go beyond strict liability, open up their testing methods to scientific scrutiny and rigor and move toward due process protections for all athletes, not just ones—like Jones—that compete for a parent company with a multi-billion dollar market valuation (and all that money can do).

Otherwise, how can we continue to trust WADA, when their notions of strict liability and refusal to engage in due process continues to end careers, cost athletes lost revenue, and ruins lives?

Yes, we need to catch cheaters. But we need to do so in a manner that is just. Otherwise, we also risk cheating—cheating ourselves of credibility, cheating the public of a trustable level of fair play, and cheating innocent athletes of justice.

Returning medals from the Olympic re-tests and restoring individuals like Pat Mendes and Cody Stanley to the field of play because of demonstrably invalid testing procedures would give WADA and doping control a temporary black eye. But that's far preferable to pushing forward with a faulty test[359] that can't distinguish cheating from accidental ingestion of contaminated products, that can't tell ingestion from re-ingestion and that—at best—only speculates as to who took what drug when and why but still imposes blanket guilt arbitrarily.

No one can or should trust a test that yields such results.

It is time for WADA and the IOC to follow USADA's lead and find a better way.

Appendix Two:
In Pat's Own Words

This appendix presents Pat's responses to specific questions asked during the ten interview sessions. I list these in no particular order, and quote directly from the transcripts. Most of the answers reflect on Pat's ten years in the sport of weightlifting and what he learned, experienced and regrets about that time.

Any edits, statements, questions or interjections attributable to this author will appear in boldface or prefaced by a note.

One: What are your all-time best numbers in weightlifting?

Snatch: 207kg
C&J 230kg
Clean: 240kg
BKSQ: 363kg (800lbs!)
Front squat: 280kg
Deadlift: 330kg for a set of four reps
Bench: 230kg
Speed squat: 250kg for a triple, all three reps completed in under five seconds
YouTube: https://www.youtube.com/watch?v=-6mRbQG-PL4

Two: Are you one of the greatest American weightlifters of all time?

Pat: That's a good question. I'll have to say no. Just cause I never performed **(at my highest level)** at a meet.

Pat: But am I the strongest American weightlifter ever? Absolutely. It's weird when you go down this road, and you try to compare yourself to different lifters to find out where you're at. **(For instance)**, do I compare myself to the 1980 U.S. Men's Team? Jeff Michaels did 187kg snatch at 110kg bodyweight, whatever the class was then. And Shane Hamman snatched 197.5kg. I think the guys coming up—CJ Cummings and Harrison Maurus—are going to blow everyone out of the water. CJ may already be the greatest American weightlifter of all time.

But I snatched more than any American ever **(and did 190kg weighing 105kg)**. Is that a good accomplishment? Being the only American to ever snatch 200+ kilos? Again, I never did it in a meet. But I would argue that I'm the best snatcher in American history.

Three: What do you think you could have lifted, if you competed for a country with a state-sponsored doping program?

Pat: I would have snatched 500 pounds (227kg). I'm just going to put that out there.

Pat: From what I've heard, someone asked Abadjiev how long it would take to produce a world champion **(from a group of established weightlifters)**. "Six months, with the right supplements" is what I heard he replied. It's not six months from ground zero; it's six months from a good lifter. I didn't have six months on drugs in 2014, but in six months of training full-time, I got into the A-session of the 2014 World Championships.

Pat: And when I started in 2007, Broz taught me how to snatch. I went from not knowing what a snatch was to snatching 200kg in 20 months. Then I fucked myself up. **(He stopped using in order to attempt the Junior National record (at the 2010 American Open) and then compete at National Championships in 2011).**

Pat: I should've just kept taking stuff. I shouldn't have only done two years. I should've trained until I was like 25 on stuff and then snatched 500lbs. You know what I mean? I'd stopped taking stuff when I was 20, and I got a 207kg snatch. I would have done it a year later if I kept going.

Pat: I think I could probably still do it **(Pat said this in summer, 2017, age 27)**.

Jim: Wow. At your weight? (He walked around at 105kg at the time of this conversation.)

Pat: No, I'd probably be like 115kg, 120kg. Actually, to be honest with you, I'd be whatever. It wouldn't even matter. I would eat as much food as I could. It'd be good food this time, not fucking milkshakes and burgers and Marie Callender's potpies. Then I would train twice a day and I would just eat and sleep and train and eat. I know I could do it.

Jim: You would only focus on the snatch?

Pat: And I would take way more drugs, like actual amounts of drugs that people take to lift those weights. Guys who squat 800lbs, they take like two grams of testosterone a week. Probably even more. I was taking 350mg a week.

Jim: but you think it could be accomplished even at your age today?

Pat: Yeah, I'm only 27 (Pat gave this interview in 2017). I think I could do it with a 360kg squat. I think now my technique is so much better that I can do it. And I would do it without straps too.

Pat: Other than that, I can't say for certain that I would have beaten lifters from state-sponsored doping countries. My competition status speaks for itself and the numbers don't lie. I wasn't the best in competition. But I never learned how to compete. At least if it was apples to apples, I could have gotten the experience, so that when I was in a competition that mattered, I would have had a good shot. I just had no experience competing **(because he had to hide all the time and taper off without the bribery or protection of a national federation).**

Pat: I also think I could have competed at the Olympics. I know that is a long shot for any athlete, but athletes have to be a little optimistic and not so critical. Underdogs win in sports. I played sports my whole life and I can remember my football coaches when we faced someone undefeated. They would say "there's still a chance." Sometimes we would win games we're not supposed to win. And I would believe them. *I think if you do that enough in life, you get success when you weren't supposed to be successful.*

Four: What do you think you could have lifted if you never took drugs?

Pat laughed in response.

Pat: I never thought of it because I would have never done this sport clean. It just doesn't make sense to me. I know that's messed up, but I viewed weightlifting as the only thing I had the chance to be great at. That's where all my strengths, all my natural abilities lined up.

Pat: I wanted to set world records. It all **(stemmed)** from this little belief in myself that I was supposed to be great at something. That's what really kept me going every day. It was my destiny to be great at something. I'm going to do something that people remember forever. That's what world records mean to me, and weightlifting is probably the worst sport to set a world record in because they get erased every 20 years **(with the change in weight classes)**. But there's still some people that remember what it was, and that's what I held onto when I trained day by day and thought "I'm destined for this for sure."

Pat: I don't know if a lot of people think like that in general. Most people are petty; they don't have this great vision of what they're going to do with their lives. That's why I felt so weird; because I even thought this way when I was young, and there was no one else around saying "I'm going to be remembered forever. I'm going to lift world records." At 18 out of high school everyone is in college wondering what to do with their lives "take this class or that class" and I said, "this is what I'm doing."

Pat: That's what happens when you decide to take stuff. That's where the mentality goes. It's why you see a lot of weightlifters that test positive never lift again, or they never come back to their glory because they don't' want to stay clean and lift. There's no reason to. That's how every world athlete I talk to responds…you can ask tons of weightlifters this…they're like "why the hell do you even lift then?" "There's no reason to lift if you're clean."

Pat: The only way I would get back into weightlifting or be really pumped about it was if you could do whatever it takes to compete. Let's just see who's the strongest. We all know we all take shit. Why does it matter? Why hold onto this fake integrity that means nothing and no one cares about? Why is it so hard for people to admit that no one cares?

Pat: People like that Michael Phelps has won 20 gold medals. They don't care what that took. If everyone does it (**PED's**), the (**notion of**) cheating's just a put on. For Liao Hui to get a two-year ban, I think that only confuses people in China. Like it's a supplement. He takes what everyone else takes.

Jim: Have you ever had another international lifter or some other country's coach talk to you about your drug regimen? Or how to manage side effects?

Pat: Maybe hint at it, but never had a real conversation of what to do, or how to do it. The only conversations I've had asked "How much do you have to pay to get a gold medal?" Like "how much did it cost to not get tested," cause at the end of the day, the only way to win is to make sure you don't get tested. They can make anyone test positive and they've proven that.

Five: Given that attitude towards doping, and trying win medals at Worlds, do you think people like Wes Kitts are suckers?

Pat: Wes Kitts? No, I don't think he's a sucker. You have to know your goals; you have to know what you want. I wanted to beat everyone, so I think you have to be very focused on the fact that if you are an American, you don't compete with everyone else. You're going to do what Americans do, lift what Americans lift, and Wes Kitts, I think he's doing awesome. He's the best in the country and anyone will probably have more financial success if you just stay clean (**in this country**), compete, win national meets, make teams, but be average in the world. You'll make more money financially; like in hindsight, as things were changing in the USA (**stipend system**) my plan was to go back to the USA and compete, like Norik (**Vardanian**), because I made a mistake. I can go clean, for America, and actually make a living with my supplement company and I would have made a lot more money and sales if I was an American weightlifter, rather than an American person lifting for Brazil and trying to beat the world.

Pat: If you're making $3,000 to $5,000 a month from your stipend, it's not bad money. But that's not why I did it. If your perspective of being good is to make that and work out in a gym and win a couple of national meets, and be on a world team, you're doing awesome. If that's all you have and that's all you want to have, it's great. But it's not that much.

So I don't think those guys are suckers. But I don't even put them in the same category as a real weightlifter, as an international weightlifter.

Pat: In Brazil, they took a different attitude towards weightlifting. They wouldn't want to take drugs. They weightlifted cause that's what they did when they were kids, and because they got paid to keep weightlifting. And it's better than living on the street or working a job at a grocery store because you get paid way more as a weightlifter. Some of them earned 3,000 to 5,000 reals a month—from the government—and then their club would pay an additional stipend. So they were ballin'. They all had the newest iPhones, which in Brazil cost twice as much as they do in the USA, and they all wear Nike and Adidas clothes, which again, cost twice as much.

Pat: When I competed for the USA and visited the OTC, the resident athletes didn't live that well. The level of stipend for US athletes was pretty low (in 2011-2014). A lot of American weightlifters I met felt sorry for themselves. But in Brazil, they enjoyed being weightlifters. They think "man, I'm a rockstar cause I get to be an athlete and lift weights for a living." If they didn't, they would be this poor guy working at a grocery store. Sure they complained about training or the coaches. But they knew the alternative, where the Americans seem like they took it for granted.

Six: What have you accomplished that you're most proud of?

Pat: I think I helped. I think my videos brought a lot of attention to the sport. Especially my squat videos. (It helped American weightlifters) to see someone else be that strong. Someone that's not a fat powerlifter wearing a suit because those were the only people squatting 800lbs at the time.

Pat: I think I'm definitely one of the first social media lifters that came on the scene. With Broz and me, we posted videos consistently and we were among the first to do it. Then Cal Strength came along. But I remember being more popular than them at the time. People still recognize me from my videos, even now when I'm doing door-to-door alarm sales.

Jim: I had a kid join my gym once and he showed me a video of you and said "Have you seen this? I want to be like this guy." He told me you're the reason he got into weightlifting.

Pat: That's funny. I think Jon North said it best. He respected me for doing my own thing and going after what I wanted. You know what I mean? As opposed to following the standards of what American weightlifting is. I wasn't scared to change countries and try to find a way to get what I wanted out of the sport. And I'm really proud that I got onto two Pan Am Games teams. Both those meets were really cool and it was the next thing below going to the Olympics.

Pat: Am I proud that I won nationals? Kind of. I'm not because I cheated so hard. It's really not that impressive that I took drugs and beat people that don't take drugs. I'll never stand on a high horse and say "yeah, I was better than everyone else."

Seven: What would have kept you from using drugs?

Pat: Criminal penalties. Drugged athletes going to prison. That's a good way to reform the system. It should apply to coaches too. Your athlete gets banned, you get banned too. Plain and simple. You get the same suspension your athlete gets. If two of your athletes test positive, it's doubled. Now the coaches would make sure their athletes aren't doing drugs.

Pat: It's an easy policy to implement. If the USA is serious about being clean, they should sign off on it. They should be the ones to start it. You can call it the "Pat Mendes policy."

NB: In 2015, Germany passed a law that would impose prison terms of up to three years on athletes that test positive for performance enhancing drugs or those found guilty of possessing performing enhancing drugs. Those caught dealing PED's would face sentences of up to ten years. These prison sentences can also apply to non-Germans caught doping at International competitions held within Germany.

NB: On October 22, 2019, the US House of Representatives passed the Rodchenkov Anti-Doping Act (RADA). This bill, now headed to the Senate, would also provide fines of up to 1,000,000 and imprisonment up to 10 years for involvement in international doping schemes.

Pat: On the flipside, USAW could grow the sport immensely by offering prize money at national meets. That would get some athletes out of the woodwork if they knew they could earn some crazy sum for winning nationals. It doesn't even have to be much; in bodybuilding, for instance, the winter earns 250 grand, but they work the entire year for that. That's like their payday.

Eight: What would you tell people if you could still coach?

Pat: I would tell people to relax. To enjoy weightlifting. Learn how to lift, then how to train, then how to focus and how to compete. Most people out there aren't making teams, and the ones that aren't need to master a process first. Kicking the wall or throwing your belt after every lift isn't making you better. It's not helping. You don't need to put such massive pressure on yourself. And you're going to get better if you don't make it such a big deal.

Pat: My mentality, especially at 2011 Worlds was that if you don't win, you're a big loser. So I felt like a big loser for a long time, and you can't perform when you feel that way. And it's more magnified when it's all you actually do for your life.

Pat: I think one of the worst things in the sport is American weightlifters really getting hung up on comparing themselves to international weightlifters. It's just not even the same. It's not even the same league. It's not even the same sport. Donnie Shankle was always angry because his entire career he did nothing but compare himself to consistently drugged athletes in state funded programs. I don't think that an American weightlifter should do that. I think Ian Wilson's really good at not trying to compare the two, I mean, he had to train with Hysen Pulaku, basically hitting the same numbers as him, but (**with Hysen**) three weight classes lighter. I got to train with them in December of 2011, and Pulaku would do 212kg C&J in training, while Ian would manage 200kg.

Jim: If you weren't banned, would you give seminars?

Pat: No. I'd rather be an online coach. I mean, I would give seminars if someone approached me. But I've seen enough seminars, and most people, you won't get much out of it, out of one day. They're really just scenester like events. People want to see and be a part of the experience of lifting heavy. I mean, the fact that Ilya and Jon North charge the same amount of money for a seminar is fucking outrageous.

Jim: In what regard?

Pat: In every regard there is! It's Ilya! That's what's crazy about the sport. There's really no standard. Ilya should cost at least $1,000 a person, for a 10-person seminar. He shouldn't even be in a room unless he's making 10-grand. He's the Olympic champion, world record holder, never beaten. And I've seen him too. He's so fucking good at teaching people how to lift. It cost me like $250 for what I learned, and I was blown away.

Nine: What would you change if you had to do it all again?

Pat: First and foremost, if we're just talking about the weightlifting, I would have liked to have been born in Kazakhstan. Be the same person, but just born in Kazakhstan. So I could have taken advantage of a state-sponsored system that really knew what they were doing. If I was born in the USA, I would have moved there, found a wife, become Kazakhstani. That's how I would rewrite the picture. I wouldn't have even tried to do anything in the United States.

Jim: At what age would you have…

Pat: As soon as I could. Like 18. If someone came to me and said "Hey, can you coach me in weightlifting, I want to break world records." I would reply, "ok, fly to Iran. Find a wife. Figure out what you need to do to be a citizen somewhere else and then go train in that country. *Don't try to do it in America.*" Again, the goal for me was never to just become a good American weightlifter.

Jim: Say you had to stay in America. Would you pick a different coach entirely, or would you pick a different coach in some senses but not in others?

Pat: If I had to go back and do it again, I think that living and training at the OTC (**which has since closed**) is probably the best place you can be in the country to train. And with Zygmunt as your coach. Either way, I would not want an American to coach me probably other than Broz.

Pat: Because the ones I've been around, they just don't get it. The thing with Broz that I respect a lot of, is if he saw a kid snatch over the national record, he would tell him to put another two and a half kilo plate on. Everyone else would say "Ok, that's good for the day, you don't want to push it." I think too many coaches here hold their athletes back because one, their mindset is "OK, we don't want to get this guy hurt," and I think Broz and I very much shared that go for broke mentality. There's a ton of value in that approach.

Jim: Are there any coaches in this country, other than Zygmunt that you respect, that you're aware of?

Pat: As far as programming, coaching-wise? Not that much. But for what they do for the sport and for what they've done? Tons. Like Dave Spitz, that guy, he's a baller, very smart, very business savvy. And he gives back a lot. Same thing with Travis Mash. I think any coach out there that's giving back and creating athletes and having a team, I have a lot of respect for them, because that involves a lot of self-sacrifice that most people aren't willing to do. It doesn't take much to make someone better, to get them from an empty bar snatch to a 70kg snatch. But it takes a ten of sacrifice to build a team and have athletes, and I respect that a lot.

Pat: I think in an ideal situation, a good coach for me has to provide a decent program, then decide on possible numbers to hit at worlds. Also, that coach has to handle all of the changing countries, and federation politics that I had to navigate myself. Dealing with that cost me too much emotionally because I had no idea what to do. I was still a young man at that point, trying to run a supplement company so that I have money to train full-time.

Ten: Do you feel like you didn't get your chance at this sport?

Pat: Well, it's my fault too in a sense because I never reached out to Broz and said "I need help with this shit. I can't do this and train, and why aren't you helping me?" And I could probably see myself not saying anything, because for me, he's already letting me live with him, he's coaching me for free and sacrificing a lot. That, and it's just always been hard for me to ask people for stuff.

Pat: I know that the couple times I've run into Zygmunt since my ban, he still talks to me, he understands—I mean, he coached Poland and all these lifters got popped under his tenure—but he knows that I worked hard, and was a good weightlifter. And I think he just sees me as lost potential.

Jim: Do you feel like you didn't really get your chance?

Pat: Yeah, of course.

Jim: And are you angry about that?

Pat: If you had asked me this three years ago, or even two years ago, probably yes. But now the curtain's kind of gone and I have a clear vision of what weightlifting really gives you, which is next to nothing. So there's not that much anger to it. And I always like to take negative things and turn them into a positive. So I see my second ban as a blessing, because now I could get married, afford a house and move across the country and live comfortably as an adult. Now I have different ventures and can expand my life. When I was weightlifting it was just weightlifting.

Pat: What do you have after weightlifting? I think that's where my perspective has changed. Because I realized I could have a shitload of stuff and different activities and be really happy without weightlifting in my life, where I didn't think that was a possibility before. I thought weightlifting was everything and I need to set world records and that was it. There was nothing else. But now, there's more. And I can live with that.

Acknowledgements

Special thanks to Kristen Erickson and Jessica Saxon for offering valuable feedback on some key chapters. Heather Hollis and Abby Manning helped select the most concise subtitle and gave suggestions for marketing the book.

Jessica Saxon, Esq., provided clarity on several of the legal issues relating to CAS cases and arbitration and strengthened the arguments in Appendix One.

Alison Miller—a fine writer in her own right—helped edit the book into its final draft.

Nat Arem from Hookgrip generously provided the cover image.

Thanks to all the members at Philadelphia Barbell for your continual trust and support.

Today Is An Important Day.

About the Author:

Jim Rutter has competed in weightlifting since 2000 and coached since 2010, achieving the rank of International Coach for USA Weightlifting. Since 2006, he has worked as a journalist in Philadelphia, writing mostly for *The Philadelphia Inquirer*. In 2009, he received a fellowship in Arts Journalism from the National Endowment for the Arts.

He owns and serves as head coach for Philadelphia Barbell Club, which has produced over 20 National and International medalists since 2017.

Endnotes:

[1] Steven Ungerleider's Faust Gold: Inside the East German Doping Machine chronicles the 25 years of doping that led to that tiny nation's incredible athletic success.

[2] https://the2doctors.net/2017/09/24/episode-23-norik-vardanian/

[3] Goldman drafted this questionnaire in 1984.

[4] The video is online here:
https://www.youtube.com/watch?v=drEWxl42-_8

[5] https://www.insidethegames.biz/articles/1060656/brian-oliver-when-doping-pays-only-one-winner-in-complex-case-of-ilya-ilyin-the-lance-armstrong-of-weightlifting

[6] See, for instance:
https://www.catalystathletics.com/article/1836/Olympic-Weightlifting-Skill-Levels-Chart/

And here:
https://www.elitebarbellclub.com/weightlifting/2018/11/7/weightlifting-class-system

For American lifters, the "master of sport" can indicate a total equivalent to medaling at senior national championships.

[7] ESPN reports on Ilya's adverse analytical results here:
https://www.espn.com/olympics/story/_/id/18122377/kazakhstan-weightlifter-ilya-ilyin-stripped-two-olympic-gold-medals

See also this article:
https://www.insidethegames.biz/articles/1060656/brian-oliver-when-doping-pays-only-one-winner-in-complex-case-of-ilya-ilyin-the-lance-armstrong-of-weightlifting

[8] These websites contain information on the positive re-tests of the Kazakh lifters:

https://www.iwf.net/2016/08/24/public-disclosures-5/

https://www.iwf.net/2016/06/15/public-disclosures/

https://www.iwf.net/2016/06/18/public-disclosures-2/

[9] In his book *Positive*, Werner Reiterer discusses the Soviet system. The central federation would host camps, bringing in promising athletes from across the Soviet Union. They would put the invited athletes on drug regimens. Those that didn't improve results by 10-15% by the end of the camp would be sent home on the assumption that they had already taken drugs and couldn't develop further.

[10] "Several years on from the scandal, Ali Moradi, the head of Iranian Weightlifting Federation then and now, claimed that the day after NADO agents tested the athletes he made a deal with a high official of the International Weightlifting Federation and NADO. He said he agreed to give up nine athletes, plus pay $400,000. In return, Hossein Rezazadeh was able to compete for the national team."

https://iranwire.com/en/features/1701

See also:
https://www.iwf.net/2006/11/24/iwf-iranian-wf-sanction-update/

[11] Two-time Olympian in the discus for West Germany Brigitte Berendonk detailed the East German program in her book *Doping: From Research to Fraud*.

[12] See further detail in this article:
https://www.vice.com/en_us/article/4xz3wj/the-rise-and-fall-of-gerd-bonk-the-world-champion-of-doping

[13] *Positive: An Australian Olympian Reveals The Inside Story of Drugs and Sport* details Reiterer's use of drugs while competing in discus for Team Australia during the 1980s. In his book, he admits to taking performance enhancing drugs over a five-year period leading to the 1988 Olympics and gives an inside account of how doping affected track and field at the time.

[14] Morgan McCullough might break that record before this book goes to print.

[15] This Vice article documents Bonk's career: https://www.vice.com/en_us/article/4xz3wj/the-rise-and-fall-of-gerd-bonk-the-world-champion-of-doping

[16] The International Weightlifting Federation eliminated the bodyweight advantage in 2016.

[17] That was sarcasm. Picture the IOC and NBC sports as Captain Renault from Casablanca. "I'm shocked, shocked to discover there's doping going on here," as they rake in billions from the excitement that Russian athletes add to the Games.

[18] After ARD's expose, an independent World Ant-Doping Agency (WADA) investigation headed by Canadian law professor Richard McLaren concluded that more than 1,000 athletes benefited from the Russian-government's doping program. While track and field boasted the most athletes assisted by the Russian government in using PED's, the much smaller sport of weightlifting finished a very close second.

[19] Some of the ARD's other documentaries, and reports by the BBC and ProPublica have shown that these types of payoffs and institutional corruption has occurred in weightlifting and track and field, among other Olympic sport.

[20] Rodchenkov admitted to switching Russian athletes over to the Duchess—a cocktail containing Trenbolone—after he developed the long-term metabolites test for Oral Turinabol.

But I'm getting ahead of myself.

https://www.sportsintegrityinitiative.com/rodchenkovs-development-turinabol-test-raises-questions/

[21] The New York Times reported that a 90-year old cyclist tested positive for Trenbolone at a Masters-level event because he ate beef liver the night before his race. And they exonerated him of the doping charge and let him keep his masters world record!

This case in particular sets a very dangerous precedent. Many athletes have tested positive for trenbolone and blamed their adverse finding on tainted beef. To my knowledge, neither the CAS nor any sporting federations have overturned any penalties or dismissed the findings for this reason.

[22] Which theoretically means more muscle fibers acting under the same nervous system signal. Once you understand that strength is a function of neuromuscular efficiency—the more motor neurons that activate when your brain tells a muscle to contract—you realize that tren potentially increases strength as well.

[23] I worry that younger athletes will read this book and think "I need to take steroids." But looking back, I can say that I've always possessed a strong affinity for the anabolic effects of drugs. The number of androgen receptors varies by individual (although politically incorrect to say—also by ethnicity), but I know that when I take steroids, my body reacts like crazy. Probably because I'm sold on it so much.

[24] You can call it "Bulgarian style" training if you want, where you max snatch, max clean and jerk and squat every session. I've heard arguments from Pendlay that true Bulgarian training required a group of lifters competing against one another like contestants on Survivor—that the pool gets smaller and smaller the more and more athletes that burn out from not being able to handle the constant intensity. Others have said that Bulgarian training required Abadjiev. Whatever. I didn't have training partners, and me and Broz didn't operate on a system.

[25] In fairness, that has since changed. The rise of Crossfit, and the concomitant growth of USAW Level 1 and Level 2 seminars (at $500/pop), has enabled the federation to dramatically increase its level of funding to athletes.
But I never saw any of that money, especially not in development.

[26] It also implies creating opportunities for athletes to train together and push one another. Glenn Pendlay has argued that the greatest aspect of the Bulgarian system—and what truly enshrined it as the Bulgarian method—involved taking the greatest (established weightlifters) from your country's system and then forcing them to all train together in such

a way that a process of elimination would occur. The athletes that pushed themselves to beat all of their teammates would eventually constitute the international team. Those that fell by the wayside would get pushed out, eliminated from the team training. Only the truly strongest—mentally and physical—would survive and thrive.

[27] https://www.mensxp.com/health/body-building/36690-the-story-of-the-world-s-most-hated-bodybuilder-and-his-exploding-arms.html

[28] To be very clear: I sold legal supplements, not controlled substances.

[29] After college, Evan would be the one that made it to the Olympics. The NFL combine also hosts a combine for bobsled and Evan switched over to that sport (his sprinting power enabled his success), and was added to the 2018 team roster as an alternate. One of the other bobsledders committed suicide, so in 2018, Taylor and I flew to Seoul to watch Evan in the Winter Olympics. I bring this story up because it doubles back on my own in an important way.

[30] https://www.youtube.com/watch?v=WK7m6I5m6gY

[31] And still hasn't done. Just saying.

[32] https://web.archive.org/web/20180801105107/http://confederation.kz/en/weightlifting/coach/person/ni-a

[33] Although parents of means can afford to send their children to very expensive academies for tennis, golf and a few other sports.

[34] Many international coaches have told me in private conversation about the role that politics plays in the selection process. To wit, I have talked to coaches from Spain, France, Italy, Canada and Cuba.

[35] The position of High Performance Director attends and oversees coaching at International competitions. However, that position does not mandate a specific yearly competition plan or training protocol for any of the athletes qualifying for Team USA.

[36] https://www.youtube.com/watch?v=uwN9SqqIRAk

³⁷ Can you imagine? The greatest snatcher of all time reduced to a bouncer at a bar at the Mall of the Americas? (Legend holds that he also worked as a circus strongman and now drives a tractor trailer.)

³⁸ Varbanov now coaches weightlifting in Toronto, where his son Alek, Jr. competes for Canada.

³⁹ Bret Contrearas interview here:
https://www.t-nation.com/training/max-out-on-squats-every-day

Jen Sinkler interview here:
https://www.jensinkler.com/brain-pick-q-a-with-john-broz/

⁴⁰   https://www.nytimes.com/2017/08/29/sports/2011-study-finds-widespread-doping-in-track.html

⁴¹ A very conservative estimate, given that people frequently conceal personally damning information on even anonymous surveys.

⁴²   https://www.nytimes.com/2013/08/23/sports/research-finds-wide-doping-study-withheld.html?pagewanted=2&_r=1&&pagewanted=all

⁴³ WADA's fancy way of saying "alleged positives" until they can test the B-samples of urine.

⁴⁴ When asked by the New York Times for his opinions, doping expert John Hoberman said the study's findings dispelled the notion that doping was a deviant behavior among a few athletes. "Either the sport is recruiting huge numbers of deviants," he said, "or this is simply routine behavior being engaged in by, more or less, normal people." He added, "That's dangerous for WADA, because that's a character issue."

⁴⁵ Other studies have found it remarkably easy to beat the drug testers in any sport: https://www.livescience.com/61747-how-widespread-olympic-doping.html

⁴⁶ https://link.springer.com/article/10.1007/s40279-017-0765-4

⁴⁷   https://www.nytimes.com/2013/08/23/sports/research-finds-wide-doping-study-withheld.html

[49] This practice still occurs today. In 2018, Armenian Tigran V. Martirosyan, who won silver at the 2008 Olympics, said "They (Armenian officials) took the samples so they could tell if we were clean or not." Martirosyan has never failed a drug test.

This report details how Armenia continued to manipulate the testing system in 2018:

https://www.sportsintegrityinitiative.com/armenian-weightlifters-used-russian-lab-cheat-olympic-drug-tests/

[50]   https://www.insidethegames.biz/articles/1056875/former-chinese-olympic-doctor-claims-10000-athletes-doped-in-1980s-and-1990s

https://www.smh.com.au/sport/chinese-olympians-subjected-to-routine-doping-20120726-22v65.html

[51] I'm sure this nonsense has completely ended in China today and the entire nation and its government has committed completely to clean sport.

[52] Seppelt discusses this facet at the segment that starts around 14 minutes in:
https://vimeo.com/146383380

[53] This document contains the new rule:
https://www.iwf.net/doc/Special_ADP_rules_Olympics.pdf

This document discusses Pulaku's positive test:
https://www.independent.co.uk/sport/olympics/other-events/albanian-weightlifter-hysen-pulaku-thrown-out-of-london-2012-after-failing-drugs-test-7984555.html

[54]

https://www.oregonlive.com/olympics/2012/07/albanian_weightlifter_fails_ol.html

[55] https://www.iwf.net/2017/01/13/public-disclosure-78/

[56] To wit: during the 2012 Summer Games in London, WADA administered over 5,000 drug tests. Only nine (9!) of those resulted in an adverse analytical finding. We now know that hundreds of athletes doped

in the lead-up to this Olympics, but they were all clean by the known testing methods at the time!

http://www.theathlete.org/Drug-Testing-In-Sports.htm

As of Jan, 2019, over 120 AAF's have been discovered on the re-tests of samples from these Games.

https://www.si.com/olympics/2019/01/18/2012-summer-olympics-doping-test-121-positive-london

[57] A process called Isotope Ratio Mass Spectrometry determines the levels of one substance vis a vis another.

[58] http://news.bbc.co.uk/sport2/hi/other_sports/cycling/5237990.stm

Despite his legal wrangling over the ratios, he would later plead guilty to doping during the Tour de France:
https://www.nytimes.com/2010/05/21/sports/cycling/21landis.html

[59] https://apnews.com/13b4b5841e854a249487cdefda841f20

[60] Carbon Isotope Ratios. This article details how CIR works to determine exogenous from endogenous testosterone:
https://www.velonews.com/2015/08/news/the-test-that-caught-tom-danielson_381086

This article suggests how underground labs are already trying to beat the CIR method:
https://www.propublica.org/article/speed-bumps-why-its-so-hard-to-catch-cheaters-in-track-and-field

[61] https://www.discovermagazine.com/health/genetic-mutant-athletes-immune-to-steroid-tests

[62] Gene UGT2B17 allows for testosterone and epitestosterone levels to be naturally low, even when doping occurs, so standard testing will not catch an athlete with this gene who is doping. **9.** Two-thirds of the Asian population has Gene UGT2B17. Only 10% of Caucasians and 7% of Hispanics have it. **10.** The percentage of positive tests in the world that contained anabolics within them: 50.6%. **11.** Some localized Asian populations, especially on the Korean

peninsula, may have upwards of an 80% group of athletes who cannot be tested for doping through T/E ratios.

[63] That might sound politically incorrect, but the New York Times reported on it.
https://www.nytimes.com/2008/04/30/sports/30doping.html?mcubz=0

https://academic.oup.com/jcem/article/91/2/687/2843517/Large-Differences-in-Testosterone-Excretion-in

[64] Another major fault in Broz' coaching. I snatched for over 16 months with straps. Using straps all the time absolutely affects how an athlete executes that lift.

[65] There's plenty of "drug-free" and popular YouTube lifters out there. Everyone knows who I'm talking about.

[66] Again, the landscape of commercially available drug tests has shifted since 2010. Back then, no random corner stores or strip mall storefront offered "any drug test now!" Plus, it had to be a company that offered the full-spectrum WADA drug panel.

[67]   https://www.nytimes.com/1987/07/24/sports/taylor-of-giants-in-a-new-book-says-he-used-cocaine-frequently.html

[68]   http://pacechronicle.com/healthandbeauty/2014/04/09/oil-changes-put-athletes-health-at-risk/

[69] https://www.nytimes.com/2005/05/18/sports/baseball/drug-rules-are-only-as-tough-as-test-monitors.html

https://www.huffpost.com/entry/devis-licciardi-whizzinator-fake-penis_n_3988031

https://www.vice.com/en_us/article/53xwm8/remembering-the-whizzinator-americas-favorite-fake-plastic-penis

https://www.npr.org/templates/story/story.php?storyId=4655618

See this round-up of positive tests from the 2004 Olympics, which hints at the use of a Whizzinator-like device:

https://www.nytimes.com/2004/08/30/sports/summer-2004-games-the-tarnished-games-doping-casts-a-long-shadow-in-athens.html

70 https://www.sportsintegrityinitiative.com/pressure-builds-on-iwf-as-corruption-claims-are-corroborated/

71 See this article, which alleges that the Greek Track and Field team was not making their athletes available for out of competition testing before the 2004 Olympics.

https://www.theguardian.com/sport/2004/feb/15/athletics.duncanmackay

72   https://www.outsideonline.com/1800151/jamaicas-anti-doping-board-resigns

See also:
The IOC allegedly buried some positive test results for that nation's athletes in 2008:
https://www.vice.com/en_us/article/8qyyea/did-the-ioc-bury-positive-jamaican-sprinter-doping-tests-its-complicated

73

https://www.telegraph.co.uk/sport/othersports/athletics/10178978/Asafa-Powell-and-four-other-Jamaican-athletes-fail-drugs-tests.html

74   https://www.espn.com/espn/otl/story/_/id/16209580/doping-whistleblowers-such-stepanovs-kara-goucher-often-left-dangling-taking-sports-bodies-governing-bodies

75 https://apnews.com/b4c133e43b9d48f9beb5c5db702522ba

76   https://www.theguardian.com/sport/2016/oct/27/wada-serious-failings-rio-2016-olympics-anti-doping

77 Since 2018, USA Weightlifting has co-opted the event and turned it into one of the three meets that comprise the American Open Series. No prize money anymore, no fun premiere sessions with top international talent.

78 By contrast, USA Weightlifting held the 2013 National Championships in a roller skating rink. Im' not kidding. Skee-ball

machines flanked the warmup area, and they had to move pool and ping pong tables out of the way to set up spectator seats.

[79] Williams also held national records in powerlifting at the time. Dude is a beast.

[80] NB: At this point, I had never failed a drug test.

[81] Want to hear something nuts? In 2017, a WADA ethics panel floated the idea of using geo-tracking devices to keep tabs on athletes. https://bjsm.bmj.com/content/52/7/456

See also:
https://www.sportsintegrityinitiative.com/future-whereabouts-secure-gps-tracking-system/

[82] Since increased to a four-year penalty.

[83] USAW has now expanded that period to six months, to avoid athletes like me that might take lots of time off to dope and then come back with massive performance gains. Also, I'm not the only American who's done that.

[84] USA Weightlifting has since disbanded its residency program at the OTC. From 2015-2017, they instead favored a vastly expanded system of direct athlete support. When the changes to the weight classes and the use of ROBI points for Olympic qualification arrived, USAW again switched gears. The new changes, in the opinion of this writer, sell short the future for the present, removing a bulk of support for youth, junior and promising senior athletes in favor of those with the greatest chance to participate in the Olympic Games.
As of this writing (2019), if you are one of the top 15 in the world in this country, you get a hefty allowance from the federation, which includes paid travel to at least one Olympic qualifier; if you are 16th, or in the top 15, but there's two other athletes ahead of you, USA gives you no money.

[85] If you don't know the story, it's none of your business.

[86] A number of athletes choose this route at the time. They paid their own rent in order to live in Colorado Springs and train at the OTC.

[87] And everyone knows his story.

[88] USA Weightlifting has since eliminated this position.

[89] https://www.catalystathletics.com/article/1743/Athlete-Selection-for-Weightlifting/
As the head coach for Poland, Zygmunt oversaw a program that tested 1,500 schoolage athletes per year. He evaluated them on performance in vertical jump, standing broad jump and bench press, plus mobility indicators such as overhead squat and front squat positions. The Polish system used measurements of femur-tibia ratio, wingspan, torso length (and relative length of the legs) as well as height versus bodyweight. Out of that original group of 1,500, Zygmunt selected TEN future weightlifters.

[90] He would find much greater success later in the 2012-2016 quadrennial, when future-Olympians Morgan King and Jenny Arthur trained at the OTC.

[91] Pat insisted in multiple conversations his belief that Rob never took any performance enhancing drugs. Pat cited his natural mobility and athleticism and said that the numbers Rob hit, while high by USA Weightlifting standards, did not ever approach international medal worthy efforts. He could clean 200kg and snatch 165kg at a time when the USA record stood at 205.5 and 165.5.

[92] Reza Zadeh: https://en.iranwire.com/en/features/1701

[93] Farah: https://www.theguardian.com/commentisfree/2017/feb/28/mo-farah-me-l-carnatine-drugs-sport
Rupp and others at NOP: https://www.letsrun.com/news/2017/05/usada-appears-highly-likely-6-nop-athletes-including-galen-rupp-dathan-ritzenhein-violated-anti-doping-rules/

[94] Success always builds this way, from one top athlete to a whole club of enthusiastic lifters. Danny Camargo's success with Mattie Rodgers built Team Oly Concepts into a well-deserved nationally known brand.

[95] You can still see that video on YouTube:
https://www.youtube.com/watch?v=wBZnxbly3so

[96] A funny side note: Even though I didn't test positive at this meet and still retain my national championship, USA Weightlifting's video

archive still features Maier's heaviest lifts from this meet; but they have purged any video of me lifting in national level competition.

97 https://www.youtube.com/watch?v=6j714Tl1bNM

98 I know from personal experience of three athletes in Olympic sport—one of whom competed at the Olympics—that this process still occurs. I'm not trying to spoil an advantage against the doping nations for any USA athlete, but I also need to make it very clear that weightlifting is very much singled out for strict, targeted out-of-competition testing by USADA. There is nothing random about who USADA decides to test. That has been admitted and confirmed.

Don't think it doesn't happen in other sports. An IAAF doping control officer tipped off a Kenyan runner about a supposed "random" OOC test: https://apnews.com/b4c133e43b9d48f9beb5c5db702522ba
99 http://www.chm.bris.ac.uk/motm/THG/THGh.htm

100 https://www.espn.com/espn/news/story?id=3312333

101 Marion Jones:
https://www.nytimes.com/2007/10/06/sports/othersports/06balco.html

Barry Bonds:
https://www.espn.com/mlb/news/story?id=1937594

Shane Mosley:
https://www.latimes.com/archives/la-xpm-2009-jan-22-sp-mosley-balco22-story.html

Bill Romanowski:
https://www.cnn.com/2013/10/31/us/balco-fast-facts/index.html

102https://academic.oup.com/jcem/article/89/5/2498/2844817

103 https://usatoday30.usatoday.com/sports/olympics/2007-02-28-catlin-drug-lab_N.htm

104 https://www.nytimes.com/2009/10/25/sports/25graham.html

105 https://www.nytimes.com/2009/10/25/sports/25graham.html

---

106 https://www.usada.org/sanction/usada-imposes-lifetime-ban-against-former-track-field-coach-trevor-graham/

107 https://www.livescience.com/58790-crispr-explained.html

108 In 2016, we would find out that dozens of international athletes in our sport managed to dope consistently and win World and Olympic medals.

109 Two years later she and Broz split up.

110 The Pan Am Games do not award medals for individual lifts.

111 It's doubtful that Brazil's anti-doping agency tested him at all during this period. I can speak from the experience of competing for that country in this regard.

112 The gender parity rule wouldn't kick in until the IWF added the 90kg weight class in 2016.

113 Donnie actually relayed this story to the author at a bar in Philadelphia in 2012.

114 Donnie is a fucking warrior.
After the snatch portion, Donnie couldn't move his neck at all. An X-ray and CT scan later showed that he broke a vertebra in his cervical spine. If he didn't make a total, USA would get ZERO men's spots for the 2012 Olympics. So Donnie let the team doctors give him two shots of Lidocaine into his fucking neck so that he could go out there and post a total. Even though he knew that Kendrick would get the spot he earned.

115 https://www.ncbi.nlm.nih.gov/pubmed/20439575

116 This type of bullshit still occurs, dressed up as "updated changes to the selection procedures with a nice new PDF for everyone to suddenly rearrange all their training plans around.

117A PUBMED subscription and an RSS feed on HGH would have alerted me to Martin Bidlingmaier's successful detection method and probably alerted me to WADA's test.

118 As of this writing, you can still see a video of it on YouTube: https://www.youtube.com/watch?v=65jovqRDaDs&t=1s

[119] This practice by USADA continues to this day. See the case of Chinese Swimmer Sun Yang, urged publicly by Travis Tygart to confess all his darkest secrets about doping in exchange for a reduced suspension.

https://www.swimmingworldmagazine.com/news/sun-yang-urged-to-spill-beans-on-darkest-secrets-in-return-for-reduced-suspension/

[120] https://www.outsideonline.com/1925761/whats-wrong-world-anti-doping-agency

[121] https://www.thelancet.com/journals/lancet/article/PIIS0140-6736%2899%2900775-8/fulltext

http://www.clinchem.org/content/55/3/445

[122] Think of it like this: in a room you have a bunch of colored lights and dimmer switches. The lights are forms of HGH. The antibodies act like the light switches. When artificial HGH is present, that particular light switch gets turned up, illuminating the room and proving that an athlete doped.

[123] However, Bidlingmaier did not contribute to the statistical analysis that yielded the decision limits used by WADA to determine a doping offence.

[124] In 2008, WADA amended its code to punish athletes that fought the charges and didn't immediately fess up to their alleged wrongdoings.

From this article: https://www.outsideonline.com/1825536/good-cop-bad-cop

Critics of the system argue that CAS teems with conflicts of interest and heavily favors the anti-doping agencies. For instance, WADA has moved to prevent athletes from exercising their right to fight charges. In, 2011, the most recent version of the WADA Code included a provision to increase the length of suspensions due to "aggravating circumstances." An athlete can avoid this extra ban by admitting "the anti-doping rule violation as asserted, promptly after being confronted."

[125] https://news.postimees.ee/1187118/mathematician-saves-veerpalu-honour

126 According to Pat Mendes: USADA said they would give him a two year ban, but he had to admit to taking HGH. Pat told me that Howard Jacobs advised him to take the deal, as they wouldn't try to get anything more than two years if he admitted use of HGH. Pat said that Jacobs said litigation would cost up to $30,000 if he didn't plea.

Pat: "I think the whole thing was they wanted to solidify that this test was real. Because it was such a new type of test and very few athletes tested positive…I basically said okay, I signed the paperwork, and they wrote the statement and I just signed off." They wanted public confirmation from an athlete that their test worked.

127 Brundage was fiercely committed to the amateur understanding of the Olympic ideal.
He begrudgingly allowed each quadrennial's organizing committee to negotiate television broadcast rights, but mostly as a way to further promote Olympism.

This paper summarizes the change in philosophical approach that occurred between the 20-year reign of Brundage and his understanding of Olympic amateurism and Samaranch's wholesale desire to transform the Olympic Games into a worldwide, fully commercialized sports powerhouse.
http://isoh.org/wp-content/uploads/2015/03/191.pdf

128   https://www.chicagotribune.com/ct-juan-antonio-samaranch-dead-ioc-president-story.html

129 https://deadspin.com/where-does-the-iocs-money-go-1822983686
See the above article for a full breakdown of the IOC's filings with the IRS for 2016.
130 To give a point of comparison; New Jersey headquartered Burlington Stores took the 500th spot on the 2016 Fortune 500 list, with net revenues of just over five billion.
https://fortune.com/fortune500/2016/search/?rank=desc

131 For a point of comparison, the United Way, which provides services in over 40 countries, raised just over $4 billion in 2018.

https://www.unitedway.org/annual-report/2018-annual-report

[132] This paragraph draws on the following sources:
http://assets.espn.go.com/oly/columns/garber_greg/1225329.html

https://www.foxnews.com/sports/ioc-and-nbc-5-things-to-know-about-the-landmark-olympic-tv-rights-deal

https://www.sportbusiness.com/2020/02/terrence-burns-la-2028-back-to-the-future-for-olympic-sponsorship/

Past and Present TOP sponsors include: Alibaba, Coca-cola, Samsung, Panasonic, Omega, Proctor and Gamble, Toyota, General Electric, Dow, Atos, AirBnB, Visa, Dow and Bridgestone.
https://www.olympic.org/partners

https://www.ispo.com/en/markets/sponsors-olympic-games-these-are-olympic-funders

For an analysis of the conflicts created by the pursuit of revenue, see:
https://www.thehastingscenter.org/doping-corruption-international-intrigue-olympic-sport-confronts-moral-crisis/

[133] Before the start of the 1998 Tour de France, police discovered a large amount of doping products and illegal drugs in a car belonging to the Festina Cycling Team. Police subsequently raided hotels hosting that year's riders, and several teams withdrew from the race entirely.
https://www.theguardian.com/sport/gallery/2008/jul/09/tourdefrance.cycling

[134]   https://www.theguardian.com/sport/2002-winter-olympic-bid-scandal

[135]   https://www.nytimes.com/2016/06/16/sports/olympics/world-anti-doping-agency-russia-cheating.html

[136]   https://www.heraldsun.com.au/sport/samaranchs-legacy-is-doping-author/news-story/31de0cf897c95f20afd73c6abfdea6fa

Also this:
https://www.independent.co.uk/sport/athletics-flo-jo-and-the-shadow-of-doubt-1200951.html

Also this:

https://www.reuters.com/article/us-athletics-johnson-smith-idUSBRE98M0PT20130923

http://www.passyourdrugtest.com/04-18-2003-news.htm

[137] USADA also originated in scandal.

Dr. Wade Exum served as director of drug control for the USOC from 1991-2000 (the year of USADA's formation). He resigned from the USOC role in January, 2000, publicly claiming that USOC leaders interfered with his fight against drug use. He filed suit against the agency and released 2,000 pages of documents. In a district court proceeding, these documents revealed that half of the positive tests from the 1980's-2000 resulted in no punishment.

Ultimately, it emerged that 114 US athletes escaped penalty after positive doping tests, including Carl Lewis.
https://www.independent.co.uk/sport/general/athletics-on-the-wrong-track-116366.html

Even Dick Pound—the former head of WADA—accused the US of running a program that enabled its athletes to check their drug-clearance times in the lead up to the 1984 Games.
https://www.ocregister.com/2009/08/01/early-effort-to-drug-test-olympic-athletes-kept-secret/
See the following articles for more information:
https://punditarena.com/features/emackenna/mackenna-monday-usada-tygart/

https://www.nytimes.com/2016/08/05/sports/olympics/lest-we-forget-the-us-too-spent-time-in-the-doping-wilderness.html
https://www.nytimes.com/2003/04/17/sports/olympics-anti-doping-official-says-us-covered-up.html

[138] http://news.bbc.co.uk/2/hi/sport/140315.stm

[139]   https://www.theguardian.com/sport/1999/feb/02/samaranch-head-anti-doping-agency

[140]   https://www.nytimes.com/2016/06/16/sports/olympics/world-anti-doping-agency-russia-cheating.html

Adam Pengilly, a British Olympian who sits on the IOC's athletes' commission has said "There are conflicts of all around the table."

[141] https://www.olympic.org/mr-richard-w-pound-q-c-ad-e

[142] https://www.nytimes.com/2016/06/16/sports/olympics/world-anti-doping-agency-russia-cheating.html?smid=tw-nytsports&smtyp=cur&_r=0

The Hastings Center provides an excellent analysis of the corruption in RUSADA here:
https://www.thehastingscenter.org/doping-corruption-international-intrigue-olympic-sport-confronts-moral-crisis/

[143] Josh Gilbert also tested positive at National Championships and received a three-year suspension. His urine showed traces of Furosemide—a masking agent and prohibited diuretic. People always speculate about a culture of doping at ABG during those early years. Here are some of Gilbert's numbers:
Oct 27, 2011: Broz posts Josh Gilbert doing a 145kg back squat (at 64kg) like it's a big deal.
April 25, 2012: Broz posts Josh Gilbert doing a 195kg back squat (at 64kg), with the caption that he performed this squat on Feb 13, 2012. So in less than 4 months, he increases his back squat by 50kg when he's already doing double body weight.
170kg deadlift on Nov 22, 2011
201kg deadlift on Jan 8, 2012
180kg FSQ on Feb 17, 2012

[144] In the car industry, a "spoon" refers to a guaranteed sale—or as close to a guarantee as anything in sales. Guys that work the finance desk, with 10 to 20 years in the industry, always have friends or clients or companies that buy cars from them. These friends go directly to the desk manager, but he can't technically sell a car or earn commission from the sale. So they pass the deal off to someone on the sales staff. Which in most cases, was me.

[145] I thought about living with him in Monte Claras; a rural area in Northern Brazil with a small main town, stone roads, a population of 400,000 and unfortunately, no weightlifting clubs.

From a training standpoint, living in Monte Claras would have solved a host of problems. Once I switched to Brazil, I would still deal with WADA, but I thought, no problem. They publish a record of all the out-of-competition tests conducted each year, by country and location. And their testers rarely ventured into rural Brazil.

I could see why; Brazil covers more square miles than the entire mainland United States, with 100 million more in population. Monte Claras is a 12-hour drive from Sao Paulo and even further from Rio; and even if the dickheads at WADA wanted to rent a Range Rover and trek up there, I could then use the Victor Conte approach and just not answer the door that day. I would have eagerly taken the odds against them showing up twice in a period long enough for me to benefit from doping again. (Why do you think American lifters do "training camps" in Bulgaria or Mexico or Korea? Same purpose, I'd wager.)

[146] The 2019 German documentary "Lord of the Lifters" would reveal that is indeed how many federations evaded detection.

[147] https://www.insidethegames.biz/articles/1033999/brazilian-teenager-among-latest-doping-cases-announced-by-international-weightlifting-federation

[148] That would change soon after.

[149] This detailed report from the New York Times presents a timeline of WADA's actions relating to the RUSADA doping scandals at Sochi and beyond:
https://www.nytimes.com/2016/06/16/sports/olympics/world-anti-doping-agency-russia-cheating.html?smid=tw-nytsports&smtyp=cur&_r=0

[150] https://www.nytimes.com/2016/06/16/sports/olympics/world-anti-doping-agency-russia-cheating.html?smid=tw-nytsports&smtyp=cur&_r=0

[151] The pair still live in hiding in Europe.

[152] nytimes.com/2016/06/16/sports/olympics/world-anti-doping-agency-russia-cheating.html

[153] According to the Stepanov's, Russia supplied performance enhancing drugs and falsified tests in exchange for five-percent of the athlete's earnings. Seppelt's documentary claimed that 99-percent of Russian athletes participated.
https://www.bbc.com/sport/athletics/30324812

[154] https://www.dailymail.co.uk/sport/article-3207651/WADA-president-Sir-Craig-Reedie-s-comfort-email-Russia-s-senior-drug-buster-reveals-toothless-clampdown-doping.html

[155] Of course the IOC wants to cross-pollinate staff at WADA. It's how they can keep a lid on the scandals they want to release (and punish) and the heroes they want to protect and keep celebrating. It's why situations arise like the 2008 Olympics, where every Jamaican sprinter *except* Usain Bolt tests positive. The other three members of the relay team don't matter as much as Puma's superstar and the darling of NBC's ratings.
At the end of the day, the IOC must answer to NBC, to the money side of the Olympics, without which they and all of their member nations and federations have no money at all. **No one at the IOC wants to return to the days of cash-poor amateurism.**

[156] https://stillmed.olympic.org/media/Document%20Library/OlympicOrg/General/EN-Olympic-Charter.pdf#_ga=2.26124477.1466056815.1586970428-1635449020.1586970428 See Page 16 for the Mission statement.

[157] Full text: https://www.wada-ama.org/sites/default/files/resources/files/wada_independent_commission_report_1_en.pdf

[158] After such obvious cheating by Russia in Sochi and in the 2010-2016 period, it's difficult to imagine a worse scenario that would necessitate the IOC banning one of the largest medal winners across all sports from the Olympics. At least not as long as the IOC wants to keep the Games interesting and want people (in certain markets) to watch it.

[159] USA at 554 athletes, Germany at 425, Australia at 421, China at 413, France at 399, Great Britain at 366, then Russia at 282. Source: https://en.wikipedia.org/wiki/2016_Summer_Olympics

[160] See the following articles:
https://www.propublica.org/article/olympics-top-investigator-secret-efforts-undermine-russian-doping-probe
Travis Tygard publicly commented that this decision would deter future whistleblowers, as it represents a punishment by the IOC:
https://www.bbc.com/sport/olympics/36878983

[161] https://www.washingtonpost.com/sports/2019/12/07/russia-olympic-ban-wada-doping/

[162] https://www.bbc.com/sport/46246496
To see just how much WADA drug their feet on the Russian doping scandal, read this interview with lead investigator Jack Robertson:
https://www.propublica.org/article/olympics-top-investigator-secret-efforts-undermine-russian-doping-probe

[163]   https://www.wada-ama.org/en/media/news/2016-07/wada-acknowledges-ioc-decision-on-russia-stands-by-agencys-executive-committee

[164] Behind the scenes, WADA and the IOC worked together to faciliate and fast-track Russia's reinstatement.
https://www.bbc.com/sport/45840481

[165] The ban imposed by WADA doesn't possess any teeth. Russian athletes still compete at all of these international events even though the country itself is technically banned.
https://www.sbnation.com/2019/12/9/21002688/russia-ban-wada-olympics-doping

[166] Nike understands this process. They have sponsored many drug cheats, including Justin Gatlin and Tyson Gay. The company continued to fund the Nike Oregon Project right up until the moment USADA gave head coach Alberto Salazar a four-year ban for trafficking testosterone (among other offenses). And why not? That project produced winners, furthering the sales revenue and public image of a near-$40 billion-dollar company. It's hard to imagine they didn't also get slowed investigations and preferential treatment when whistleblowers like Kara Goucher revealed Salazar's dirty tricks to USADA and the FBI.

https://www.espn.com/espn/otl/story/_/id/16209580/doping-whistleblowers-such-stepanovs-kara-goucher-often-left-dangsling-taking-sports-bodies-governing-bodies

[167] Taylor later put this to rest by referring to Broz as "very paternal," a term I know he hates.

[168] If you know, you know. And despite SafeSport, it's more common than you think.

[169] See the coverage, starting here:
https://www.washingtonpost.com/wp-srv/investigations/poker/people.html

Allegedly, this part of Nat's life formed the back story for the movie *Runner, Runner*, in which Justin Timberlake portrayed Nat's role in the poker scandal.

https://en.wikipedia.org/wiki/Runner_Runner

[170] I emailed Phil Andrews at USAW. He worked at the organization, but not yet in his current position of CEO. I asked Phil to remove me from the testing pool. My ban expired and I wanted to bypass any regulations that enabled USADA to come knocking at all hours or keep me stuck in America on Whereabouts. Funny thing about Whereabouts; once you test positive, the rules still require you to register your location, so if you start using again, they can pop you a second time and doubly mar your reputation. Ask Sonny Webster how that feels.

[171] A year later we expanded the line to include a hydration supplement, an intra-workout fuel, a mental focus formula as well as t-shirts and programming.

[172] Wada and USADA also use a Carbon-Isotope Ratio test (which is far more expensive). This test claims it can distinguish naturally produced testosterone that the body makes via the food an athlete eats from pharmaceutical testosterone. The test looks for ratios of carbon isotopes; pharmaceutically produced testosterone allegedly contains primarily one isotope of carbon (C-17) while so-called naturally produced testosterone derives from food that consists mainly of the C-16 isotope. However, studies have already shown flaws with this understanding as the differing diets of populations around the globe—not to mention the soil and

nutrients available to the local plants—affects the ratio of C-16 and C-17 in the food ingested.
See: https://www.ncbi.nlm.nih.gov/pmc/articles/PMC2784500/
Again, just like the flawed test for HGH, WADA and USADA continue to use a test with built in assumptions that make the test less valid than either organization believes.

[173] Dr. Magdolna Trombitas

[174] That rule had changed. We heard rumors that Lu Xiaojun found that out when USADA reps met him at the airport before he conducted some seminars in the USA.

[175] Phil Andrews relayed to this author and USAW Coach Walt Neubauer that he had this conversation with Ajan. Andrews told Walt and I about it over lunch on December 8, 2018, while the three of us were in Ecuador, ironically enough, representing Team USA at the Tamas Ajan Cup.

[176] Former WADA head Dick Pound has expressed concern that the following sports are corrupt, regarding doping: cycling, tennis, soccer, track and field and soccer:
https://www.dailymail.co.uk/sport/othersports/article-2384113/Dick-Pound-Doping-widespread-sport.html#ixzz3LRLJg8MN

For USADA head Travis Tygart's take on FINA (Swimming's international governing body) trying to run its own doping, see:
https://www.swimmingworldmagazine.com/news/travis-tygart-to-fina-you-cant-have-fox-guarding-henhouse-hand-over-anti-doping-to-truly-independent-orgs/

[177] There is evidence that the UCI instructed WADA lab doctors to help prominent cyclists beat the EPO test, if not outright cover up evidence of doping:
https://www.cyclingnews.com/news/lausanne-laboratory-gave-armstrong-key-to-beating-epo-test-says-tygart/
See also:
https://www.outsideonline.com/1795306/tygart-wada-head-helped-armstrong-beat-epo-tests

[178] https://www.telegraph.co.uk/athletics/2020/06/08/lamine-diack-solicited-31m-bribes-court-hears-start-corruption/

According to the Telegraph, Diack admitted accepting at least one million in bribes.
https://www.telegraph.co.uk/sport/othersports/athletics/12059112/Lamine-Diack-admits-soliciting-1m-from-Russia.html

[179] Headed by Dick Pound, Richard McLaren, and Jack Robertson

[180] https://web.archive.org/web/20160121075247/https://wada-main-prod.s3.amazonaws.com/resources/files/wada_independent_commission_report_2_2016_en.pdf

[181] https://www.si.com/more-sports/2016/03/24/cas-upholds-russian-doping-suspensions-reallocated-olympic-medal

[182] This article provides a concise, damning analysis of how much the doping affected the results of those World Championships and the London Olympics:
https://www.sportsintegrityinitiative.com/german-documentary-raises-questions-over-doping-and-athlete-privacy/

[183] Ashenden's scientific work helped develop the biological passport that enables WADA and other antidoping agencies to track longitudinal blood and urine data over time.
His CV: http://d3epuodzu3wuis.cloudfront.net/R042.pdf
See also:
https://www.theguardian.com/sport/2015/nov/28/iaaf-athletics-doping-scandal

https://www.sportsintegrityinitiative.com/open-letter-from-dr-ashenden-to-lord-coe/

[184] Ashenden provided this analysis to ARD journalist Hajo Seppelt for his documentary *Doping—Top Secret: The Shadowy World of Athletics*. View here: https://vimeo.com/146383380

[185] To understand the difficulty here, see the analysis provided by Peter Vigneron in Outside Magazine:
"When a marquee athlete tests positive, many international sports organizations—the UCI, the IAAF, the International Triathlon Union—may find themselves in the unenviable position of destroying the career of a world-famous athlete. Or, in Russia's case, an athlete critical to the country's identity. Until Seppelt's report, the IAAF's conflict of interest

had been largely theoretical. I was not aware of suspicions that the IAAF accepted money to make doping positives go away, and the organization had shown integrity by banning a number of big-name athletes in the past several years.

The IAAF's current role in anti doping can't be overstated. Most countries, including Ethiopia and Kenya, cannot afford an independent anti-doping agency. So they depend entirely on IAAF to oversee testing. (Because USADA is well funded and independent, IAAF only occasionally tests American runners away from competitions.) An allegation of corruption in the IAAF, then, means that the one agency keeping an eye on the world's best runners has now lost its claim to independence and integrity."
Vigneron provides more insight here: https://www.outsideonline.com/1928046/why-russian-runner-doping-scandal-matters

[186] From the BBC Panorama video that also covered the Track and Field allegations: https://www.dailymotion.com/video/x6uc4up

[187] https://www.flotrack.org/articles/5060656-seb-coe-knew-of-russian-doping-allegations-in-2014

[188] Recent inquiries have revealed further conflicts of interest in Coe's role at World Athletics vis-à-vis his business dealings. Coe was an ambassador for Nike while running for Presidency of the IAAF. During his successful presidential campaign, the IAAF awarded Eugene, Oregon the 2021 World Championships…without a vetting process.

Coe has been accused of other conflicts of interest by members of British Parliament. For instance, Coe is the executive chairman of CSM Sports and Entertainment, which has profited from deals made with Japanese conglomerate Dentsu, which owns the commercial rights to World Athletics.
https://www.dailymail.co.uk/sport/sportsnews/article-8445327/World-Athletics-president-Sebastian-Coe-rejects-conflict-interests-claims-business-dealings.html

[189] See an interesting discussion of the ethical and historical issues that complicate the perpetuation of these world records:
https://fivethirtyeight.com/features/track-and-field-may-scrap-its-records-because-of-doping-scandals-is-that-a-good-idea/

[190] For a full analysis of the "unbeatability" of some of these records, see: https://sportsscientists.com/2016/08/world-records-fossils/

[191] I'm not saying that track and field athletes aren't still attempting to beat—especially on the women's side—the long-standing world records in the shorter races or field events. I'm saying that the testing for the drugs that enable world record performances in those events has made it impossible to use the drugs that made those world records happen in the first place. No one will ever again get away with taking a yearly regimen of testosterone derivatives (such as Turinabol) that the East Germans and Soviets took in the 1970s and 1980s. No one today can do anything but micro-dose with testosterone, which athletes back then took in 100s of cc's per week.

[192] For instance, the scandal-plagued history of Nike Project Oregon. Whistleblower Kara Goucher first alerted USADA to potentially rule-violating and unethical use of TUE's and other tactics as early as 2013 (after going to the FBI with these allegations in 2011).
See: https://www.womensrunning.com/culture/people/goucher-on-alberto-salazar-doping-violations/

In June 2015, ProPublica and the BBC released a documentary on those shady tactics. Then USADA began a full investigation that resulted in a coach Alberto Salazar receiving a four-year ban in 2019! In the meanwhile, both Galen Rupp and Mo Farrah both won Olympic and World Championship medals while competing for Nike Project Oregon. I think it's a fair question to ask what USADA knew and when did they know it? And did they sit on any of that information?
https://www.propublica.org/article/former-team-members-accuse-coach-alberto-salazar-of-breaking-drug-rules
https://www.nytimes.com/2019/10/06/sports/salazar-doping-nike-oregon-project.html

[193] I personally had this process verified to me by Regis Becker (the current head of Safe Sport) and Leo Totten. Both recalled serving as the Team Manager for Team USA at International competitions and having to carry "the brown paper bag" full of $10,000 in American cash for the Team USA registration fee.

[194] Getting into the "A" session at a World Championships is a real pissing match in certain weight classes. National federations must

declare an entry total for each of their athletes when registering them for international meets. Often, a federation will enter a total far in excess of what that lifter has ever posted in a qualifying meet. By entering something high, the federation ensures their athlete will lift in the A session and also ups the ante for every other country.

At the Verification of Final Entries (VFE) meeting (that typically takes place the day before the competition begins), any federation can also change the entry total for any of their competitors.

After the VFE, we discovered that a 401kg total would have guaranteed a spot in the 105kg A session, and the coaches didn't need to go as high as 406kg.

[195] Pat's actual words on this subject: "In hindsight after coaching a few people and looking at my career, its something you do at the very ground stage of weightlifting. When you're heading to a World Championship, you shouldn't be doing stuff like that anymore because the whole idea is basically to learn how to fight with heavy weights and really your body does learn what it's really like to lift the true max through those attempts. And you do become a better lifter, but to actually apply that, you'll have to make a lot of those attempts over and over again. Like there's very few people, if any, who go into a meet missing their opener six or seven times in a week.

[196] The IOC would rescind all four of those golds after the doping re-tests in 2016. But somehow Kazakh cyclist Alexander Vinokourov won Gold at age 39 after a long career in the most doped sport in history (cycling) and multiple appearances in the most doped sporting event in the history—the Tour de France.

Vinokourov competed for Team Astana, one of the most repeat offenders of doping in cycling history. He got popped in 2007 (when a much younger man) and then he wins gold in 2012 at 39? I don't buy it.

See: https://www.theguardian.com/sport/2015/feb/27/astana-doping-cycling-troubled-team

And then the Kazakh triple-jumper wins gold but doesn't get popped? C'mon. Olga Rypakova has the third best indoor triple jump of all time. Do the fucking re-tests on all the IAAF World Championships from 2001-2015 if you're really serious about clean sport!

[197] Doping re-tests of Ilya's B-samples from the 2012 and 2008 Olympics alleged that he took banned substances to win Gold medals at those events.

[198] Chinshanlo is also eligible for the 2021 Olympics after serving only a TWO-YEAR ban for her positive re-test from the 2012 Olympics. She recently competed in the 2019 World Championships—where two kilograms heavier in the new weight classes—she took fourth with a 93kg snatch and a 120kg C&J. Turinabol sure does help with those bigger C&J's.

[199] https://www.espn.com/espn/feature/story/_/id/21596079/how-teenager-cj-cummings-help-rescue-weightlifting

[200] Tygart claimed that Armstrong offered USADA this donation in 2004.
https://www.usatoday.com/story/sports/cycling/2013/01/08/lance-armstrong-doping-usada-donation/1818065/
See also:
https://www.youtube.com/watch?v=S7Rw_QGfEJ8
Armstrong had given the International Cycling Union two separate donations of $25,000 and $100,000, which Tygart referred to as a "clear conflict of interest."
https://www.cyclingnews.com/news/mcquaid-reveals-armstrong-made-two-donations-to-the-uci/

[201] It's worth noting that the Congressional mandate that established USADA only called for that organization to cover amateur athletic activities in sports governed by the USOC.

[202] I can provide a full breakdown of USADA's revenue from 2013-2019. USADA publishes all this information on their website.

[203] It's worth noting that around the same time the UFC partnered with USADA, the UFC also created a new program to educate athletes on how to train and cut weight properly and prevent and recover from injuries. They hired Jeff Novitzky as Vice President of Athlete Health and Performance to oversee that operation.
Novitzky's former job? He worked for the federal government. His two biggest cases? Taking down BALCO and the doping investigation that brought down Lance Armstrong; during the latter investigation, he worked closely with Travis Tygart.
Talk about a potentially massive conflict of interest! Especially when Novitzky earns $500,000 a year salary from the UFC! When you know all the tricks of the prosecution, you can earn a killing working for the defense.

See also: https://sports.yahoo.com/news/ufc-hires-usada-to-employ--best-anti-doping-policy-in-sports-220648544-mma.html
https://www.outsideonline.com/1896686/big-fish
https://www.usatoday.com/story/sports/ufc/2015/10/14/jeff-novitzky-ufc-anti-doping-program-balco-barry-bonds/73737912/

[204] USADA conducted drug tests for the Floyd Mayweather-Shane Mosley bout on May 1, 2010:
https://www.usada.org/announcement/mayweather-vs-mosley-professional-boxing-testing-program-statistics/
Since 2010, USADA conducted testing on professional fights for multiple boxing promotions.

[205] https://www.sbnation.com/longform/2015/9/9/9271811/can-boxing-trust-usada
See also this blog entry "USADA's Conflict of Interest Problem" by University of Colorado at Boulder professor and sports governance expert Roger Pielke, Jr. which outlines ethical issues involved in USADA's interactions with professional boxing fight promoters.
https://leastthing.blogspot.com/2013/02/usadas-conflict-of-interest-problem.html
And here:
http://leastthing.blogspot.com/2015/09/usadas-moonlighting-gets-it-in-trouble.html

[206] In USADA's own words: "By the afternoon of Friday, October 19, 2012, USADA had reported out to the NYSAC the A and B sample results for the October 3 sample and the preliminary A sample results for the October 10 and October 16 samples. Clenbuterolwas detected in three of the four samples that had been reported by the laboratory to USADA by that time."
From: https://www.usada.org/wp-content/uploads/USADAs-Detailed-Correction-to-SB-Nation-Article-by-Tom-Hauser.pdf

[207] https://slate.com/technology/2012/07/dietary-supplements-at-the-olympics-why-athletes-risk-false-drug-charges.html

[208] The UFC and its fighters must receive licenses from the Athletic or Gaming Commissions of states where they want to host a fight. These gaming commissions sometimes weigh the results of doping tests—when they are informed of them—in their decision to grant a license to a fighter before an event.

[209] From a conceptual standpoint, there is no third-party in the relationship between USADA and the UFC that guarantees that they can act like an "independent testing agency." The UFC directly pays USADA to test its athletes. It's not like those fees go through the government or are authorized by Congress. USADA provides the UFC with a service, and there's nothing independent about it.

[210] Note that USADA began testing UFC athletes during the second half of 2015. Total tests for UFC athletes in 2015 included 238 OOC and 115 in-competition tests. Third-party revenue increased over $1.5 million from 2014 to 2015. But the next year, the first-full year of testing, USADA administered 2,289 tests on UFC athletes (1,971 OOC and 318 IC).

[211] https://ufc.usada.org/testing/results/sanctions/

[212]   https://www.mmafighting.com/2019/10/28/20937260/nate-diaz-blasts-made-up-usada-drug-testing-issue-it-was-all-just-a-big-old-bunch-of-bullsh-t
If you believe Chael Sonnen, USADA gave Diaz *two* apologies: https://www.youtube.com/watch?v=GqH4fwUi9yo

[213]   Jeff   Novitzky   interview: https://www.youtube.com/watch?v=7v_vNb9NodQ

[214] See:
https://ufc.usada.org/usada-ufc-announce-advancements-ufc-anti-doping-policy/
https://www.mmafighting.com/2019/11/25/20979630/usada-unveils-significant-revisions-to-ufc-anti-doping-policy-nate-diaz-jon-jones
And: https://www.espn.com/mma/story/_/id/28161474/ufc-revises-drug-policy-combat-contaminated-supplements

[215] The two major revisions, which the UFC announced Monday, are the adoption of a "UFC prohibited list," which sets threshold limits on what constitutes a positive drug test for several banned substances, as well as a list of "certified supplements" that offer immunity to athletes in the event they are found to be contaminated.
Since the UFC partnered with USADA and launched its year-round drug testing program in 2015, a significant percentage of the cases involving failed drug tests have ultimately been linked to the ingestion of

contaminated legal supplements, according to UFC senior vice president of athlete health and performance Jeff Novitzky.
See: https://www.espn.com/mma/story/_/id/28161474/ufc-revises-drug-policy-combat-contaminated-supplements

Also: https://www.bloodyelbow.com/2019/11/25/20982220/ufc-new-usada-rules-drug-testing-tainted-supplements-get-out-of-jail-free-card-novitzky-mma-science
In a summary of the changes to UFC policy listed on the USADA website, the drug testing organization notes:
Without limitation of other evidentiary methods, an *Athlete* shall bear *No Fault or Negligence* in an individual case where the *Athlete*, by *Clear and Convincing* evidence, demonstrates that the cause of the *Adverse Analytical Finding* was due to a (i) *Contaminated Product* or (ii) *Certified Supplement*. In such a case, there will be no Anti-Doping Policy Violation based on the *Adverse Analytical Finding* and the *Athlete* will not be permitted to compete in a *Bout* until, based on follow-up testing, the *Prohibited Substance* is no longer present in the *Athlete's Samples* (or below the applicable *Decision Concentration Level* for such *Prohibited Substance*, if any) or no appreciable performance advantage is obtained from the presence of the substance.

In a nut shell, if fighters are found to have ingested PED's from either a certified supplement or unknowingly from a contaminated product (food or beverage—not a non-certified supplement), they won't be punished. However, they will not be allowed to compete until the substance has passed from their system.

[216] This concept provides a threshold for a prohibited substance; if the athlete's sample reports a concentration below the threshold, they shall be "managed" by USADA as atypical findings, rather than as adverse analytical findings. This sounds like a technicality, but it is a huge change. Atypical findings are used to flag an athlete's sample for further investigation. Adverse analytical findings indicate that an athlete has committed an anti-doping rule violation.

[217] https://link.springer.com/article/10.1007%2Fs11930-016-0089-7

[218] There is partial justification for this change regarding hydrochlorothiazide:
https://onlinelibrary.wiley.com/doi/abs/10.1002/dta.2499

But the WADA Code does not specify any detection concentration thresholds in its document that specifies thresholds in other substances:
https://www.wada-ama.org/sites/default/files/resources/files/td2019dl_v2_finalb.pdf
The most recent WADA prohibited list (2020) still lists hydrochlorothiazide as a banned substance:
https://www.wada-ama.org/sites/default/files/wada_2020_english_prohibited_list_0.pdf

[219] Selective androgen receptor modulators have been found to contaminate pre-workouts and other supplements in many notable cases in recent years, including a case involving a teenage athlete in USA Weightlifting.
Again, under the aegis of "strict liability" the athlete bears responsibility for anything ingested, including unknowingly contaminated supplements.

Clomiphene is also used widely by athletes as part a post-steroid protocol to re-start their body's own natural production of testosterone. There is little reason why an otherwise healthy male under 40 should need to take this drug.

[220] WADA is making amendments to its 2021 revised (and forthcoming) Code that will attempt to deal with meat contamination regarding Clenbuterol, even though WADA has stated that "it did not have any scientific means to distinguish whether failed drug tests for clenbuterol have resulted from contaminated meat or genuine doping."
https://www.insidethegames.biz/articles/1079924/wada-publishes-stakeholder-notice-regarding-meat-contamination
Clomiphene is prescribed to men as part of testosterone replacement therapy treatments.
https://www.ncbi.nlm.nih.gov/pubmed/16422830
[221] Again, why are fighters or strength athletes or athletes in other Olympic disciplines taking trenbolone and zilpaterol? Because those drugs absolutely enhance performance.
A second question: why is any human being given a pass on the injection of a substance meant primarily for beef cattle? There have been few documented cases of trenbolone contamination in meat.
I should also note that the alleged concern is meat contamination; that large scale companies (Tyson is the largest user of this product in the USA) continue to give this drug to their cattle too close to slaughter.

I should further note that a French company produces this drug; yet under French regulations, no cattle farmers in France can give it to their cows.

222 See: https://www.usada.org/sanction/us-weightlifting-athlete-north-receives-sanction-rule-violation/
See also: https://www.floelite.com/articles/5039878-jon-north-holds-the-awf-grand-opening-promotional-lifting-expo

223 The USADA agents only knew that Pat would attend the AWF event because Jon North posted about it on his Instagram.

224 A member of the Team USA delegation for the 2019 Junior Pan Ams (held in Cuba) told me they saw discarded syringes in the trash cans of the training hall locker room. Senior level athletes from Cuba trained in that facility during the Junior competition.

225 See this article for a detailed explanation of Rodchenkov's double-dealings regarding the development of the test for long-term metabolites of Oral Turinabol and the central role he played in assisting cheating in Russia.
https://www.sportsintegrityinitiative.com/rodchenkovs-development-turinabol-test-raises-questions/

226 'Detection and mass spectrometric characterization of novel long-term dehydrochloromethyltestosterone metabolites in human urine'; can be viewed here:
https://www.docdroid.net/6um5m7W/vdocumentssite-detection-and-mass-spectrometric-characterization-of-novel-long-term-dehydrochloromethyltestosterone-pdf

227 The WADA independent observer report noted that 4,125 of the 11,470 athletes in Rio — or roughly 36% — were not tested in 2016 prior to the Games. That includes 1,913 in high-risk sports such as track and field and weightlifting among others.
https://www.wada-ama.org/sites/default/files/rio2016_io_team_report_26102016.pdf

228 See for instance: https://www.youtube.com/watch?v=gV8CIKaw86w

229 https://www.ncbi.nlm.nih.gov/pubmed/17045758

[230] Science has already shown that fat tissue stores dozens of noxious substances and toxins, and that these re-appear in a person's system during fat loss, sauna sessions and high intensity exercise that burns fat for fuel.

[231] It's worth noting that in 2018, Mateus would receive a four-year ban for oxandrolone metabolites.
Sanction notice: https://www.iwf.net/2018/12/23/public-disclosure-122/

[232] As an example of this protection, iranwire.com claimed that in 2006, doping officials from Iran's National Anti-Doping Organization surprised the Iranian weightlifting team at a camp. The DCO's tested 11 athletes, including Hossein Reza Zadeh. Nine of the 11 tested positive, but not Reza Zadeh.
Iranwire.com claims that Ali Moradi, the head of the Iranian Weightlifting Federation gave up those nine athletes and $400,000 to get Reza Zadeh cleared.
https://iranwire.com/en/features/1701

[233] https://www.bloodyelbow.com/2019/12/2/20991293/jon-jones-claims-innocence-again-after-usada-changes-im-just-god-gifted-with-solid-work-ethic
As of this writing, athletes Grant Dawson and Muslim Salikhov have also been cleared of ADPV's resulting from repeated AAF's for M3 in their urine.
https://www.espn.com/mma/ufc/story/_/id/26143964/salikhov-cleared-doping-case-similar-jones

[234] UFC had already suspended Jones for six months after he committed a felony hit-and-run in April, 2015; the other car was driven by a pregnant woman. Jones allegedly fled the scene on foot. The UFC stripped him of his title and suspended him (reinstating him about six months later):
https://www.espn.com/mma/story/_/id/12783425/jon-jones-stripped-light-heavyweight-title-suspended-ufc

[235] Jones received a one-year suspension for this doping offence.
From USADA's website: "Jones, 29, tested positive for the presence of two prohibited substances, clomiphene and letrozole, following an out-of-competition urine test on June 16, 2016. Clomiphene and letrozole are both Specified Substances in the class of Hormone and Metabolic Modulators and are prohibited at all times under the UFC Anti-Doping

Policy, which has adopted the World Anti-Doping Agency Prohibited List. Under the UFC Anti-Doping Policy, the standard sanction for a policy violation involving a Specified Substance is a one-year period of ineligibility."
https://ufc.usada.org/jon-jones-receives-doping-sanction/
Note that Jones claimed the positive test stemmed from his use of Tadalafil, an erection dysfunction medication that contains neither clomiphene nor letrozole.
See:
https://www.espn.com/mma/story/_/id/25608180/jon-jones-complicated-legacy-mma-greatness-personal-trouble

[236] A few interesting things to note from Jones' first anti-doping policy violation:
Jones hired Howard Jacobs to represent him. Jacobs must work harder the more he gets paid.
Jones tested positive in July, 2016 for clomiphene and letrozole, both banned substances.
He claimed to have taken a tainted supplement, and a three-member arbitration panel, operating under the principles of due process, found him to be negligent but not guilty.
Under the strict liability rule, however, USADA sentenced him to a one-year ban.
https://www.espn.com/mma/story/_/id/17993398/jon-bones-jones-suspended-one-year-failed-drug-test

[237]   https://www.mmafighting.com/2017/8/22/16187202/jon-jones-failed-drug-test-at-ufc-214

[238] The official arbitration report claims the suspension reduction followed from Jones providing "substantial assistance" to USADA; in other words, he may have snitched. (UFC commentator Cael Sonnen doesn't think so, but Cormier and others certainly do).
See: https://www.mmanews.com/chael-sonnen-it-appears-jon-jones-isnt-a-snitch/
See: https://mmajunkie.usatoday.com/2018/09/daniel-cormier-jon-jones-scumbag-for-being-usada-snitch
It should also be noted that a similar case, involving a weightlifter who received a non-analytical violation (meaning, he didn't' test positive for drugs), got a reduction of only 24 months (of a 48-month suspension) for *snitching*, i.e., providing substantial assistance to USADA.

See: https://www.usada.org/sanction/michael-zoda-accepts-doping-sanction/

[239] Do I need to remark how bad the optics look on this one? McLaren showed some serious stones to go after doping committed by Russian federal police. But in this decision, he embarrassed himself with hypocrisy and inconsistencies.
See: https://fitnessvolt.com/28528/jon-jones-return/

[240] FROM THE MCLAREN ARBITRATION REPORT:
https://ufc.usada.org/wp-content/uploads/FINAL-Award-Jones-and-USADA.pdf
"On his return from the foregoing suspension, the athlete was tested on the 6th and 7th of July and the results were negative. He also had five negative tests within five (5) months prior to his positive test. On the 28th of July, 2017, the day before his headliner title bout in UFC 214, the athlete gave a urine sample. That sample was later reported as an adverse analytical finding ("AAF") by the World Anti-Doping Agency ("WADA") accredited Sports Medicine Research & Testing Laboratory (SMRTL). The laboratory AAF was for the M3 Metabolite of a prohibited anabolic agent, which may be found in any of oral Turinabol, dehydrochloromethyltestosterone, Halodrol, methylclostebol or promagnon. **The Laboratory did not use a quantitative measurement for its analysis because the particular substance is not a threshold one.** The sensitivity of the method used by SMRTL to detect the M3 metabolite is extremely high due to the advance analytical methods used to detect prohibited anabolic agents. The concentration of the M3 metabolite was extremely low at between 20-80 picograms/milliliter (pg/ml). A picogram is one trillionth of a gram (i.e., 0.000 000 000 001 gram). Neither the parent drug, oral Turinabol nor the short and/or medium-term metabolites of oral Turinabol were found in the athlete's urine sample."
Section 3.7 of the same:
"Both USADA and the Athlete and his representatives have diligently sought to determine the source of his positive test for the M3 metabolite without success. However, at all times during USADA's investigation, USADA found the athlete and his representatives to be open, response and helpful."
Section 3.12:
"Pursuant to the arbitration portion of the Agreement it is necessary to determine if the period of the Athlete's maximum ineligibility of eighteen (18) months can be reduced any further down to the minimum level of

ineligibility of twelve (12) months. Any such reduction under Article 10.5.2 of the UFC ADP would be based upon the Athlete's degree of Fault."

Under Section Five: Factual Background: Section 5.1: "The Athlete took a number of steps to determine the source of his positive test for the M3 metabolite. He submitted to multiple interviews by USADA in 2017 and 2018 which focused on the supplement products being used by the athlete in 2017. He identified 14 supplements he was using in 2017 in advance of his positive test. None of these supplements has a Prohibited Substance identified on the label of the product.

The 14 supplement products he was using in 2017 were laboratory tested to attempt to identify the presence of prohibited anabolic agents or any of their metabolites. **None of the supplements submitted for testing demonstrated the presence of any prohibited anabolic agents or related metabolites**."

AUTHOR'S NOTE: I have to point out that for any Olympic athlete, this burden of proof would 100% fall on them. The athlete or her lawyer would have to find the supplements in question, find an unopened container from the same batch, then PAY for the lab tests themselves. They would not get USADA to be their errand boy in a situation like this, because under the notion of strict liability, they would be automatically assumed guilty for putting any of these supplements in their bodies.

I know of the father of one young athlete who went through this process to prove his *teenage* daughter's innocence and it cost him over $10,000.

[241] In Section 7: Issue, section 7.1 of his decision, McLaren asks:

(i)   Does the source of the Prohibited substance have to be identified as a necessary condition for the application of any discretion under Article 10.5.2 (of the USADA-UFC ADP) to reduce the period of ineligibility?

(ii)   And then in (ii) he asks, "If not, then what is the appropriate period of reduction based upon the degree of fault?

In Section 7.17 of his decision, McLaren writes **"I find that all of the evidence available to me leads me to conclude that the violation was not intended nor could it have enhanced the Athlete's performance. There was absolutely no intention to use Prohibited Substances on the part of the Athlete."**

In all seriousness, McLaren should never arbitrate an anti-doping case again. He's clearly corrupt on the UFC's behalf to even ask this question. The fact that UFC pays his arbitration company, and probably cut them a HUGE check, explains this decision

I wonder, if McLaren, **reading about Jones recent arrest for a DUI and a weapons charge**—and knowing that Jones is a convicted felon—regrets writing the lines in Section 7.19:
"I find the Athlete to have been a truthful witness who recognizes his past mistakes and has learned from them...Throughout listening to the testimony, I found the Athlete to have been a very credible person who was well intended and well meaning,"
Except of course when he snorts cocaine, flees the scene after injuring a pregnant woman with his car, and commits a DUI and a weapons charge after serving his probation for a previous felony.

[242] Section 5.3 of McLaren's report discusses Jones' admitting that he used cocaine during this period.

[243] Jeff Novitzky has actually publicly stated that they have considered this theory as to why Jones originally tested positive for Turinabol metabolites in 2017. See: https://mmajunkie.usatoday.com/2018/12/microdosing-weight-cutting-tainted-cocaine-ufc-232-jeff-novitzky-on-jon-jones-theories

[244] USADA's revised policies for the UFC also shifted the designation of many recreational drugs from Prohibited Substances to Substances of Abuse, including cannabis, fentanyl, methamphetamines, Ecstasy, and cocaine (really not setting the bar that high for these professional athletes).
See: https://ufc.usada.org/wp-content/uploads/UFC-Prohibited-List-2019.pdf

For practical purposes, the term Substance of Abuse means that as long as the athlete can show (by preponderance of evidence), that the violation (say, cocaine use) does not enhance the athlete's performance in a fight, then they may not face any punishment at all, but may have to attend a substance abuse training program at their own cost.
https://ufc.usada.org/wp-content/uploads/UFC-anti-doping-policy-EN.pdf

[245] Full text of the arbitrator's decision: https://ufc.usada.org/wp-content/uploads/FINAL-Award-Jones-and-USADA.pdf

[246] See: https://fitnessvolt.com/33477/jon-jones-vada-test-results-turinabol/

And: https://www.bjpenn.com/mma-news/ufc/jeff-novitzky-says-turinabol-has-been-detected-on-several-jon-jones-tests-dating-back-to-august/

[247] https://www.mmafighting.com/2018/12/23/18154375/nevada-commission-wont-license-jon-jones-after-abnormal-drug-test-finding-ufc-232-moves-california

[248] NB: The Voluntary Antidoping Agency tested Jones at his weigh-ins and discovered a low picogram level of M3.
See: https://fitnessvolt.com/33477/jon-jones-vada-test-results-turinabol/
[249] The California State Athletic Commission (CSAC) gave Jones' permission to fight after Nevada revoked his license. See:
https://www.usatoday.com/story/sports/ufc/2018/12/23/jon-jones-drug-test-ufc-232-moving/38789897/

[250] https://mmajunkie.usatoday.com/2018/12/jon-jones-drug-test-atypical-result-ufc-232-moved-to-los-angeles-gustafsson-dana-white

Rodchenkov and Sobolevsky's original paper speculated that the longest metabolites, M3, would be detectable for about 50-60 days. See:
https://www.docdroid.net/6um5m7W/vdocumentssite-detection-and-mass-spectrometric-characterization-of-novel-long-term-dehydrochloromethyltestosterone-pdf

[251] https://www.mmafighting.com/2018/12/29/18160041/the-science-of-bones-an-in-depth-look-at-jon-jones-drug-test-findings-why-hell-be-able-fight-ufc-232

[252] There are only THREE WADA-accredited labs in all of North America: Montreal, Salt Lake City, and Los Angeles.

[253] https://www.mmafighting.com/2018/12/29/18160041/the-science-of-bones-an-in-depth-look-at-jon-jones-drug-test-findings-why-hell-be-able-fight-ufc-232
At the time of the arbitration report for Jones' July 2017 adverse finding, McLaren wrote in his report that there is no peer reviewed scientific literature firmly establishing urinary excretion patterns or interindividual variability for the M3 metabolite.
See the full report here: https://ufc.usada.org/wp-content/uploads/FINAL-Award-Jones-and-USADA.pdf

Eichner, whose lab analyzed Jones' tests, wrote that the "most likely" cause of the long-term metabolite of the steroid Turinabol (4-chloro-18-nor-17β-hydroxymethyl,17α-methyl-5α-androst-13-en-3α-ol (M3)) still being in Jones' system was due to "residual levels from a previous exposure." The low levels of the M3 metabolite were "not indicative of further exposure," he wrote.

"There is no evidence that DHCMT has been re-administered," per the document obtained from the commission.

[254] https://sports.yahoo.com/one-50-millionth-grain-sand-banned-substance-found-jon-jones-system-determined-not-new-usage-232215579.html

[255] https://www.mmafighting.com/2018/12/27/18158305/jeff-novitzky-reveals-that-usada-first-found-adverse-findings-in-jon-jones-drug-tests-back-in-august
See also this tweet: https://twitter.com/shaunalshatti/status/1078397146745823232

[256] https://mmajunkie.usatoday.com/2018/12/jon-jones-drug-test-atypical-result-ufc-232-moved-to-los-angeles-gustafsson-dana-white

[257] Again, a detection concentration threshold stipulates that a prohibited substance or its metabolites or markers must be present *above a specified level*, in order for the presence of that substance to be considered as an Adverse Analytic Finding that could lead to an anti-doping policy violation.

[258] In 2018, a proposed study sought to look at the validity of the long-term metabolites for determining an AAF:
https://www.wada-ama.org/sites/default/files/resources/files/17c02mp_dr._parr_summary.pdf

[259] https://www.mmafighting.com/2018/12/27/18158305/jeff-novitzky-reveals-that-usada-first-found-adverse-findings-in-jon-jones-drug-tests-back-in-august
And also here for more detail on the levels of picograms in Jones' system:
https://www.ocregister.com/2019/02/28/ufc-235-jon-jones-tests-positive-for-picograms-again-why-it-does-and-doesnt-matter/

---

[260] Under Section 20.5 of the original WADA code: roles and Responsibilities of National Anti-Doping Organizations, section 20.5.2 reads:

National antidoping organizations must: "adopt and implement anti-doping policies which conform with the (WADA) code."

https://www.wada-ama.org/sites/default/files/resources/files/wada_code_2003_en.pdf

It is not, as Tygart suggest, that USADA develops new rules for certain profitable and popular sports in North America and then he hopes that these changes serve as a model for WADA or other sports to implement.

To quote Tygart directly:
"We're thrilled with these changes and hope it becomes the model for all sports organizations," USADA CEO Travis Tygart told ESPN.

Of the changes, Tygart told MMA Fighting: "The changes to the policy we're all really excited about, it's a great evolution of the program and we're actually hopeful other sports who are interested in protecting clean athletes more effectively and creating fairer systems, this will be the model for it and something we've been pushing both the World Anti-Doping Agency (WADA) and other programs for the past couple of years to try and do something along these lines."

[261] https://www.mmafighting.com/2019/11/25/20979630/usada-unveils-significant-revisions-to-ufc-anti-doping-policy-nate-diaz-jon-jones

[262] http://www.espn.com/espn/feature/story/_/id/21596079/how-teenager-cj-cummings-help-rescue-weightlifting

[263] If USADA hadn't tested these athletes, it likely would have been business as usual, in the same pattern of bribery and undisclosed positive tests pointed out by Hajo Seppelt's documentary "Lord of the Lifters."

[264] And only one of five that have appeared in EVERY Olympics.

[265] https://www.usatoday.com/story/sports/olympics/2014/05/07/nbc-olympics-broadcast-rights-2032/8805989/

[266] This excellent article by Dr. Ross Tucker on the Science of Sport website illustrates the connection between doping methods and World records in track and field. Tucker's article explains why many women's world records in particular, will never be broken.

https://sportsscientists.com/2016/08/world-records-fossils/

[267] https://www.sportsintegrityinitiative.com/testogel-doctors-british-cycling-tues-false-perception-of-cheating/

[268] https://www.prweek.com/article/1525349/a-bumpy-road-ahead-british-cycling-next-the-team-formerly-known-sky

https://www.independent.co.uk/sport/cycling/team-sky-british-cycling-doping-allegations-richard-freeman-testosterone-package-a8727756.html

[269] https://www.dailymail.co.uk/sport/othersports/article-4373912/Jamaican-sprinters-face-doping-scandal.html
See also: https://www.reuters.com/article/us-olympics-bolt-medal/bolt-loses-relay-gold-after-jamaicas-carter-tests-positive-idUSKBN1591RH
And: https://www.telegraph.co.uk/athletics/2017/04/03/ioc-accused-failing-investigate-positive-drugs-tests-including/

[270] https://www.bbc.com/sport/athletics/44299586
https://www.bbc.com/sport/athletics/26974788

[271] Victor Conte believes Bolt is dirty like the rest of the Jamaican team:
https://www.japantimes.co.jp/sports/2015/08/11/more-sports/conte-says-coverup-protected-big-stars-seoul-games/
and
https://www.youtube.com/watch?v=eNCK_PWtOoE

[272] https://ethics.harvard.edu/blog/economics-corruption-sports-special-case-doping
By contrast, the construction industry accounted for only 4.1% of US GDP in 2018:
https://www.statista.com/statistics/248004/percentage-added-to-the-us-gdp-by-industry/

[273] Indeed, the IOC established WADA in 1998 after the Festina scandal at the Tour de France. The reason? They feared that sponsor money would dry up if the public thought the Games were dirty.

https://www.nytimes.com/2016/06/16/sports/olympics/world-anti-doping-agency-russia-cheating.html
Quoting Robert Weiner, a former spokesman for WADA and, previously, the United States Office of National Drug Control Policy.

[274] While USADA performs this task as a service for athletes like Jon Jones, I know of one USAW athlete who ingested a contaminated supplement. Her father had to remortgage the family home to pay for lawyers and testing fees to clear his teenage daughter's name.

[275] As a result of many positive tests, the IOC changed the sport of weightlifting to provisional status, and mandated that the IWF rehabilitate its approach to doping. The IWF suspended nine nations and their weightlifters from participating in any international meets for a full year as part of their show to "get tough" on doping. Whether or not a country received a year suspension depended on how many positive results the IOC and WADA found in those re-tests of their athletes' urine. This punishment affected both doped and non-doped athletes in these countries, without any sense of scrutiny or fairness.
https://www.espn.com/olympics/weightlifting/story/_/id/20872097/russia-china-nine-weightlifting-countries-suspended-year

[276] https://www.iwf.net/anti-doping/reanalysis/

[277] Note that they have not done a blanket re-test of all track and field athletes from 2008 or 2012 Olympics or from the world championships from 2001-2011, all of which we know are suspect.

[278] In WADA Code Appendix, "Definitions," WADA defines **Strict Liability**: The rule which provides that under Article 2.1 and Article 2.2, it is not necessary that intent, fault, negligence, or knowing use on the athlete's part be demonstrated by the anti-doping organization in order to establish an anti-doping rule violation.

[279] On March 18, 2017, USADA tested Amy Hay after she won her weight class at the 2017 American Open Series I. Hay's urine tested positive for the SARM Ostarine. In arbitration with USADA, Hay claimed that her then-boyfriend put the banned substance in her water bottle.
From the arbitration:

The Panel did not hear testimony from Hay's weightlifting coach, Greg Everett (Everett) and thus these factual determinations are based solely on the testimony and credibility of Hay and DF (the boyfriend). Hay and DF testified that on the evening before the March 18 competition, DF took one of his ostarine capsules and emptied a small amount of its contents into one of Hay's water bottles that she drank that evening. DF sabotaged her supposing this would somehow implicate Everett, who DF thought was a terrible individual."
Under the concept of strict liability, Hay still received a reduced sentence of 18 months.
For USADA's announcement: https://www.usada.org/sanction/amy-hay-granted-reduced-sanction-doping/
See the arbitration here: https://www.usada.org/wp-content/uploads/AAA-Award-Amy-Hay-redacted.pdf
I should point out that in the arbitration, USADA argued it was important to expose the boyfriend/now-husband's true identity and to make it known to his employer.

[280] Several other players tested positive for long-term metabolites of Oral Turinabol in 2015 and 2016, including Chris Colabello, Daniel Stumpf, Alec Asher and Boog Powell. All received suspensions and all said they don't know why they tested positive.
https://www.foxsports.com/mlb/story/cody-stanley-162-game-ped-suspension-turinabol-ken-rosenthal-070916

"Stanley, 27, made his major-league debut last season, appearing in nine games for the Cardinals. He would be the second player to receive a lifetime ban, joining former Mets pitcher Jennry Mejia.

"I will never apologize for something I didn't do," Stanley said in a formal statement through the players union. "We will not stop searching for why all of this has happened."

An independent arbitrator rejected Stanley's appeal of his second positive test on Thursday, triggering his 162-game suspension. Minor leaguers who tested positive for Turinabol have admitted to using tainted supplements, baseball officials say, but Stanley and the others have offered no such explanations.

From: https://www.foxsports.com/mlb/story/cody-stanley-162-game-ped-suspension-turinabol-ken-rosenthal-070916

[281] To present all the facts: Stanley had previously served a 50-game suspension for tamoxifen and methylhexanamine, the latter a stimulant found in many commercially available pre-workouts.
https://www.foxsports.com/mlb/story/cody-stanley-162-game-ped-suspension-turinabol-ken-rosenthal-070916

[282] Are we expected to believe that *while suspended*, and in between February and May, Stanley intentionally ingested oral Turinabol, knowing that he was serving a ban for that same substance?

[283] Stanley's arbitration panel must not have included someone as sympathetic to his cause as Richard McLaren.

[284] He also doesn't, by himself, sell millions of pay-per-views or command a sizable fan base—instead, as a first-timer, he can serve as an example by MLB, whose image has been shattered by legions of drug cheats in the past three decades.

[285] It's crucial to note that he only tested positive for the metabolites and never the parent compound or short-term metabolites, which would absolutely show ingestion or re-ingestion.

[286] East German pharmaceutical company Jenapharm first developed and sold Oral Turinabol in the 1960s, shortly after its discovery. The East German State-Sponsored Doping Program began administering it to its athletes, most of whom remained unaware that they were taking an anabolic steroid.
https://www.lvdfitness.com/blogs/the-compound/what-is-turinabol-dhcmt
After the fall of the Berlin Wall and the release of documents related to the state-sponsored doping, many athletes filed lawsuits against Jenapharm:
https://www.espn.com/olympics/news/story?id=2048448

[287] https://www.lvdfitness.com/blogs/the-compound/what-is-turinabol-dhcmt

[288] Rodchenkov and Sobolevsky's original paper did not by itself include a longitudinal study that determined exactly or even gave a rough-estimate of how long M3 or any of the other metabolites continue to be detectable in urine. The 50-60 days was speculation on the their part.

---

[289] WADA or USADA's use of any test carries an implicit presumption that they have vetted the test.

"A similar presumption operates in sports drug cases where, while the onus is on the sporting organizations to prove that someone committed a doping offence, there is a presumption that the testing has been carried out correctly, with the onus then being on the athlete to prove otherwise."

Noted here by Bangor University Law Professor and Doping Law expert Chris Davies:

https://www.austlii.edu.au/au/journals/UNDAULawRw/2012/2.pdf

[290] https://www.sherdog.com/news/news/Grant-Dawson-Cleared-for-UFC-Norfolk-Needs-Additional-Drug-Testing-for-Nevada-License-170337

[291] Recall Novitzky's former position working for the federal government on investigations that took down BALCO and Lance Armstrong.

[292] https://www.mmafighting.com/2018/12/29/18160041/the-science-of-bones-an-in-depth-look-at-jon-jones-drug-test-findings-why-hell-be-able-fight-ufc-232

[293] https://www.ocregister.com/2019/02/28/ufc-235-jon-jones-tests-positive-for-picograms-again-why-it-does-and-doesnt-matter/

[294] Salikhov is one of many cases that lend evidence to the "pulsing theory," that the long-term metabolites appear after some tissue (likely fat tissue) releases them from storage. That none of Salikhov's tests showed parent compound or short-term metabolites indicates that he was not ingesting Oral Turinabol. In other words, these pulses of long-term metabolites come from their storage, *somewhere*, in his system.

[295] https://www.mmafighting.com/2019/3/4/18250707/ufcs-muslim-salikhov-cleared-by-usada-in-doping-case-similar-to-one-involving-jon-jones

[296] https://www.mmafighting.com/2017/8/22/16187202/jon-jones-failed-drug-test-at-ufc-214

[297] The first offence was for clomiphene and letrozole in 2016, for which Jones served a one-year ban.

From USADA's website: "Jones, 29, tested positive for the presence of two prohibited substances, clomiphene and letrozole, following an out-of-competition urine test on June 16, 2016. Clomiphene and letrozole are both Specified Substances in the class of Hormone and Metabolic Modulators and are prohibited at all times under the UFC Anti-Doping Policy, which has adopted the World Anti-Doping Agency Prohibited List. Under the UFC Anti-Doping Policy, the standard sanction for a policy violation involving a Specified Substance is a one-year period of ineligibility."

https://ufc.usada.org/jon-jones-receives-doping-sanction/

Note that Jones claimed the positive test stemmed from his use of Tadalafil, an erection dysfunction medication that contains neither clomiphene nor letrozole.

See:

https://www.espn.com/mma/story/_/id/25608180/jon-jones-complicated-legacy-mma-greatness-personal-trouble

[298] https://ufc.usada.org/wp-content/uploads/FINAL-Award-Jones-and-USADA.pdf

WADA Code in Articles 10.4 and 10.5 has a specific requirement to establish likely source. However, the case law has in restricted circumstances found that the identification of a source was unnecessary to obtain the reduction of a sanction. There are four cases where proof of source was found to be unnecessary for an athlete to obtain a reduction in sanction.

THOSE FOUR CASES ARE:

Mauricio Fiol Villanueva v. FINA, CAS 2016/A/4534: athlete could prove absence of intent without the establishment of the source of a Prohibited Substance where the athlete's demeanor, character and history allow for such a finding.

Arijan Ademi v. UEFA, CAS 2016/A/4676 agreed with Villanueva "that it is possible for an athlete to discharge his or her burden of proving lack of intent without establishing the source of a Prohibited Substance. In particular, the Panel in Ademi focused on the testimony provided by the Player, which was supported by the evidence of the athlete's physiotherapist and the Club doctors.

WADA v. World Squash Federation & Nasir Iqbal, CAS 2016/A/4919, upheld that an athlete could prove lack of intent without identifying the source of the Prohibited Substance.

FINA v Cox, FINA Doping Panel 07/18: determined that "the athlete had met her burden of proving that her ADRV was not intentional, despite the fact that she could not establish the likely source of the Prohibited Substance. These factors included the athlete's own testimony, evidence heard from others which supported the evidence tendered by the athlete, and that no evidence was tendered" (by the Prosecution) "to contradict or undermine the athlete's using the prohibited substance. Citing Villanueva, the Panel in Cox noted that demonstrating evidence of the source of a Prohibited Substance will be extremely helpful in a case, but is not absolutely essential.

[299] McLaren's total and forthright belief in Jones' word surprises given that McLaren arbitrated Jones' *second* doping offence, and given Jones' criminal record and admission to cocaine use during the arbitration process.

[300] It should be noted that Brian Ahrens, the head of the UCLA Olympic Analytical Lab (also WADA-accredited) has also publicly agreed with Eichner, Fedoruk and Bowers' conclusions regarding the presence of long-term metabolites of Oral Turinabol in Jones' urine.

[301] https://sports.yahoo.com/one-50-millionth-grain-sand-banned-substance-found-jon-jones-system-determined-not-new-usage-232215579.html

[302] Fedoruk joined USADA in 2011 as Science Director and is responsible for providing scientific expertise to drive USADA's science, testing, results management, and supplement areas. As a Canadian, he was responsible for science and medical issues during his tenure at the Canadian Centre for Ethics in Sport, Canada's anti-doping agency. As a member of the Organizing Committee for the 2010 Vancouver Olympic and Paralympic Winter Games, he managed anti-doping testing, education, and laboratory analysis challenges before and during the Winter Games. He holds a Ph.D. in Pathology and Laboratory Medicine from the University of British Columbia.
The above, directly quoted from: https://www.usada.org/about/meet-our-team/matt-fedoruk/

303   https://www.mmafighting.com/2018/12/29/18160041/the-science-of-bones-an-in-depth-look-at-jon-jones-drug-test-findings-why-hell-be-able-fight-ufc-232

304 All of these statements from:
https://www.mmafighting.com/2018/12/29/18160041/the-science-of-bones-an-in-depth-look-at-jon-jones-drug-test-findings-why-hell-be-able-fight-ufc-232

305   https://www.mmafighting.com/2018/12/29/18160041/the-science-of-bones-an-in-depth-look-at-jon-jones-drug-test-findings-why-hell-be-able-fight-ufc-232

306   https://www.mmafighting.com/2018/12/29/18160041/the-science-of-bones-an-in-depth-look-at-jon-jones-drug-test-findings-why-hell-be-able-fight-ufc-232

307 Jones was tested five times in a span of 23 days in February. A USADA test on Feb. 1 came back negative, as did a Feb. 9 VADA test ordered by the CSAC. NSAC tests on Feb. 14 and 15 came back positive, the first for 40 picograms and the second for 20 picograms. On Feb. 18, a VADA test ordered by Nevada came back negative. https://www.ocregister.com/2019/02/28/ufc-235-jon-jones-tests-positive-for-picograms-again-why-it-does-and-doesnt-matter/

Here is a fuller history of Jones' drug testing from December, 2018 to February 23, 2019:

- Dec. 28: M3 metabolite (VADA for CSAC)
- Dec. 29: Clean (USADA, CSAC)
- Jan. 6: M3 metabolite (VADA for CSAC)
- Jan. 7: M3 metabolite (VADA for CSAC)
- Jan. 13: Clean (VADA for CSAC)
- Feb. 1: Clean (USADA)
- Feb. 9: Clean (VADA for CSAC)
- Feb. 14: M3 metabolite (NAC)
- Feb. 15: M3 metabolite (NAC)
- Feb. 18: Clean (VADA for NAC)
- Feb. 23: Pending (USADA)

Source: https://www.mmafighting.com/2019/2/28/18245093/two-jon-jones-drug-tests-come-back-atypical-cleared-to-fight-at-ufc-235-by-nac

[308] You can watch the entire four-hour discussion here: https://mmajunkie.usatoday.com/2019/01/khabib-mcgregor-jones-nsac-hearing-live-video-stream

[309]

https://www.desmoinesregister.com/story/sports/mma/2019/01/29/jon-jones-license-ufc-235-anthony-smith-drug-testing/38974069/

[310] The members of the NSAC jointly impressed me with their commitment to fairness and justice in this situation. All of them clearly did their homework on the issues involved, and they all brought relevant and insightful questions to bear on the evidence presented to them by Eichner and others from USADA.

Watching the hearing conveyed the strong sense that this commission was not going to just roll over for The UFC, no matter how much money that organization pours into Nevada's economy.

[311] In December 2015, then 23-year-old Dylan Scott became a member of the International Tennis Federation and played matches at the Futures and Challenger levels. Scott played only high school tennis and worked as an insurance adjuster when he returned to the sport. He claimed that from June 2014 to September 2015, he ingested a supplement called "Quad" that he purchased at a Total Nutrition store in Coral Gables. Over that period, Scott claimed to have taken 4-5 bottles of this substance.

Scott competed in five Futures and 1 Challenger tournament during 2016 and 2017, eliminated from most in the first round. In early 2017, Scott began training with Dominik Hrbaty, who focused on increasing his levels of fitness for competition (during which time, he lost a good deal of weight). On July 8, 2017, the ITF drug-tested Scott at a tournament in the Czech Republic. His urine tested positive for the M4 metabolite of DHCMT in the amount of 80 picograms. The ITF issued him a four-year suspension, which he appealed to the CAS. https://www.doping.nl/media/kb/6065/CAS%202018_A_5768%20Dyland%20Scott%20vs%20ITF%20%28S%29.pdf

[312] In fairness, I must add that Cristina Ayotte, the head of the Doping Control Laboratory in Montreal (a WADA-accredited lab) testified that there is no evidence that the metabolites are sequestered in fat.

From a standpoint of scientific curiosity, I have to ask why no one is clear on whether or not the long-term metabolites are lipophilic or not. Experimentally, that is a very simple question to answer. Reduce some DHCMT to its long-term metabolites and then see if they dissolve in oil or not. Given that we know that DHCMT can be readily made into an oil-based injectable form, it seems very likely that its metabolites would also be highly lipophilic.

[313] https://mmajunkie.usatoday.com/2018/12/microdosing-weight-cutting-tainted-cocaine-ufc-232-jeff-novitzky-on-jon-jones-theories

In his opening statements to the NAC in January, 2019, Jones' lawyer Paul Greene mentioned that one of the theories is that the metabolites "come out when you drop weight," something experienced at inconsistent intervals by fighters, weightlifters, track and field athletes, and combat sports participants. Novitzky also fielded this theory back in 2018, arguing that the M3 metabolite "may be hiding in the fat tissues surrounding organs and maybe having a pulsing effect, where it's released at certain times, and other times, you can't detect it."

[314] https://www.researchgate.net/publication/328110011_HPT-Axis_Effects_and_Urinary_Detection_Following_Clomiphene_Administration_in_Males

[315] https://www.scielo.br/scielo.php?script=sci_arttext&pid=S0103-50532010001200008

[316] During five tests over a period of a few months in 2019, Jones tested positive three times for metabolites of Oral Turinabol and twice didn't show any metabolites.

This indicates that the body is releasing these metabolites at differential rates related to his training.
https://mmajunkie.usatoday.com/2019/02/jon-jones-ufc-235-two-adverse-drug-test-findings-three-negative-anthony-smith-nsac

[317] Marnell: OK, that leads to my second question: We have tried to introduce consistency into our regulations as it pertains to anti-doping, not only what's on the list, but strict liability first offence or fourth offence. So how do we deal with this? How can we be as fair and consistent as we can while also understanding that the war on drugs and

the science of the war on drugs has just changed in the hour or two that we've held these hearings, and it will continue to change. Do you have any advice, or recommendations or thoughts on how this commission should look at the idea of pulsing or residual regardless of the drugs, as new science introduces itself? The safe play is to just stick to the regulations and say "have a nice day" (strict liability). The more aggressive play is to look at these residual effects and find a way to look at them and adopt them, but that opens pandora's box or could, depending on how its done. You're the foremost expert in the world, we trust you more than anybody else in this room today.

[318] According to Daniel Eichner's own statement in support of Jon Jones and The UFC, this test does not indicate the use of Oral Turinabol. (He said, and I quote, "these low levels do not indicate re-ingestion.")

[319] Jones' urine hasn't shown any of the parent molecule (oral Turinabol) or any of the short-term metabolites *which would absolutely be present* if he had taken Turinabol again between any of those 12 testing dates over that four week period. Meaning: the presence of long-term metabolites does not prove ingestion of Turinabol.

[320] From the WADA Code:
2.1 Presence of a Prohibited Substance or its Metabolites or Markers in an Athlete's Sample
2.1.1 it is each athlete's personal duty to ensure that no Prohibited Substance enters his or her body. athletes are responsible for any Prohibited Substance or its Metabolites or Markers found to be present in their Samples. Accordingly, it is not necessary that intent, fault, negligence or knowing use on the athlete's part be demonstrated in order to establish an anti-doping rule violation under Article 2.1.

[Comment to Article 2.1.1: An anti-doping rule violation is committed under this Article without regard to an Athlete's Fault. This rule has been referred to in various CAS decisions as "Strict Liability". An Athlete's Fault is taken into consideration in determining the Consequences of this anti-doping rule violation under Article 10. This principle has consistently been upheld by CAS.]

2.1.2 Sufficient proof of an anti-doping rule violation under Article 2.1 is established by any of the following: presence of a Prohibited Substance or its Metabolites or Markers in the athlete's A Sample where the athlete waives analysis of the B Sample and the B Sample is not analyzed; or, where the athlete's B Sample is analyzed and the analysis of the athlete's B Sample confirms the presence of the Prohibited Substance or its Metabolites or Markers found in the athlete's A Sample; or, where the athlete's B Sample is split into two bottles and the analysis of the second bottle confirms the presence of the Prohibited Substance or its Metabolites or Markers found in the first bottle.

[321] For a legal discussion of the conceptual difficulties in applying comfortable satisfaction see:
https://sportslawnews.wordpress.com/2015/12/13/comfortable-satisfaction-the-issues-inherent-in-a-middle-ground-evidentiary-burden/
And:
https://digitalcommons.mainelaw.maine.edu/cgi/viewcontent.cgi?article=1320&context=mlr
The latter article discusses USADA's case and the CAS ruling against American sprinter Tim Montgomery, in which Montgomery's refusal to testify—a Fifth Amendment right—was viewed by the CAS as "corroborating evidence" tipping the balance of probabilities against him.

[322]   https://www.espn.com/mma/story/_/id/28492523/grant-dawson-faces-nsac-licensing-issue-removed-ufc-246-card

[323] A well-executed system of testing of youth and junior athletes in development can help with this process—meaning, test them at 15, 17, at 19, at 20, then again in their first senior international competitions a few years after. Knowing that they had no OT metabolites in their system as youth and juniors, means you never saw the parent compound, and if you then see it later, you will know that they at some point *possibly* ingested OT intentionally and are thus more likely to deserve an ADRV. But even then—given that Jones and others—sometimes tested negative for long-term metabolites only to test positive a few days or weeks later does not help us with this situation as most competitive athletes in Olympic sport are not tested with great enough frequency to know what is merely a pulse, and what is a first time positive.

Statistically speaking, we may—in any given urine test—be getting a "pulse free" situation of Oral Turinabol.

[324] See Catlin's bio for a list of his pioneering work in anti-doping:

https://thecatlinperspective.wordpress.com/2017/05/29/dr-don-h-catlin-and-performance-enhancing-drug-tests/

[325] Schänzer once authored a study that discovered a banned precursor to the steroid nandrolone in the toothpaste used by a German track and field athlete and his wife.
https://onlinelibrary.wiley.com/doi/full/10.1002/dta.2761?af=R

[326] From here: https://thecatlinperspective.wordpress.com/2016/08/04/the-rio-olympics-the-russian-doping-scandal-dietary-supplements-and-banned-substances-in-sport/
Don Catlin, the founder and former head of the WADA-accredited Anti-doping lab at UCLA has also stated that in his opinion, many of these low level M3 "positives" result from contaminated supplements. On his blog "The Catlin Perspective," he argues that
"The testing method for DHCMT was improved in the last few years with the detection of long-term metabolites extending the detection window from several days to several months. Perhaps that is one reason. Unfortunately, the drug remains prevalent online and has been seen as a contaminant in dietary supplement products as well. If the drug infiltrates the raw material supply for supplements, it could lead to trace amounts of contamination that the new urine-testing methodology would be more likely to expose."
"As for the potential sources of DHCMT, unfortunately it is not hard to find. A quick google search for supplements that contain DHCMT or oral turinabol brings up at least ten different websites where you can buy the drug in pill form. It is clear that oral turinabol remains available, likely through raw material providers in China or elsewhere. Unfortunately, many of these raw material providers also offer legitimate and legal supplement ingredients to the supplement marketplace, leaving open the real possibility for inadvertent contamination of benign products."

[327] Now I realize that Catlin holds a stake in the "contamination theory" being true, as he and his son run the Banned Substances Control Group, which certifies supplements, suppliers and manufacturing facilities as being contamination free. But Catlin, unlike say, Dick Pound or McLaren, has also provided an unwavering honesty and integrity in his public statements about doping and the success of efforts to combat it in amateur and professional sport.

---

328 McLaren was very clear on his belief in Jones' innocence based only on Jones' testimony. In Section 7.17 of his decision, McLaren wrote "I find that all of the evidence available to me leads me to conclude that the violation was not intended *nor could it have enhanced the Athlete's performance.* **There was absolutely no intention to use Prohibited Substances on the part of the Athlete.**"

329 https://www.foxnews.com/sports/facing-possible-lifetime-ban-cody-stanley-is-living-every-players-nightmare

330 See, for instance:
Clenbuterol:
https://www.usada.org/spirit-of-sport/clenbuterol-and-meat-contamination/
https://www.wada-ama.org/en/media/news/2019-05/wada-publishes-stakeholder-notice-regarding-meat-contamination
https://www.si.com/olympics/2018/09/27/will-claye-positive-test-clenbuterol-usada-cleared-tainted-beef-case

Trenbolone and Zilpaterol:
https://www.nytimes.com/2019/01/08/sports/cycling-steroids-tainted-meat.html
https://www.usada.org/sanction/carl-grove-accepts-public-warning/
https://www.jenrhines.com/journal/2018/9/10/positive-doping-tests-from-tainted-meata-wake-up-call
https://www.reuters.com/article/us-beef-usa-korea/south-korea-suspends-some-u-s-beef-imports-over-feed-additive-idUSBRE99802620131009
http://jamaica-gleaner.com/article/sports/20171104/mexican-boxer-claims-eating-meat-caused-positive-drug-test

331 https://www.lawinsport.com/topics/item/u-s-weightlifting-athlete-abby-raymond-accepts-sanction-for-anti-doping-rule-violation

332 The Holy Arbiter of Truth himself.

333 https://thecatlinperspective.wordpress.com/2016/07/31/colabello-oral-turinabol-and-the-mlb-positive-drug-tests/

334 I'm willing to entertain an understanding in which scenarios three and four share some overlap. But even in that case, the balance of probabilities is not overwhelmingly in favor of the athlete cheating

simply on the basis of the presence of oral Turinabol metabolites. Again, if all the urine shows is picogram levels of long-term metabolites, we must give extra weight to Eichner's testimony and the statements from Catlin and arbitration decisions by Richard McLaren favoring the athlete and the potential for contamination.

[335] Section 3.2.4 of the WADA Code, argues that WADA's own processes should not be allowed to violate principles of natural justice such as unequal treatment under the law.

[336] In those situations, I would stipulate that we must pay careful attention to past testing for Oral Turinabol.

[337] Why are you punishing any Olympic or amateur athlete for the presence of metabolites when the science shows that they didn't take it recently enough to have a performance enhancing benefit?

[338] A possible solution to this conundrum would be to amplify the punishments for any athlete showing the parent compound or short-term metabolites of steroids like Turinabol or stanozolol. For instance, apply a mandatory four-year ban to knock them out of an Olympic quad. We must also make strides to root out sources of the contamination in the supplement and food industries.

[339] At least until we have more conclusive data and longitudinal excretion studies that can conclusively say these metabolites last no longer than this amount of time.

[340] If that's the way WADA wants to encourage people to microdose with Oral Turinabol, so be it.

[341]   https://thecatlinperspective.wordpress.com/2016/07/31/colabello-oral-turinabol-and-the-mlb-positive-drug-tests/

[342]   https://www.insidethegames.biz/articles/1073680/olympic-medallist-iovu-facing-lifetime-ban-as-iwf-announce-eight-more-doping-violations

[343] The remainder of the article explains exactly what I mean in this sentence: WADA took a new test and applied it uncritically to stored urine samples without fully vetting the test's ability to show evidence for an anti-doping rule violation.

[344] Ayotte, for instance, has publicly—in the arbitration of Dylan Scott case—stated her disagreement with how the Jones' case has been handled. But she only has her surmises and opinions and no real data to contradict the data that Eichner and Fedoruk have presented under oath.

[345] See Chapter 12 of this book for a fuller discussion of the Veerpalu case and WADA's errors in applying a new test for HGH.

[346] https://www.espn.com/olympics/skiing/story/_/id/6890892/andrus-veerpalu-receives-3-year-doping-ban-using-hgh

[347] https://news.err.ee/106881/after-veerpalu-ruling-all-eyes-on-wada

[348] Both of these scientists worked on Veerpalu's successful acquittal. At the time, Fischer worked as a Senior Researcher at the Estonian Genome Center and Donald Berry chaired the Department of Biostatistics and Applied Mathematics at the M.D. Anderson Cancer Center, where he pioneered the use of statistics in developing clinical trials.

[349] https://chance.amstat.org/2014/09/doping/

[350] There is evidence from a number of longitudinal studies and data from (doping cheats) individuals that the M3 metabolite can be detected for a very long period of time. (1:44:35)
When asked under oath how long the metabolites would last, Eichner—the head of the WADA lab in Salt Lake—said "it would depend on the amount of exposure, the frequency; he noted that it depends on how much administration and we "don't know" is what he concluded.
Eichner: "I think saying 'no idea' is a little harsh, we don't know exactly how long it is but in the last four or five years, we've been involved in dozens of cases and have longitudinal data on individuals, the important thing to remember is that these aren't controlled experiments where they're (the subjects) are locked in a room and we know exactly what they're taking or not taking.
Through experience with other cases, and looking at the longitudinal data, there is definitely evidence that the M3 metabolite can be detected for a very long period of time.

[351] Remember the swimming pool-drop of water analogy for picograms? Any time an athlete takes one Turinabol pill, that ingestion leads to a

swimming pools worth of metabolites. The body stores them. They come out over long periods of time and not in a linear fashion.

352 Those are her exact words.

353 Again, her exact words. This type of argument is not scientific but speculative, at best. And a shameful way to testify in a court decision that affects a young athlete's future.

354 Again, her exact words.

355   https://www.vice.com/en_us/article/4xz3wj/the-rise-and-fall-of-gerd-bonk-the-world-champion-of-doping

356 The bottom line: WADA's is operating on a lot of unfounded assumptions about the behavior of long-term metabolites of oral Turinabol and what those metabolites mean for anti-doping.

357 Again, WADA answers to no one, with only the CAS to provide a route for appeals. The CAS is an organization of lawyers, many connected to the sports industry with serious conflicts of interest. Both WADA and the CAS are funded, staffed and organized by the IOC. The IOC answers to no one but its carefully cultivated image and subsequent billion-dollar revenue stream.
For   a   further   discussion: https://www.outsideonline.com/1925761/whats-wrong-world-anti-doping-agency

358 WADA knows the test is problematic and as recently as 2018, they commissioned a study to examine the detection window further: https://www.wada-ama.org/en/resources/research/controlled-administration-trial-of-oral-turinabol-metabolite-confirmation-and

Yet they still continue to re-test the stored samples!

359 WADA should not use this test until they have done long-term longitudinal excretion studies on the long-term metabolites with a variety of populations, and also test for greater excretions of the metabolites during pre-competition weight cutting, sauna-ing and fat-burning sessions on athletes.

Otherwise, they must throw the test out

And they have to do it with levels of DHCMT taken by athletes, not a male in his forties taking one tablet and then seeing how long it lasts. Like give 20 athletes 20-40mg a day for six months or so, then see three years later if you're still seeing M3 metabolites. Because that's what the drug regimen looks like—or even better, go test the urine of a former track and fielder from Russia or a weightlifter from Armenia that hasn't competed in a while. Then run them on the track or make them do CrossFit for two to three weeks and see if their fat cells release Turinabol metabolites.